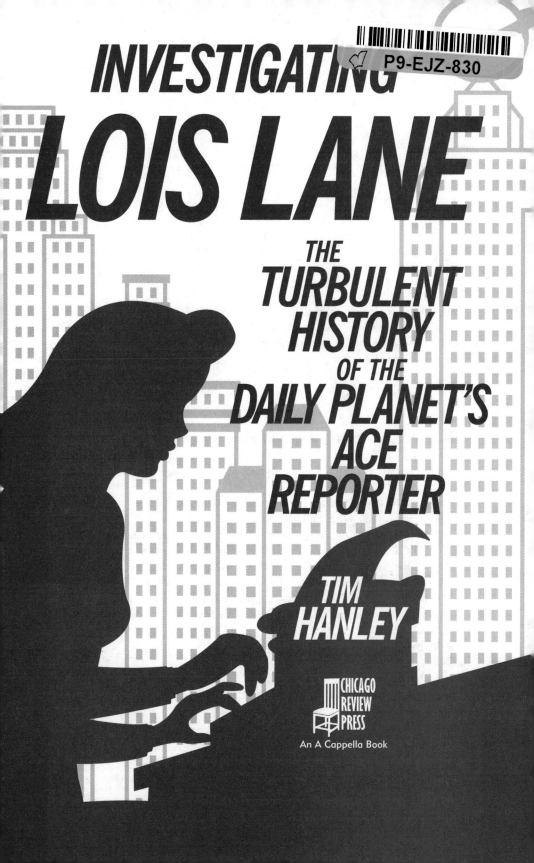

INVESTIGATING
LOIS LANE

THE TURBULENT HISTORY OF THE DAILY PLANET'S ACE REPORTER

TIM HANLEY

CHICAGO
REVIEW
PRESS

An A Cappella Book

P9-EJZ-830

Copyright © 2016 by Tim Hanley
All rights reserved
Published by Chicago Review Press Incorporated
814 North Franklin Street
Chicago, IL 60610
ISBN 978-1-61373-332-5

Library of Congress Cataloging-in-Publication Data
Names: Hanley, Tim, author.
Title: Investigating Lois Lane : the turbulent history of the Daily Planet's
  ace reporter / Tim Hanley.
Description: Chicago : Chicago Review Press, [2016] | Includes
  bibliographical references and index.
Identifiers: LCCN 2015041161 | ISBN 9781613733325 (paperback)
Subjects: LCSH: Lane, Lois (Fictitious character) | Comic books, strips,
  etc.—United States. | Women in literature. | Women in popular
  culture—United States. | BISAC: SOCIAL SCIENCE / Popular Culture. |
  LITERARY CRITICISM / Comics & Graphic Novels. | COMICS & GRAPHIC
  NOVELS / Superheroes. | SOCIAL SCIENCE / Feminism & Feminist Theory.
Classification: LCC PN6725 .H36 2016 | DDC 741.5/973—dc23 LC record
  available at http://lccn.loc.gov/2015041161

Unless otherwise indicated, all images are from the author's collection
Front cover design: Tim Hanley
Interior design: PerfecType, Nashville, TN
Cover and interior layout: Jonathan Hahn

Printed in the United States of America
5 4 3 2 1

To Russell, June,
George, and Betty

Contents

Introduction

*L*ois Lane was nearly killed in *Adventures of Superman* #631. This was hardly out of the ordinary for Lois. For seven decades, she'd survived all manner of death traps as gangsters, super-villains, and alien invaders tried to do away with her. Lois was a perpetual damsel in distress, and for vast swaths of her history she existed only to be captured and call out for Superman, who would swoop in to save her from certain doom.

But this 2004 issue of *Adventures of Superman* was different. This time, Superman was too late. Lois was in the sights of a sniper, and Superman arrived only after she'd been shot through the chest. The circumstances were also unusual. Lois wasn't lured into an obvi-ous trap, nabbed while recklessly snooping around for a story that would get her on the front page of the *Daily Planet*, or ensnared by one of the other innumerable ploys that comic book writers used to put her in peril. In this story, Lois was the hero.

As part of an ongoing story line written by Greg Rucka with art by Matthew Clark and Renato Guedes, Lois was embedded with American troops overseas. America was at war with the fictional country of Umec, and Lois covered the conflict for the *Daily Planet*. An explosion and sniper fire rocked her unit, and when the initial attack waned, Lois noticed that one of the soldiers was still alive and needed assistance. Ignoring the warnings of a fellow reporter sheltered with her in a safe zone, Lois ran to the soldier and dragged him to safety, but was shot in the process.

This issue is considered one of the most iconic Lois Lane stories ever written. In the year of its release, Greg Rucka was nominated for Best Writer at the Eisner Awards, the comic book industry's highest honors, and DC Comics recently reprinted the story in a special collection that celebrated Lois's seventy-fifth anniversary. The bravery displayed in this story reflects a view of Lois common in the Modern Age of superhero comics, in which many consider her to be as much of a hero as those who wear capes and tights.

Rucka in particular is a big fan of Lois, saying of her, "She's the woman that Superman falls in love with—think about who that woman has to be." Superman, he points out, "is a guy who's seen wonders we'll never see and Lois is, to him, one of those wonders." Bryan Q. Miller, a writer for the *Smallville* television show and comic books, is similarly effusive, declaring that "Lois embodies everything about the human spirit that [Superman] aspires to protect and preserve. She's his grounding element—the thing that reminds him not only what he's fighting for, but why." Miller succinctly sums up his feelings about the character: "Lois Lane is Clark Kent's Superman."

Lois is Superman without the superpowers. She's not faster than a speeding bullet or more powerful than a locomotive, but she is just as committed to truth and justice through her tireless reporting, and just as willing to put herself in harm's way to help someone. Lois is reckless and passionate for all the right reasons, and while that sometimes gets her in trouble, it only further endears her to her legions of fans. To those who grew up reading her comics or watching her various live action and animated incarnations, Lois Lane is a beloved icon and role model.

However, this image represents Lois at her best, and her many comic book appearances haven't always reflected this heroic ideal. Lois's history is one of constant contradiction. As a normal human woman in a world of superheroes written and drawn primarily by men, Lois was subject to unrelenting gender stereotypes that undermined her image as a fearless reporter. Her story follows two competing models: that of an independent, progressive woman and that of a limiting concept of womanhood.

The perpetual duality of Lois Lane creates an ebb and flow in her overall narrative, and each era of the character is rife with complications. She embodies the progress and struggles of American women, an ongoing cycle of advances and setbacks. Lois may not be bulletproof, but she always bounces back, and her resilience throughout this incredible journey has rightfully afforded her a place in the pantheon of today's superhero icons.

The Ambitious Sob Sister

Action Comics #1 hit newsstands in June 1938 and changed the entire course of the comic book industry. The book was an instant hit; the cover featured a man wearing a cape and lifting a car, while inside was the debut story of a character who would go down in history as a tireless crusader for truth and justice. This hero was fearless and brave, quick to stand up to evildoers when no one else would, and unflappable in the face of danger. Her name was Lois Lane.

Lois was a reporter at the *Daily Star*, a "sob sister" relegated to the lovelorn column but keen to find a big scoop and make it to the front page.* Her editor, George Taylor, and her associate, Clark Kent, were more hindrance than help, but Lois persevered. She fought for every assignment she got, even stealing tips when she had to, and over the years she endured kidnappings, fires, and explosions all in the pursuit of a good story. *Action Comics* and its spinoffs sold millions of copies each month, and Lois Lane was soon a household name.

---

* A sob sister was a female reporter who wrote sentimental stories or, as in Lois's case, advice columns for women. While they weren't seen as the equal of male reporters, the rise of sob sisters in American newspapers at the turn of the twentieth century was an important step that gave women a voice in the primarily male domain of journalism.

Superman was there too, of course, receiving most of the attention, but it's easy to stand up to bad guys when you're bulletproof. Although Lois had none of the advantages of Superman or even Clark Kent, she was just as driven in pursuit of her goal. She was determined to be a star reporter, but it was a long road to the front page.

Creating a Legend

Before *Action Comics* debuted, the comic book industry was still finding its way. In the mid-1930s, several publishers began to reprint newspaper comic strips as comic books, on paper so poor and for a price so low that they were meant to be thrown out after they were read. The books were popular, and soon publishers began to commission original stories. Young creators jumped at the opportunity, hoping to strike gold with a new character that they could transition into a lucrative daily newspaper strip with one of the major syndicates. There were humor stories, detective yarns, and tales of adventure, but comic books didn't really take off until the dawn of superheroes.

National Comics found some success with *Detective Comics* in 1937,* and publisher Harry Donenfeld directed editor Vin Sullivan to launch another series the following year to be called *Action Comics*. Sullivan compiled a new cast of characters—boxer "Pep" Morgan; Scoop Scanlon, Five Star Reporter; Zatara, Master Magician—but he was missing a cover story. Max Gaines, the publisher at National's sister company All-American Publications, forwarded him an old pitch about a costumed hero named Superman, and Sullivan liked what he saw. He took a chance and put Superman on the cover, and everything changed from there. The book was a smash, and soon every publisher wanted its own superhero.

---

* *Detective Comics* originally starred characters like Gumshoe Gus and Cosmo, the Phantom of Disguise. It took two years before the series premiered its most iconic character, the Bat-Man.

The creators of Superman were two young men from Cleveland named Jerry Siegel and Joe Shuster.* They had been pitching several versions of the character for years before he first appeared in *Action Comics* #1. Siegel was an avid fan of pulp and science fiction novels and wrote his own stories from a young age, creating his own fanzine, *Cosmic Stories*, in 1929, when he was just fifteen years old. He met aspiring artist Joe Shuster in high school, and the two teamed up on a new self-published magazine they titled *Science Fiction: The Advance Guard of Future Civilization*. Siegel wrote prose stories and Shuster provided illustrations.

The earliest incarnation of the Man of Steel appeared in the magazine's third issue, in a 1933 story called "The Reign of the Super-Man." The titular character was a villain who resembled a prototypical Lex Luthor, and there was no Lois Lane involved. Siegel and Shuster soon reworked the character, dropping everything but the name and turning him into a hero. They switched from prose to comics and pitched the character to every publication they could think of, both as a newspaper strip and as a comic book.

The duo sold a few of their other stories to an early National venture, *New Fun*, in 1935, starring characters like the swashbuckling Henri Duval and the supernatural Doctor Occult. They also had a regular feature in *Detective Comics* with their adventuring hero Slam Bradley. All the while, Superman remained frustratingly unpublished.

Finally, Vin Sullivan offered them the cover story of *Action Comics* #1, and the duo churned out thirteen pages as quickly as possible. They sold the rights to Superman to National for $130 and a contract to continue making Superman stories, a decision they later came to regret. But in 1938, they were overjoyed to debut Superman after five years of reworking and rejection.

---

* Shuster was born in Canada and moved to Cleveland when he was nine, and we Canadians claim him as our own. Historica Canada aired a "Heritage Minute" television commercial chock-full of errors that gave Shuster full credit for creating Superman in 1931, Canada Post recently issued a set of Superman stamps, the national mint put out a set of Superman coins, and the Canadian comic book awards are called the Shusters. Our connection to Joe Shuster and Superman, however tenuous, is a real source of pride for Canadians.

Superman was Kal-L, a baby sent from the doomed planet Krypton to Earth, where he was adopted by human parents.* He grew up to become Clark Kent, a reporter at a major metropolitan newspaper, originally known as the *Daily Star*. His Kryptonian physiology gave him superpowers, and Superman used those powers to fight evil and help those in need. In *Action Comics* #1, Superman convinced the governor to order a stay of execution for a wrongly convicted inmate on death row, confronted a man who was beating his wife, stopped a gang of kidnappers, and investigated a corrupt senator. As his alter ego Clark Kent, he also had a date with his coworker, the tenacious and ambitious reporter Lois Lane.

The earliest version of Lois had been added to the Superman story during the constant revisions prior to the property landing at National, at some point around 1935. Films starring female reporters were popular in this period, and Siegel and Shuster drew inspiration from this trend. Film scholar Deac Rossell writes that "the newspaper film genre was the only place where an actress could portray a role that stood on equal footing with men," and many great female characters came out of these movies. They also had a lot in common with Lois: Margaret Banks, played by Carole Lombard in 1929's *Big News*, was a sob sister, while Ellen Garfield, played by Bette Davis in 1935's *Front Page Woman*, worked for the *Daily Star*.

These hardworking, fast-talking women were determined to show that they belonged in the unwelcoming, male-dominated newspaper business. Ellen Garfield declared to her boyfriend, a rival reporter, "I'm going to prove I'm as good a reporter as any man." Timmy Blake, played by Joan Blondell in 1937's *Back in Circulation*, was described as a "scoop-hunting news hawk," while Torchy Blane, originally played by Glenda Farrell in a series of films beginning with 1937's *Smart Blonde*, was called "the lady bloodhound with a nose for news" and a "headline hunter, trouble hunter, man hunter."

---

* The details of this origin were tweaked over time. Clark's initially nondescript parents became farmers Jonathan and Martha Kent by the early 1950s, and "Kal-L" was changed to "Kal-El" a few years later.

Torchy Blane was a major influence on Lois Lane, cited specifically by Siegel in interviews years after Lois's creation. She was a determined reporter who never let anything or anyone stand in her way. In *Smart Blonde*, her police lieutenant fiancé told her, "No, you wait here. This rathole is no place for a woman." She immediately replied, "But I'm a newspaperman!" and followed him into the building despite his warnings. Torchy jumped onto moving trains to get interviews, talked her way onto murder scenes, and was always just ahead of her fiancé as they investigated the same crimes.

Lois's last name also had a Torchy Blane connection. Siegel was a fan of the actress Lola Lane, particularly the ring of her name, and Lola Lane went on to replace Glenda Farrell in 1938's *Torchy Blane in Panama*. The writer borrowed her surname and the alliteration for his own female reporter.*

For her first name, Siegel turned to his past. Lois Amster was Jerry Siegel's high school crush; he even published a romantic poem about her in the school newspaper in hopes of earning her affection. It didn't work, nor did he create much of a lasting impression with Amster. Decades later, when she was asked about inspiring Lois Lane, all Amster could remember about Siegel was that he stared at her a lot and occasionally wore his pajamas to school. But Siegel remembered her. A damsel in distress in one of his first comics, "Doctor Occult" in 1935's *New Fun*, was named Lois Amster, and the first name later became legendary in *Action Comics* #1.

During Lois Lane's first story, while reluctantly on a dinner date with Clark Kent, Lois was approached by a tough customer named Butch Mason who demanded a dance. Clark was too cowardly to stand up to Butch, so Lois announced that she was going to leave. Butch declared, "Yeah? You'll dance with me and **like** it!" So Lois slapped him and walked out of the restaurant. An irate Butch tried to get revenge by kidnapping Lois, but Superman stopped him. The

---

* There are other possible antecedents for Lois's last name. Siegel and Shuster had used it before: a female villain in "Federal Men" from *New Comics* #2 in 1936 was named Kate Lane. Another striking coincidence can be found in Paul Gallico's short story "Solo Job," about a female reporter named Sally Holmes Lane. It was first published in *Cosmopolitan* in 1937 and may have stuck in Siegel's memory.

Man of Steel returned Lois to the city and said to her, "I'd advise you not to print this little episode." Yet Lois was in her editor's office the very next morning insisting that she saw Superman.

Lois's first appearance showcased the ambition that would be the core of the character for the next seventy-five years. She was sick of reading sob stories and writing advice for the lovelorn, and the second she got wind of a big story she pounced, despite the warnings of a superhero she'd just seen dismantle a car and dispatch a gang of thugs. Lois wanted to be on the front page.

Siegel and Shuster gave Lois the potential to achieve her dream, putting her in a situation that was atypical for women in the workplace in 1938. Working women were still a rarity, making up less than a quarter of the workforce. Most of these women were in jobs that had little room for advancement, such as clerical and secretarial work. Lois may have started out in the lovelorn column, but she was writing for a major newspaper and had access to the editor to pitch other stories. From her very first appearance, Lois seized every chance to move up the ladder.

Action Comics #1 also eschewed a common limitation for women at the time by having Lois be entirely unattached. Most of the women in the newspaper films of the 1930s were married or in serious relationships with marriage just on the horizon. Lois's main inspiration, Torchy Blane, was engaged. Torchy wasn't just a "newspaperman"; she had one foot in the stereotypically feminine realm of marriage and domesticity. Engagement also implied a degree of control. As much as Torchy might outsmart and disobey her fiancé, once the wedding ring was on her finger she would be a married woman, and the understanding was that this meant things would be different.* Lois had no such attachments whatsoever.

Siegel and Shuster had a track record for creating capable female characters in *Detective Comics* before they got the *Action Comics* gig. Their Slam Bradley stories featured an array of women who could keep up with the adventurer and hold their own in a fight. Another

---

* At most major newspapers in the 1930s, when a female reporter got engaged it was assumed she would soon be moving on to housewifery. She wasn't fired so much as everyone, herself included, just knew that she was now done in the newspaper business.

feature, "Spy," starred Bart Regan and Sally Norris as secret agents who traveled the world stopping villainous plots. Originally, Bart was the spy and Sally was his tagalong girlfriend, but Sally earned her way into the spy program by helping Bart and proved that she was just as skilled a secret agent as he was. Sally was in no way a damsel in distress; she was an equally capable companion. Romance was a part of most of these stories, and occasionally Siegel and Shuster's female characters needed rescuing, but ultimately they were well-rounded, talented women. Lois Lane continued this trend, and in her first appearance she was the picture of brassy defiance of the status quo.

A Rock and a Hard Place

Having made *Action Comics* an immediate smash hit, Superman helmed the leadoff story for every issue after the series debuted. *Action Comics* was soon followed by an eponymous solo series that starred Superman in every story. Between the monthly *Action Comics* and *Superman* quickly shifting from quarterly to bimonthly, Superman was a regular presence on the newsstands.

In the first few years of Superman's meteoric career, Lois appeared in slightly fewer than half of his many stories. While the ambition that defined her first appearance remained, Lois's characterization was quickly limited. She wasn't there to be a well-rounded character, with her own skills to display and goals to be achieved; instead she became a plot device, chasing stories to end up in dangerous situations so that Superman could save her.

In the second issue of *Action Comics*, Lois was researching a story in a foreign country when she was framed for treason; Superman stopped her from being executed. In *Action Comics #5*, Superman swooped in and grabbed Lois from her car just as it was about to be destroyed by an onslaught of water from a demolished dam. This trend continued whenever Lois appeared: Superman deflected the bullets of scads of gunmen, foiled multiple kidnappings, and prevented the destruction of dirigibles, planes, and various other aircraft, all to rescue Lois.

Before long, Lois was little more than a damsel in distress, a role that defined one of the major conventions of the nascent superhero genre. It wasn't enough to just let a hero display his skills; a damsel in distress always reinforced the hero's greatness with grandiose pronouncements. When Clark or Lois got commended for a story they uncovered, Lois always immediately pointed out, "All the credit should go to **Superman!**" While witnessing one of Superman's feats, Lois exclaimed, "He was colossal!" In that same issue she compared Superman to Clark, saying "He's grand! He's glorious! He's terrific!—He's everything you're not! Brave, bold, handsome—superb!"

If Lois's declarations seemed especially effusive, it was because she'd fallen madly in love with Superman, and it only took three issues. In her second appearance, Lois remained focused on journalism, asking Superman, "What manner of being are you?" By her third appearance, the Man of Steel had won her over. After Superman saved Lois from the destroyed dam in *Action Comics #5*, all of her journalistic aims fell by the wayside. She exclaimed, "Oh, I could kiss you! As a matter of fact, **I will!**" And so, despite Superman's protests, she did. As Superman flew her back to town, Lois said, "The first time you carried me like this I was frightened—just as I was frightened of you. But now I love it—just as I love you!" As Superman flew off so Clark could call in the story, a smitten Lois pleaded, "**Don't go!** Stay with me . . . always . . ."

From then on, a lovestruck Lois was the norm whenever Superman was around. This wasn't a development of Lois's character so much as an extension of her primary purpose as a damsel in distress. It added extra relish to her pronouncements of his greatness, but more practically it also gave the writers another way to put Lois in dangerous situations, as she chased after her elusive love.* She was so keen to see Superman again that in one issue she stole Clark Kent's scoop to meet up with two men who claimed to be Superman's managers. They were con men and the meet quickly went sour, but the real Superman arrived to save Lois when the con men threw her out a window. As he left she desperately inquired, "But when will I see you again? I must see you! I must!" When Superman performed

---

* Jerry Seigel remained the primary writer for Superman comics during this period, but Don Cameron and Bill Finger occasionally wrote Superman stories as well.

as a strong man at a local circus, Lois was there on opening night. A panel showed her face alight with excitement, her hands clasped together in glee as she gushed, "I'm going to see him again!—**Superman**, my dream-lover!" When she tried to meet Superman after the show, she was captured and held at gunpoint by a saboteur before the Man of Steel intervened.

Back at the newspaper, Lois remained ambitious but couldn't get any traction. Two years after Superman first appeared, the *Daily Star* was renamed the *Daily Planet*, and the editor of the paper changed from George Taylor to Perry White. Things remained the same for Lois, though; she was still the paper's sob sister, answering letters from the lonely hearts in the lovelorn column. Even after four years of finagling scoops and following leads with Clark, she still wasn't a full-fledged reporter, and her career goals were often treated like a joke. In *Superman* #18 in September 1942, Clark greeted Lois with the rather patronizing "Poor Lois! Still giving out advice to the lovelorn."

While the lovelorn column was Lois's regular job, it was also used as a punishment for full-time reporters. When Clark was late for work, the editor gave Lois the big assignment and made Clark the sob sister for the day.* When Lois was made editor for a day in another issue, a job she later called "too much for me," she made Clark write the lovelorn column, devaluing her own position. Even Lois knew that there was no lower job at the *Daily Planet* than her own.

Lois and Clark's antagonistic relationship highlights the third key component of the comics' damsel-in-distress role: a love triangle in which the damsel is in love with the superhero and has no interest in his alter ego. The hero can't reveal his secret identity, and so the unwitting damsel is left frustrated and in the dark. Lois performed each aspect of her role to the utmost, not only being madly in love with Superman but also absolutely *hating* Clark Kent.

She had good reason for the latter. Both Lois and Clark had dual identities; Lois saw herself as an ace reporter, but everyone else

---

* Unfortunately for Lois, Clark ended up getting the front page story anyway. Superman showed up when her investigation took a dangerous turn, and somehow Clark had the story written by the time she got back to the office. Weird coincidence.

saw her as a sob sister. While her life was one of constant frustration, Clark's dual life was one of constant ease. He outscooped Lois at every turn, using his superpowers to beat her to the story over and over again. It was usually Lois who found the story in the first place; she'd barrel headfirst into dangerous situations and find the diamond smugglers or the spy ring, often ditching Clark to do so. The only problem was that she always got caught. By the time she was rescued and returned to the *Daily Planet*, Clark was already there, story in hand, having used his superspeed to rush back to the office and type up a report. This happened so frequently that Lois could barely contain her frustration. She called Clark a "spineless worm" and later declared, "Oh, how I hate Clark Kent!—I tell you, he deliberately set out to take my job from me!"

The Man of Steel only exacerbated the situation, practically taunting Lois in both of his identities. As Superman flew off after saving Lois from mad scientist Lex Luthor, she called out, "Thanks for a swell news story!" Superman slyly replied, "Don't thank me yet! I have a hunch Clark Kent will get the story into print before you do!" Back at the *Daily Planet* after another adventure, Lois was miffed at being outscooped again, but Clark told her, "Just be satisfied that **Superman** got you out of that mess alive!" In *Action Comics* #64, Superman left Lois tied to a chair after she was captured by the Toyman, and when Clark showed up later he refused to untie her until he'd typed up the story. Superman had Clark's back and Clark had Superman's, leaving Lois entirely on her own.

The superhero's only real trouble was maintaining his secret identity when he needed to switch from Clark to Superman, and he had an easy solution for that. When Lois and Clark were trapped in a burning cabin, he put Lois in a hypnotic trance so that she wouldn't remember him smashing through the barn roof to free them. On multiple occasions, Clark knocked Lois unconscious by touching a specific nerve so that she wouldn't see him transform into Superman. Lois didn't even have to be conscious to serve her primary function as a damsel in distress.

This unfortunate truth was epitomized in a story in *Superman* #4. Clark had already knocked out Lois earlier in the story so that he could take down a malicious duo away from her prying eyes, but after he revived her, a plane crash left her in a coma. Superman spent the rest of the story carrying her limp body from adventure to adventure, saving Lois from a pterodactyl, a giant rodent, Lex Luthor's chemical vat, and the sinking of a floating city. She was unconscious the entire time, doing nothing and speaking no dialogue until she woke up at the end of the issue. And, of course, the issue ended with Clark Kent's byline on the *Daily Planet*'s front page story.

Lois's struggles at the newspaper were reminiscent of the travails of real-life female journalists across America. In 1936, Ishbel Ross published *Ladies of the Press*, a history of female journalists, in which she concluded, "They are remarkable only because they are exceptions." An average big-city newspaper in the 1930s, with thirty to fifty reporters on staff, typically employed only two or three women, and rarely in high-profile positions. The *New York Times* didn't have a woman in its city room until Kathleen McLaughlin in 1935; she later said of her treatment in her early days, "You could have cut the ice with a sword," and that to her coworkers, "I just wasn't there, for months on months." When Lois first appeared in 1938, only two female reporters had won a Pulitzer Prize for journalism since the award's creation in 1917.*

In 1930, roughly fifteen thousand women were writing or editing newspapers in the United States, and a decade later that number had increased by only a thousand. World War II quickly changed that. With so many men gone to war, and many of the remaining male reporters off covering it, women flooded the newspaper business and were soon getting front page stories left and right. This boom coincided with the changing fortunes of Lois Lane, whose persistence finally began to pay off.

---

* There are multiple Pulitzer Prize categories for journalism, and well over fifty individual winners were named in this twenty-year period. The two women winners were Minna Lewinson of the *New York Times*, who shared the Meritorious Public Service Award with Henry Beetle Hough in 1918, and Anne O'Hare McCormick, also of the *New York Times*, who won the Correspondence Award in 1937. It was another fourteen years before a third woman, Marguerite Higgins of the *New York Herald Tribune*, won a Pulitzer Prize for journalism.

The Tide Turns

Lois Lane's limited role wasn't the result of deliberate sexism on the part of her writers and artists but was instead the inevitable consequence of her position in the Superman comics. Superman wasn't just the star of *Action Comics* and *Superman*; he quickly became one of the biggest stars in the world, inspiring a slew of imitators and catapulting DC Comics* into the forefront of the comic book industry. He was so well known and central to DC's identity that the company's entire comic book line was soon branded with a logo that read "DC: A Superman Publication," regardless of whether Superman was actually in the book. It's no wonder that the character was placed at the center of every story he appeared in, to the detriment of his poorly fleshed-out supporting cast. Every other character, including Lois, was there solely to best feature the wildly popular Man of Steel.

Siegel and Shuster imbued Lois with several positive and progressive traits in *Action Comics* #1, but those same traits were subsequently used to make Lois the archetypal damsel in distress. She remained tough and ambitious, just trapped in a limited role. However, with Lois appearing regularly in multiple series, her many damsel-in-distress story lines sporadically and unintentionally added new dimensions to Lois, and their accumulated weight slowly helped her depiction evolve. She grew from a plot device to an increasingly well-rounded character who ultimately became an ace reporter with adventures of her own.

Lois chased stories into dangerous situations so that Superman could save her, but this oft-repeated scenario also showcased and reinforced her bravery. Lois boldly stepped in front of speeding police cars, forcing them to stop so that she and Clark could tag along with the officers. When an explosion ripped through a bank or a

---

* National Allied Publications originally published Superman stories through their Detective Comics Inc. imprint before officially merging both divisions into National Comics. Then National combined with All-American Publications to become DC Comics in the early 1940s.

warehouse, Lois never shrunk back in fear. Instead, she ran toward the building to find out what happened.

While her investigations usually led to her capture and her inevitable rescue, she was tough and never gave up. Lois's response to interrogation was to exclaim, "You'll not get one scrap of information out of me!" When she was tied to a chair in a building set to explode and Superman was nowhere to be found, she shimmied over to a telephone, knocked it off the table, and had the operator patch her through to the *Daily Planet* while she lay sideways on the floor with her head pressed against the receiver. Superman saved her in the end, but her own resourcefulness made it possible.

Lois also had a soft spot for children, but even this seemingly stereotypical trait served to add another dimension to the character. Her concern allowed her focus to widen beyond simply getting a story, and her compassion shone through. Lois and Clark visited an orphanage in *Superman* #3, and they suspected that the children housed there were being abused and forced to work. They left when they were unable to find any solid evidence, but a troubled Lois later tossed and turned in her bed and ultimately got up in the middle of the night to sneak back into the orphanage and investigate further. Similarly, in *Action Comics* #27, a boy told Lois about abuses at a rehabilitation house for children, and she and the boy broke in to look for evidence. In both instances, Lois got into serious trouble, almost dying in a fire in the first and ending up bound and gagged in a basement prison in the second.

Lois again put herself in peril to help kids when the children's section of a stadium began to collapse. She was underneath the area, with chunks of concrete falling all around her, and Superman was momentarily paralyzed, unsure of whether to save Lois or the kids. Lois made matters easier by calling out from the raining debris, "Never mind me!—**Save those children!**" After Superman dug her out of the rubble, Lois nearly died from her injuries while at the hospital, before Clark gave her a transfusion of his super-blood to revive her.

The blood transfusion was one of the very few useful things Clark Kent did in the comics' Golden Age. While Superman was a hero to all, as Clark he acted like a bumbling coward so that no one would suspect his true identity. This also kept Lois's romantic focus on Superman and not Clark, maintaining their integral love triangle. She had no interest in a "weak-kneed pantywaist" like Clark, so his fainthearted wimp routine kept the triangle intact. In this way, the conventions of her damsel-in-distress role again benefited Lois as a character: because she worked alongside Clark so often, she came off looking very good in comparison to his apprehensive ways.

Clark was always hesitant to pursue a story or confront a villain, so Lois had to take charge and do the hard work herself. While readers knew that Clark was playing reticent so that he could come back as Superman, Lois was still depicted as an assertive woman who took the lead. Clark got stories the easy way because he was Superman; Lois got stories because she was a go-getter and pursued a lead with all her might, even if it meant dragging Clark along or ditching him all together.

Clark's general ineptitude also resulted in Lois showcasing new and interesting skill sets. When Clark was too timid to talk his way into a club suspected of illegal gambling in *Action Comics* #32, Lois got dressed up and altered her appearance so the doorman wouldn't recognize her, then walked right into the secret gambling room. When Perry White sent Lois and Clark to cover the opening of a ski resort in *Superman* #32, Clark could barely stay upright on the ski slopes or the skating rink, while Lois acquitted herself handily at both sports.

As *Action Comics* and *Superman* continued and Lois tirelessly finagled her way into story after story only to be outscooped by Clark, things finally began to turn around at the *Daily Planet*. Lois got her first front page story in *Action Comics* #27, more than two years after her first appearance. It was about the rehabilitation home for children that Lois broke into with her young friend to search for evidence of abuse, a much-deserved scoop for Lois after that adventure took a dark turn. However, while Lois's first story was a momentous occasion, Lois herself downplayed it. When Clark congratulated her on her scoop, she replied, "Not **my** scoop, Clark! After all, it was your suspicions that got us onto the right trail!" She gave all of the credit to Clark, even though she'd done most of the legwork.

More scoops for Lois followed, occasionally at first, but the pace picked up. Her lovelorn column faded away and she made it to the front page more and more. Even then, Clark sometimes still came out on top, like when Lois's story about a used car racket was trumped by Clark's scoop that the duped car dealers were donating their subpar cars as scrap metal for the war effort. A frustrated Lois exclaimed, "**Why** do you always manage to come out ahead?" But her plaintive cries diminished as the years passed, and by *Action Comics* #85 in 1945, Lois was getting so many stories that Perry White warned Clark "to wake up—or hunt for a new job!"

At this point, Jerry Siegel and Joe Shuster were no longer working on Superman comics. The books still bore their names, but Siegel had been drafted in 1943; he worked in public relations for the army instead of serving on the front lines. Shuster had ceased to be a regular contributor to the comics years before. Not a fast artist to begin with, his increasingly poor eyesight slowed him down further, and with multiple Superman comics and a regular newspaper strip in production, Shuster's art contributions were minimal. The duo focused primarily on the daily newspaper strip, while new writers and artists took their place in the comic books and continued the evolution of Lois's role, at a slightly quicker pace.

A significant component of this evolution was Lois's increase in scoops, but she still wasn't getting full credit for her work. Every story she published involved Superman in some way, and the comics often implied that she wasn't getting front page stories because of her own hard work so much as because Superman was benevolently stepping aside as a favor to her. Clark had kept her down initially, and now Superman was helping her get ahead; either way, her career wasn't hers but rather was dependent on the whims of the Man of Steel.

Then came "Lois Lane, Girl Reporter." From October 1943 to February 1944, twelve comedic strips starring Lois Lane appeared alongside the regular, full-color *Superman* Sunday newspaper strip. Drawn by Wayne Boring, the four-panel strips served to fill up some space and give the *Superman* team less work to do when they were behind on their deadlines. They were gag strips; in one, Jimmy Olsen was smitten with a young woman and burst into Lois's office, declaring, "Lois, love has kicked me in the face . . . even if it doesn't show!" to which Lois immediately replied, "It shows!" None of the strips featured Superman.

In May 1944, "Lois Lane, Girl Reporter" appeared again, this time as a four-page story in *Superman* #28. Written by Don Cameron with art by Ed Dobrotka, the story began with Jimmy Olsen musing, "Gosh, Miss Lane, you're an elegant reporter, but you gotta admit you wouldn't get most of your big scoops if it wasn't for **Superman** . . ." Lois replied, "After all, Jimmy, I **do** get **some** stories on my own!" Lois was then sent off to report on a man who was about to commit suicide by jumping off the ledge of a tall building. Lois climbed out onto the ledge to talk to the man, and was unimpressed with his story of heartbreak.* As she stamped her feet in annoyance at the man's idiocy, the ledge crumbled and Lois plunged toward the ground. She immediately declared, "I could sure use **Superman** right now!!" But the Man of Steel never arrived. Instead, Lois reached out and grabbed a giant banner that read ELECT ROBERTS, wryly observing, "I must remember to give Mr. Roberts my vote!" The banner slowed her fall, and a series of well placed awnings helped her land in a police net, safe and sound. Lois saved herself and got a front page story, the suicidal man survived, and Superman was nowhere to be found. The story ended with Jimmy Olsen saying, "I gotta hand it to you, Miss Lane—you're terrific even **without Superman!**"

"Lois Lane, Girl Reporter" ran for thirteen installments over the next two years, following the same formula: Lois investigated a story, got into a dangerous predicament, saved herself, and got a front page story, all without any help from Superman. A lovesick potential suicide was her least threatening assignment. In the tales that followed, Lois exposed and often captured all manner of thieves, swindlers, gangs, and counterfeiters. She was creative in her handling of these villains: she lit mob goons' pants on fire with a blowtorch,

* The man was about to kill himself because he had given his girlfriend a heart-shaped box of nougats for her birthday and she fed them to her dog. Lois's reaction was apt: "Why, you grade-A boob, you! Do you mean to say you'd jump eight stories over a thing like **that**?!?"

beat up a gang of swindlers with a wet mop, and pelted pirates with watermelons from atop a cliff.

The solo feature was an empowering step for the character, though its title demonstrated that Lois's role was still far from equal. It dubbed her a "Girl Reporter," a description that now seems oddly gendered but was common at the time. Lois was even referred to as such years later when *Superman's Girl Friend Lois Lane* premiered in 1958.* The term is an example of *othering*, by which male is the default and female is a noteworthy aberration. It's a distinction that suggests inferiority; note that the term is not "woman" but "girl," which implies childishness. Clark Kent was never called a "boy reporter."

Perhaps owing to its gag-strip origins, "Lois Lane, Girl Reporter" was initially more comedic than the Superman stories it accompanied, but by the final appearance of the feature in *Superman* #42, the storytelling in the rest of the book had evolved to match its light-hearted tone. The cover showed Superman playing five instruments at once as Lois conducted the music, and inside Superman battled witches and imps, a sea monster, and a villain with a top hat and a monocle. The series had shifted toward a juvenile sensibility, with villains like the Toyman, the harebrained "accidental magicians" Hocus and Pocus, and a mysterious being from another dimension named Mister Mxyztplk.† The comic book industry was still years away from the innocuous adventures that characterized its censorship-fearing Silver Age, but Superman had already moved from hardened criminals to lighter fare.

This shift in tone led to some fun, silly adventures for Lois outside of "Lois Lane, Girl Reporter." In one, from *Action Comics* #60 in May 1943, attributed to Jerry Siegel and George Roussos, Lois was

---

* The terminology wasn't limited to Lois either. In *Superman* #108 from September 1956, Clark Kent reported on female police officers in a story titled "The Girl Cops of Metropolis." Throughout the story, Clark described them with a gendered modifier: they were "policewomen," "lady cops," "girl Sherlocks," and "female sleuths," their gender front and center every time they were mentioned.
† The name "Mxyztplk" was later changed to "Mxyzptlk," which is clearly far easier to remember and pronounce.

hit by a truck and dreamed that she was Superwoman. She stopped a domestic dispute, saved Clark, later saved Superman, and then convinced Superman to marry her. She was quite disappointed to wake up in the hospital and realize that her engagement was just a dream.

A similar story, published four years later in *Superman* #45 and attributed to Alvin Schwartz and John Sikela, showed the subtle evolution of Lois's role. Superman had gotten himself into a tricky situation in which he had to make Lois think that she had superpowers in order to protect his secret identity, so he zoomed around faster than she could see to help her fly and punch through walls. Thinking she was Superwoman, Lois immediately captured a gang of "cold, violent, inhuman" brutes (with Superman's secret help) and got a front page story out of it.* In just a few short years, Lois went from trying to parlay her superpowers into marrying Superman to instead using them to get a big scoop. She was an ambitious reporter from her very first appearance, and after nearly a decade her ambition had paid off.

---

* Clark later convinced Lois to give up her superpowers when no one would dance with her for fear of her stepping on their toes with her super strength. When Clark then asked the "depowered" Lois to dance after he'd shunned her before, she slapped him across the face and shouted, "Well—here's my answer! No! You men who try to keep women weak and defenseless—I hate you!"

1a

Joe Shuster's Lost Lois

The history of superhero comic books is littered with writers and artists who never got the recognition they deserved for creating characters that continue to make millions of dollars for their publishers. For every Bob Kane, whose name is perpetually attached to Batman, and Stan Lee, who cameos in every Marvel film, there's a Bill Finger, Jack Kirby, or Steve Ditko who goes largely unrecognized by the general public and the corporations who own the characters, despite massive and often more significant contributions to the genre. Writing and drawing mainstream superhero comics was, and continues to be, simply work for hire, and only the very lucky or the particularly business savvy have received much in the way of credit or residuals for their creations.

Jerry Siegel and Joe Shuster were initially unconcerned that they had sold the rights to Superman outright in exchange for $130 and a ten-year contract to continue making comics. Then Superman became a megahit. Siegel and Shuster kept producing comics for DC, but when Siegel returned from the war he learned that DC had published a story based on his pitch for a new Superboy character without giving him credit or any money. With their work contract about to expire, Siegel and Shuster sued DC for ownership of both Superman and Superboy. They ultimately settled the suit, and DC kept both characters while Siegel and Shuster split $94,000 between them, a great deal of which went to their lawyers.

Siegel continued writing comics at different publishers, and even returned to DC a decade later, but Shuster soon disappeared. With his increasingly poor eyesight and a chronic wrist problem, it seems that he couldn't keep up with the frenetic pace required for monthly comic books. Shuster's settlement money didn't last long and he eventually fell into poverty, taking freelance art jobs when he could and living in a small apartment in New York City. When the musical *It's a Bird . . . It's a Plane . . . It's Superman* opened on Broadway in 1966, Shuster couldn't even afford tickets. He often walked over to the Alvin Theatre to watch the audience file into the show, but he never saw it himself.

Shuster's is a sad tale of a man whose work inspired legions of fans and built fortunes for several companies while he languished in obscurity, but there may have been even more tragedy between the lines. A close look at Shuster's life and comics suggests a story of heartbreak as well, dating from the dawn of Lois Lane.

Lost Love

In 1935, a Cleveland high school student named Jolan Kovacs placed an ad in the *Plain Dealer* offering her services as a model. Jerry Siegel had just added an early version of Lois Lane to his continually evolving Superman pitch, and Joe Shuster thought he would benefit from a live model to best capture this new character. Shuster replied to Kovacs's ad, and a few weeks later she was posing for him and Siegel at Shuster's apartment. In a 1983 interview, Shuster definitively declared, "To me she was Lois Lane." Kovacs returned for more sessions, and she went on a few dates with Shuster before moving to Chicago to pursue modeling in a bigger city. Shuster and Kovacs kept in touch via letters, and she was always encouraging when publishers rejected Superman, urging Shuster to keep on trying.

Flipping through the art in the early issues of *Action Comics*, a reader might easily assume that Lois Lane appeared in every single issue. However, a closer look at the text shows that this wasn't the case; Lois was in fewer than half of the stories in the first few years of the series. But when she wasn't around, she was replaced by a variety of brunettes who looked just like her. Some were damsels in distress, some were villains, but they were all doppelgängers of Lois Lane. So too was Sally Norris in "Spy," along with several of the women romanced by Slam Bradley in Siegel and Shuster's *Detective Comics* stories.

These similarities were partly due to Shuster's limited art skills and the conventions of the art form. While he drew a wide variety of male characters, Shuster's female faces all looked fairly similar. Unless the woman was considerably older or meant to be ugly, his female faces were practically interchangeable. This was true of many Golden Age superhero artists, and remains a common problem in comic book art even today.

Nonetheless, this preponderance of brunettes with the same hair-cut and facial features is striking. In Shuster's earlier work on "Henri Duval" and "Doctor Occult" in *New Fun*, the female characters were often blonde. Shuster hadn't known Kovacs for long when these comics were drawn, but a couple of years later, after the two had dated and Kovacs had moved to Chicago, the vast majority of his female characters followed a pattern modeled on her. This hints at a certain degree of pining on Shuster's part.

Furthermore, nearly every fictional female reporter before Lois Lane was blonde. Connie Kurridge from the newspaper strip *Connie* and Sally Holmes Lane from the short story "Solo Job" were both blonde. So were Carole Lombard, Bette Davis, Joan Blondell, and Glenda Farrell; three of the first Torchy Blane films were actually called *Smart Blonde*, *The Adventurous Blonde*, and *Blondes at Work*. Newspaperwomen and blondeness went hand in hand, yet Shuster made Lois a brunette, like Kovacs.

A decade after they parted ways, Shuster and Kovacs met up again in New York City. Kovacs had changed her name to Joanne Carter, the last in a series of different professional names she had tried out in the modeling world. She had moved all over the country pursuing modeling, from Chicago to Boston to New York, but it never worked out for her. She spent part of World War II in California building ships and was briefly married. Shuster had stayed in contact with Kovacs over the years, regularly trading letters with her as she moved across America. On April 1, 1948, a cartoonist's ball was held at the Waldorf-Astoria in New York City, and Kovacs happened to be in town. Shuster invited her to go with him, and she accepted.

It must have been a pleasant change of pace for Shuster to have a date with an old flame. He and Siegel had recently lost Superman to DC Comics for good, and their new collaboration, *Funnyman*, was about to flop. Still flush with his settlement money from the lawsuit, Shuster went all out. It was a costume ball, and Shuster rented Kovacs a ball gown so that she could dress up like Dixie Dugan, a Hollywood showgirl from a long-running newspaper strip. Jerry Siegel was also at the ball and was pleased to see Kovacs again. Then, at the end of the night, Kovacs left with Siegel.

Things escalated quickly after that. Siegel was married with a young son, but that was soon over; his wife, Bella, filed for divorce in July, citing "gross neglect of duty and extreme cruelty." Siegel agreed to her terms and gave her sole custody of their son. Siegel and Kovacs got married in October, just over six months after reuniting at the cartoonist's ball. Siegel and Shuster barely spoke to each other for the next twenty-five years. Whether this falling out was due to tensions over the DC lawsuit, the failure of *Funnyman*, Siegel and Kovacs's marriage, or some combination thereof is unknown, but the famed duo was no more.

By the mid-1950s, a down-on-his-luck Shuster had found a new, albeit rather seedy, gig providing illustrations for the kinky bondage and torture magazine *Nights of Horror*. He did art for lurid prose stories with titles like "The Bride Wore Leather," "Satan's Doorway," and "Patriarch of Sin." All told, Shuster illustrated sixteen issues of the cheaply produced series and was paid in cash under the table.

The contents of these magazines were a far cry from Superman's adventures. The scenes Shuster drew featured scores of scantily clad men and women in all manner of elaborate BDSM and torture scenarios. The stories were heavy on sadism; there were whippings, stabbings, chains, threats with hot pokers, iron maidens, and red ants poured into honey-smeared underpants. Murder was common. There were also sporadic lesbian and interracial liaisons, as well as a great deal of bodice ripping and occasional nudity.

Setting aside the sordid circumstances, Shuster's *Nights of Horror* illustrations were some of the best work of his career. His Superman art often looked rushed and unfinished, likely owing to the breakneck timetable of the comic book industry. With *Nights of Horror*, his work was carefully rendered in more detail. The linework was solid, the faces were expressive, and his layouts effectively communicated the shocking scenarios.

There were also familiar faces scattered throughout the art. A fellow with a whip bore a striking resemblance to Clark Kent, a Lex Luthor look-alike used an oar to paddle a woman on a bed of spikes, and Jimmy Olsen's double, complete with bowtie, got an innocent young gal hopped up on reefer. These men appeared occasionally, but far more common was Joe Shuster's muse.

Craig Yoe, who discovered this lost art and published it in *Secret Identity: The Fetish Art of Superman's Co-creator Joe Shuster*, writes that when he showed the images to comic book historian Ron Goulart, he immediately noted that "most of the women look like Lois Lane." Lois was all over *Nights of Horror*, from being injected with a hypodermic needle in "The Strange Loves of Alice" in the first issue to being suspended ominously over spikes in "The Flesh Merchants" in the final issue. There were a few older women and some blondes every so often, but the majority of the female characters in *Nights of Horror* were dead ringers for Lois Lane. Some scholars argue that Shuster was trying to get back at DC Comics by depicting their beloved characters in lurid settings, but the preponderance of Lois over the other Superman doppelgängers suggests a more specific fixation.

The sudden demise of *Nights of Horror* ended Shuster's brief fetish art career. In the summer of 1954, a gang of street youths known as the Brooklyn Thrill Killers were arrested and charged with two murders. The ringleader was Jack Koslow, a Jewish Nazi enthusiast with a Hitler moustache, and when he revealed that he was a fan of *Nights of Horror*, the publication quickly became enmeshed in the story. Within a few months, the series was banned, there was a mass burning of the remaining issues of *Nights of Horror*, and Shuster was out of a job. Luckily, he had drawn the art anonymously and his name never came up during the massive public outcry that followed the gang's capture.

Shuster's financial trouble and his hypothetical heartbreak reached a happy conclusion in the mid-1970s. The Siegels were having money problems as well, and it was the former Jolan Kovacs who reached out to Shuster about talking to DC Comics and their corporate owners, Warner Bros. Siegel and Shuster were reunited, and whatever past problems had plagued them and Kovacs were set aside as all three became fast friends again. Their campaign to get recognition and restitution for creating Superman was supported by several big-name creators at DC, most notably Neal Adams, who led the charge. Wanting to avoid bad publicity with *Superman: The Movie* on the horizon, Warner Bros. granted both creators a lifetime pension worth tens of thousands of dollars per year, and put the "Created by Jerry Siegel and Joe Shuster" credit back in their monthly Superman comics.

Joe Shuster passed away in 1992 at the age of seventy-eight, and Jerry Siegel died in 1996 at the age of eighty-one. The estates of both men later filed lawsuits against DC and Warner Bros. to regain the rights to Superman, but after an up-and-down decade of legal battles both claims ultimately failed. Shuster married once, and very briefly, in the 1970s. He had no other significant romantic relationships.

2

Lois Lane on Screen, Part 1

Superman became more than just a comic book behemoth, quickly taking over American pop culture. In the decade following his debut, Superman spawned multiple comic book series, a radio show, cartoons, a novel, live action films, and innumerable toys and games. He was even a giant balloon in the Macy's Thanksgiving Day Parade in 1940, floating over millions of spectators as fifty handlers marched him toward Thirty-Fourth Street.

Lois Lane didn't have a parade balloon, but she appeared in every other Superman property of the 1940s and '50s. No female comic book character has starred in as many adaptations as Lois, and each version added a new dimension to the character. As popular as the comics were, radio and film reached a massive audience as well, and the comics often incorporated popular elements from Superman adaptations. This was especially true with the radio show, and Lois's audio adventures may have played a role in her comic book progress at the *Daily Planet*.

The Adventures of Superman Radio Show

The Superman radio show launched less than two years after the premiere of *Action Comics* #1, and it was soon a massive hit. It began in syndication in February 1940; its fifteen-minute episodes were prerecorded and sent to local stations for broadcast to young fans. In 1942 a national radio network, the Mutual Broadcasting System, picked it up, and the program then went out live three days a week. Later, as its popularity grew, it was upped to five days a week. At its peak, *The Adventures of Superman* was heard by 4.5 million listeners per episode and was the highest-rated children's radio program in the country.

The program starred Bud Collyer as Clark Kent/Superman, and he made a clever distinction between his dual roles. As Clark, Collyer spoke in a soft tenor voice, and when he switched to Superman he dropped his voice to a deeper baritone and spoke more declaratively. It was a particularly effective tactic on a radio show, but the trick has been used in several portrayals of Superman since then.

Lois was initially played by Rolly Bester, first appearing in the seventh episode of the series. She wasn't at all fond of Clark, and in their first on-air interaction she greeted him with, "Well, Mr. Star Reporter, couldn't you find anything to do but come and horn in on my story?" Villains captured her in the next installment, and she had little to do until Superman rescued her a few episodes later. A different damsel in distress replaced Lois for the next story arc, and when she returned weeks later she was voiced by Helen Choate. Lois and Clark were sent to do a story on a prison, and Lois was again captured, this time during a prison break.

Joan Alexander debuted in June 1940 as the third voice for Lois. Whereas Bester's and Choate's takes on the character had been somewhat harsh, particularly toward Clark, Alexander smoothed out the rough edges. Lois remained a keen, assertive reporter, but her interactions with Clark were less abrasive, and instead of competing against each other, they often worked together on stories.

Alexander had to fight to keep her job, but she was clever. When the show's director, Robert Maxwell, fired her early in her run, Alexander bought a wig to disguise herself and showed up at the audition for her replacement. The producers unknowingly rehired her, and she remained a fixture on the show for the next decade. Collyer in particular was happy about her return; he found her to be a consummate professional, able to read a script cold and nail the performance straight away.

The Adventures of Superman added several notable elements to the Superman mythos that were then integrated into the comic books. The *Daily Planet*'s editor, Perry White, appeared for the first time on the radio show, as did the newspaper's copyboy, Jimmy Olsen. Kryptonite made its first appearance on the radio as well, along with a few of Superman's superpowers. The radio show's opening narration even had a long-lasting impact, debuting such memorable catchphrases as "Look! Up in the sky! It's a bird! It's a plane! It's Superman!"

As for Lois Lane, she resembled her Golden Age comic book incarnation in many ways, but there were some key differences, especially in the early years of the series. She was still a zealous reporter, and chasing after a story often got her into trouble, but her damsel-in-distress role was less pronounced. Lois often fought back ferociously against her captors. In one episode in which she was kidnapped to be framed for murder, she dodged her guards and ran straight for a window, only to be tackled before she could jump through it. They had to drug her to stop her from trying further escapes.

Superman was less of a presence as well. He was characterized as an urban legend, so his interactions with the main cast were rare. When Lois was captured, it was usually Clark or the police who rescued her, often after some sly heroics from Superman. The effusive praise and love for Superman that quickly took over Lois in the comics was far less of a factor on the radio, simply because she didn't see him very much.

At the *Daily Planet*, radio Lois got to skip the years of treading water that her comic book counterpart endured. She was sometimes sent out on stories to capture the "women's angle," but she was never a sob sister for the lovelorn column. While it took two years for Lois to get a front page story in the comics, it only took her six weeks on the radio. In the series' twentieth episode, Lois phoned in the prison break story before Clark could by rushing to the telephone while Superman was still sorting out all of the bad guys. Her first radio scoop predated her first comic book scoop, in *Action Comics* #27, by more than five months, and Lois's reporting prowess on the radio may have had some influence on the rise of her reporting career in print.

As in the comic books, however, the radio program frequently introduced Lois as a "star girl reporter," and the treatment of the character reflected this subordinate role. The term was both a compliment and a put-down: Lois was a great reporter, for a girl. Clark was a great reporter, full stop, and clearly the best reporter at the *Daily Planet*. When Lois and Clark investigated stories, the people they talked to were always familiar with Clark and his track record of getting to the bottom of odd occurrences, so they were happy to let him help. Lois had no such notoriety. While they often co-investigated mysteries, if Lois found a clue that pointed to a particular person as the culprit, the listener could be sure it was a false lead. Clark would then find the clue that led them to the real culprit.

As the series went on, Lois's nose for news began to cause trouble, including one story that spurred the series' longest arc. When Lois learned about a museum's plan to dispose of a chunk of Kryptonite by dumping it in the ocean, she sensed a scoop and wrote up the story. Clark warned her not to disclose details of the disposal lest Superman's enemies go after it, but she didn't listen. As a result, the Scarlet Widow stole the Kryptonite and sold it to four of Superman's worst enemies. Superman spent weeks battling villains and his life was in grave danger, all because Lois didn't sit on the story.

Lois was also often relegated to the background of big stories, including one of Superman's most well-known radio outings, recently returned to the public eye thanks to a mention in Steven D. Levitt and Stephen J. Dubner's bestseller *Freakonomics*. The writers of the program wanted to teach good citizenship to their young listeners, and so in 1946 Superman tackled the Clan of the Fiery Cross, an analogue of the Ku Klux Klan. The sixteen-part story was billed as an "exposé of fanatical and un-American bigotry"; Superman protected an Asian family from the hate group and ultimately dismantled the organization's entire Metropolis branch.* Jimmy Olsen and Perry White played big roles in the story, but Lois appeared in just two of the sixteen episodes, and only because Jimmy and Perry had been kidnapped and Clark needed somebody else to talk to. In fact, most of Lois's dialogue involved her being incredulous at the threat of the clan and insisting that they'd never try to kidnap Perry or Jimmy. Her reporter's instincts weren't always spot on.

Ultimately, although the series made very clear that she was no Clark Kent, Lois was a brave and tenacious reporter who was much more than a mere damsel in distress. A girl reporter, however problematic the term, was nonetheless a constant female presence in a male-dominated field. Joan Alexander stayed on the program until the end of its run in 1951, and all told, the series aired more than two thousand episodes.

Fleischer Studios / Famous Studios Cartoons

Not content with a massive radio success, DC Comics wanted to bring Superman to movie theaters as well. They contacted Fleischer Studios, an animation studio best known for their Betty Boop and Popeye the Sailor shorts, but the Fleischer brothers, Max and Dave, weren't terribly interested. Producing a Superman cartoon would be complicated and time-consuming, and their entire business was already mired in troublesome levels of dysfunction due to the brothers' feuding. Half to scare away DC and half to make it very worth their while if they ended up making the cartoons, Fleischer Studios proposed a budget of $100,000 per cartoon short, four times what

---

* "The Clan of the Fiery Cross" was not only a well-told story that vehemently criticized racism and bigotry at every turn (Perry White called the clan members "lamebrains and diseased minds"), it also portrayed the organization as a complete sham. The group's leader, the Grand Imperial Mogul, freely admitted that he didn't care at all about racial purity, and that the clan was simply a way for the folks at the top to make vast sums of money selling memberships and robes to dumb racists. Critiquing both racism and capitalism was a bold move in 1946.

their cartoons usually cost. DC was keen for the big screen, and after a bit of negotiating, both sides settled on a rate far above the studios' usual fee. Work began immediately.

What made Fleischer Studios unique was their lifelike cartooning, which was created through a process called *rotoscoping*. They filmed a live action version of their cartoons first, with actors going through all of the movements called for in the story, and then their animators drew overtop the actors to capture their realistic motion. This was trickier with Superman; their actors couldn't fly or lift an entire building. But they mimicked the actions as best they could, and the animators made artistic corrections and filled in the gaps.

All of the Superman cartoon shorts starred Bud Collyer as Superman/Clark and Joan Alexander as Lois Lane, reprising their roles from the radio show. The shorts were beautifully animated in a bold art deco style, and they featured rousing scores by Sammy Timberg. The first ten-minute short, simply called *Superman* but also known as *The Mad Scientist*, premiered on September 26, 1941. In its most action-packed scene, Superman saved a building from toppling over after it was hit by a devastating energy ray, and punched the ray itself all the way back to the weapon's source at the villain's hideout, which was then destroyed. Audiences were thrilled; the cartoon was seen by over twenty million people and nominated for an Academy Award.

The short was also a great showcase for Lois Lane. It began with the *Daily Planet*'s editor calling Lois and Clark into his office to follow up on Lois's lead concerning a mad scientist who was sending threatening letters. When the editor wanted Clark to go with Lois to follow up on her lead, Lois interjected, "But, Chief, I'd like the chance to crack the story on my own." Before the editor even had a chance to think it over, Lois rushed out of the office with a "Thanks, Chief!" leaving Clark looking flummoxed.

The cartoon then cut to Lois in full aviator gear, strapping on goggles as she settled into the pilot's seat of a small propeller plane. She took off, flying herself to the mysterious island where the mad scientist's energy ray was housed. The plane's lights alerted the scientist, and Lois was captured soon after she landed. Superman later arrived and freed her, but the short ended with a shot of a new edition of the *Daily Planet* featuring a cover story by Lois Lane as her editor enthused, "Congratulations, Lois! That was a great scoop!"

For the first nine Superman animated shorts, all produced by Fleischer Studios, Lois was similarly adventurous and successful. When a dinosaur came to life at a museum, instead of fleeing with the panicked crowds and museum workers, Lois ducked into a phone booth to call in the story even as the building collapsed around her. In another short, Clark told Lois to stay put as he called in the story of a giant robot that was stealing priceless jewels. While Clark was in the phone booth, Lois crept up behind the robot and climbed into its cargo hold so that she would return with the robot to its operator and find the real perpetrator of the crime. Lois didn't have much time for Clark generally, and often got rid of him so that she could get a scoop on her own; when the *Daily Planet* sent the duo to cover an exploding volcano, Lois stole Clark's press pass in order to have the story to herself.

Not only did Lois not listen to Clark, she didn't listen to Superman either. As she raced after the escaped dinosaur rampaging through the city, Superman told her to return to the office and she replied, "And miss the best story in years? Swell chance!" After narrowly saving Lois from the beast's monstrous jaws while she was trying to get a good picture of it, Superman again told her to stay put, but her only response was a sarcastic "Yes, milord."

Superman didn't need to be so worried, because Lois handled herself well. She was on board a train carrying a billion dollars in gold when robbers attacked, and she grabbed one of the goons' tommy guns to shoot at their automobile, which was driving alongside the tracks. After a machine gone haywire pulled an asteroid toward Earth in another episode, Lois stayed with the machine despite the danger and ultimately shifted it into reverse once Superman sorted out the wiring. When a gorilla escaped from the local zoo, Lois didn't run away; she stayed to get some pictures and ended up saving a little girl. Lois was tough as nails even when she was captured; in one episode, her captors suspended her over a vat of molten metal because she wouldn't answer their questions, and she still refused to help them.

On top of her heroics, Lois also got more big scoops. Eight of the nine Fleischer Studios cartoons ended with Lois getting the front page story of the *Daily Planet*, and the one short that didn't, *The Magnetic Telescope*, instead *began* with a front page story by Lois. Even Clark was impressed with Lois's reporting prowess; after the dinosaur adventure, he told her, "You showed plenty of courage getting that monster story, Lois!" Clark appeared in all of the shorts, but he was busy as Superman, and his bylines were few and far between. Lois was the undisputed star reporter.

But that soon changed.

After producing the first nine Superman shorts, Fleischer Studios underwent a dramatic overhaul. Max and Dave were no longer on speaking terms, and their latest full-length feature, *Mr. Bug Goes to Town*, flopped in December 1941.* The studio was in a difficult financial position with its primary backer, Paramount Pictures, and Paramount eventually forced both brothers to resign in early 1942 and took control of the company, renaming it Famous Studios.

Famous Studios produced eight more Superman shorts of comparable quality and style, but there were two significant differences. First, the United States had entered World War II, so now Superman faced off against Axis forces and plots. The new shorts had titles like *Japoteurs* and *Secret Agent*, and one ended with an irate Hitler and the wartime anthem "Praise the Lord and Pass the Ammunition."

Second, Lois's involvement in the shorts quickly diminished. Her roles in the first two Famous Studios cartoons resembled her past appearances, but in fragmentary ways. In *Japoteurs*, Lois snuck onto the test flight of a huge aircraft that was then taken over by Japanese stowaways. She radioed in the hijacking, but she didn't get a front page story out of it. In *Showdown*, Lois didn't have much to do other than follow the main story and ride around with the police, though she did get a front page scoop. However, it was her last.

Lois spent the third Famous Studios short trapped in a Japanese prison, not doing much of anything until she was ultimately rescued from a firing squad by Superman. Lois was captured more often in

---

* *Mr. Bug Goes to Town*'s release was unknowingly ill-timed, as it premiered two days before the Japanese attacked Pearl Harbor.

this second run of cartoons, and had less to do before tangling with the bad guys inevitably ended badly for her. While she still fought back when she could and held up well under interrogation, her story-chasing didn't result in any success. Instead, Clark got front page headlines while Lois got nothing.

In the series' penultimate short, *The Underground World*, Lois finally had a good story to bring to her editor. While investigating some newly discovered caves, Lois stumbled onto a subterranean race of bird people. The bird people captured Lois and her companion and were about to submerge them in a boiling liquid as some sort of avian ritual sacrifice, but Superman showed up just in time to save them both. As her editor read her report, he commented, "It's really a great story, Lois," and then he casually lit the pages on fire as he added, "but no one would ever believe it." The short ended on a shot of the story burning in an ashtray.

Lois's shocked expression as her manuscript burned was the final shot of her in a Famous Studios cartoon. Lois didn't appear at all in *Secret Agent*, the last short. In fact, Lois wasn't even mentioned. Instead, Superman helped a blonde undercover agent who had infiltrated a group of German saboteurs. It was a fitting end to the Famous Studios shorts, which had diminished Lois's role to the point of cutting her out entirely.

Due to the high costs of production and waning interest from theaters, Famous Pictures only made eight Superman shorts before moving on to other properties. The seventeen total shorts, particularly the early ones produced by Fleischer Studios, are today regarded as some of the best comic book adaptations of all time, and they remain hugely inspirational for those who work on Superman in a variety of media. Modern creators and fans often cite Lois's depictions in the Fleischer cartoons as examples of the character at her best, an empowering, tough-as-nails antidote to her less inspiring comic book incarnation at the time.

Adventures of Superman Television Show

By the early 1950s, radio was old news and television was starting to catch on as a new, exciting medium across America. Always eager to expand the Superman brand, DC began to develop a Superman TV show. They'd already had some success with a live action Superman via two serial films produced a few years earlier.

The serials, *Superman* and *Atom Man vs. Superman*, were produced by Columbia Pictures and starred Kirk Alyn as the Man of Steel. Each episode was about fifteen minutes long, designed to air before matinees in theaters. Each serial consisted of fifteen episodes, making it the equivalent of a four-hour film. The budget on the serials was small, and the creators cut costs by awkwardly animating Superman's flying sequences. Luckily, subpar specials effects were expected by the kids who flocked to the matinees; the Superman serials played in theaters all across the country, even theaters that didn't usually show serials, setting box office records.

Noel Neill played Lois Lane in both serials, and she faced the same problems that her comic book counterpart had endured a decade before. In *Superman*, released in 1948, Lois was an established reporter who went after big, dangerous stories, only to be outscooped by newcomer Clark Kent. No matter what she did, Clark came out on top. Lois snuck into a mine after an explosion, hoping to find the trapped miners and get a story out of it, and not only was she caught in another mine blast but Clark got the story. She tried to get rid of Clark on multiple occasions, ditching him on the side of the road and later letting him borrow her car and then reporting it stolen, all to no avail.

Lois's quest for big scoops wasn't helped by the fact that she was captured repeatedly, and that villains used her journalistic keenness against her. An exclusive interview turned into a kidnapping, and when she followed up on a tip she stole from Clark, it was actually a trap. *Superman*'s Lois was determined and competitive, and belligerent to Clark and to any bad guys who crossed her path, but she could never get any real traction and was constantly frustrated.

Atom Man vs. Superman, which premiered two years later, carried on in a similar vein. While the rivalry between Lois and Clark had calmed somewhat, there was still a lot of scoop-stealing, and Lois was peeved at Clark for beating her to a story on multiple occasions. Nonetheless, they collaborated on a plan to have Lois pretend to be fired so she could go work for the news organization recently established by paroled criminal genius Lex Luthor. Clark strongly suspected that Luthor was Atom Man, the mastermind of a series of recent crimes, and so Lois infiltrated his news operation to investigate. Her journalistic instincts proved to be off, though; after working there for a few days, Lois decided that Luthor was on the level, but ultimately Clark was proved correct.

The second serial also brought in Lois's infatuation with Superman, which hadn't come up in the first. On more than one occasion, Superman performed a great feat and Lois sighed, "Isn't he wonderful?" After Superman picked up Lois's news truck and saved her from an oncoming flood, her companions expressed their awe while Lois stared at Superman adoringly, a big smile on her face, as she cooed, "It was easy, for Superman."

When *Atom Man vs. Superman* hit theaters in 1950, serials were well on their way out of fashion and work on the Superman TV series was already underway. The executives at DC wanted to have full control of the series, so they hired Robert Maxwell from the *Adventures of Superman* radio show to write an hour-long pilot to shop around to networks and sponsors.

For the role of Superman, there are differing reports as to why Kirk Alyn didn't return. Some say that Alyn wasn't interested in reprising the role and turned it down, others that Alyn wasn't happy with the money so DC looked elsewhere, and still others that the producers wanted to go in a new direction and Alyn was never seriously considered. Whatever the case, the show's creators ultimately turned to the amiable George Reeves. Reeves had played a small part in *Gone with the Wind* in 1939, then bounced around a couple of studios before he was drafted into the war in 1943. He found work harder to come by after the war, and by the time Superman came up, Reeves's most critically acclaimed performance, a costarring role in the war drama *So Proudly We Hail!*, was nearly a decade past. Like many actors in the 1950s, Reeves didn't have a high opinion of television and was much more interested in movies, but he was nearing forty years of age and film roles had dried up. He took the part despite his reservations.

Lois Lane was played by Phyllis Coates, a former chorus girl turned actor. Born Gypsie Ann Evarts Stell in Wichita Falls, Texas, Coates went to UCLA and soon found her way into show business, landing a contract with Warner Bros. in 1948 at the age of twenty-one. She amassed a number of small, often uncredited roles before trying out for Lois, and ended up winning the part after the producers considered more than three hundred women for the role.

When Reeves met Coates for the first time on set, he was still concerned that he was slumming; he greeted her by saying, "Well, babe, this is it: the bottom of the barrel." However, regardless of his trepidation about the project, Reeves and Coates became friends and would stay in contact long after Coates left the program. Reeves also insisted that they share top billing, using his influence to ensure that each of the early episodes of *Adventures of Superman* would end with "Starring George Reeves and Phyllis Coates."

But first came the pilot episode, "Superman and the Mole Men," a science fiction adventure that took a dark turn. While researching a story on the world's deepest oil well, Lois and Clark discovered that the drill had broken into the subterranean home of a diminutive mole-like species. The harmless mole men climbed up the shaft to explore the surface, frightening the local townspeople. An angry, armed mob formed to kill the mole men, but Superman stepped in to protect them. Ultimately, Superman returned the mole men to their home and the mole men destroyed the oil well, ending the conflict.

Financed by DC on a tight budget, "Superman and the Mole Men" featured production quality barely a step above the serials, but the performances were winning, particularly Coates as Lois. She played the character as tough and focused, with a little bit of snark when it was called for. Her Lois was keen for a good story, refusing to let Clark out of her sight when he tried to investigate the mine on his own. She also took a lot of convincing from Superman before she agreed not to send in the mole men story, as her journalistic integrity conflicted with the wisdom of not spreading further panic.*

---

* Coates also premiered what would become a signature move for her Lois when she let out an ear-piercing shriek after she was surprised by her first sighting of the mole men.

Later in the pilot, Lois stood strong against the armed mob, and when the ringleader tried to move her out of the way she declared, "I can get out of the way by myself if I feel like it, but I just don't feel like it." As the ringleader reached out to grab her, Lois fought back, yelling, "Take your filthy hands off me!" and "Why, you dirty coward!" It took two other mob members to pull her off the ring-leader and keep her restrained, and she then stomped on the foot of one and elbowed the other in the stomach as she escaped their hold.

Lois also got to deliver the very last line of the pilot. As she stood alongside Superman and watched the oil well burn, she remarked, "It's almost as if they were saying, 'You live your lives, and we'll live ours.'" It was a bit of a corny ending, but getting to say the closing line while the man whose name was in the title of the show stood silently is no small accomplishment.

DC was excited about the pilot and immediately moved into production on a full season of *Adventures of Superman*, even though they hadn't yet found a network or a sponsor. The cast expanded to include John Hamilton as Perry White, Jack Larson as Jimmy Olsen, and Robert Shayne as police inspector Bill Henderson. The twenty-four-episode season was shot in black and white, and very quickly. Each episode was budgeted at only $15,000, and the season shot at a pace of roughly five episodes every two weeks. Often episodes would be shot simultaneously; for example, every scene set in Perry White's office for a block of episodes was recorded on the same day, and then they'd move on to the next location. The actors were often overwhelmed by the whirlwind pace; luckily Reeves had a photographic memory that helped him keep his dialogue straight, but Hamilton often needed his scripts right in front of him while they shot a scene, disguised as papers on Perry's desk.

Robert Maxwell had creative control over the season, and after working on the wholesome Superman radio show for so many years, he may have wanted to try something different in this new medium. The episodes were surprisingly dark for a show based on a children's comic book; following the science fiction pilot, the style shifted to a true crime aesthetic, complete with robberies, kidnappings, and gangsters. The program was violent, and even Superman crossed the line on occasion. In "The Stolen Costume," a felonious married couple learned that Clark was Superman and tried to blackmail him. Superman refused to make a deal, and instead flew the couple to a remote cabin at the top of a snowy mountain where they'd be forced to live out the rest of their days where no one would ever find them. Not wanting to stay there forever, the couple decided to climb down the icy mountain and quickly plummeted to their deaths, all because Superman wanted to protect his identity.

In the midst of this dark environment, Lois Lane more than held her own against the myriad gun-toting villains who crossed her path. Coates's Lois was kidnapped often, but never without a fight; she went down kicking and screaming every time, against goons twice her size. It's a testament to Coates's commitment to Lois's physicality that in one scene where Lois was fighting back against a gangster, Coates got in a little too close and was accidentally knocked out by an errant blow.

Lois was hardly a helpless damsel in distress, not content to just sit and wait for Superman to rescue her. When smugglers who were transporting criminals across the border into Canada captured her, she was locked in a cabin with another woman who was hysterical with grief because the smugglers had killed her husband. Lois calmed down the woman, got the full story about the smugglers, snuck out of a back window, evaded the guards, and reached a phone booth, where she was able to get a message to Clark at the *Daily Planet* offices.

That sort of bravery was common for Coates's version of Lois. Despite threats against her life, she testified in the trial of a mob boss, detailing a series of articles that she'd written exposing his racket. In another episode, a cave-in at a coal mine trapped an old man deep underground, and when Lois heard about the rescue plan she was unsatisfied with the slow timetable and immediately set out to rescue the man herself. When told to wait, she responded, "And do nothing? Not me."

Back at the *Daily Planet*, Lois had no time for Clark's opinions. While the two were collegial but competitive, duking it out to get big scoops, Reeves played Clark as a bit of a smug know-it-all, always ready to dole out advice even when it wasn't wanted. He often called Lois a "good girl" and cautioned her to stay away from dangerous stories, but she never listened. Lois brushed him off after one such warning by saying, "I'm a big girl now, Clark. Don't worry." If Lois wasn't going to listen to mobsters with guns when they told her to stay put, she certainly wasn't going to listen to Clark.

Coates said of her take on Lois, "I played her tough and direct," and television historians agree. Allan Asherman calls her Lois "one of the strongest women characters in early American TV," while Gary Grossman characterizes her as a "tough, independent woman." Compared to what her comic book counterpart was up to at the time, this depiction was a stark change of pace.

When the filming of the first season wrapped in 1951, *Adventures of Superman* had yet to be picked up, and the cast and crew went on to other jobs figuring that nothing would come of the show. A full year later, Kellogg's agreed to sponsor the show, just as they had with the Superman radio show, and the program began airing in syndication in September 1952. It swiftly gained such a following that Coates dyed her hair blonde so that she wouldn't be recognized on the street so often.

The cast was surprised to be called back to film a second season, but unfortunately Phyllis Coates had booked other jobs during the long break, and she turned down twice her original salary to return as Lois. Her decision was partly professional, because she'd committed to filming a new pilot, but Coates later revealed that there were other factors at play. There was a lot of drinking on set; Reeves in particular was always sipping on something, though he held his liquor well and his drinking rarely affected production. Others indulged as well, but Coates's family had a history of alcoholism and she decided it was prudent to take herself out of that environment.

Noel Neill, who'd played Lois in the Columbia serials, was quickly tapped to replace Coates. The producers were familiar with her work, so they skipped auditions; they simply called her up and offered her the part, which she accepted. Neill had a particular affinity for the role, because her father had been a newspaper editor in Minneapolis when she was a child, and Neill wrote articles for publications like *Women's Wear Daily* when she worked as a model. Her modeling led to Bing Crosby discovering her, and Neill performed as a singer and dancer before Paramount signed her to a film contract. She starred in several westerns and teen movies, but Lois Lane was her defining role.

Neill's take on Lois replaced Coates's cool focus with a warmer disposition. She was always quick to smile, and her occasional confrontations with Clark and Perry over stories rarely had much edge. Whereas Coates, and Joan Alexander before her, had played Lois with a slightly formal, neutral accent that was reminiscent of the upper-class mid-Atlantic accent common in films of the 1930s and 1940s, Neill kept her homespun midwestern accent. The overall effect was a gentler, homier Lois Lane; comics historian Tom De Haven writes that Neill "softened the role to the point of wide-eyed innocence."

This new approach to the character fit in well with the show's second season, because Neill wasn't the only new face at *Adventures of Superman*. The architect of the gritty first season, Robert Maxwell, was replaced by Superman's comic book editor, Whitney Ellsworth. He took the program in a lighter direction that was more in keeping with the comics, upping the comedy and making the villains less threatening. Some people weren't impressed, including the departed Coates, who later said that Ellsworth "turned it all to pudding." But the show became even more popular. At its height, the program was watched by 91 percent of households with children under twelve.

Neill's Lois was still an ambitious reporter, stealing Clark's tips and trying to get ahead of him on big stories, but the tone of her investigations had changed. They were presented more as harebrained schemes than legitimate journalism, and they often involved Lois teaming up with the young and dull-witted cub reporter Jimmy Olsen. The two well-intentioned goofballs hatched their schemes and set off to uncover big stories, only to end up captured nearly every time. They'd bypass the police to set up their own trap for criminals or sneak into a dangerous locale, only to have their reckless plans backfire on them. Tellingly, when Superman inevitably rescued them his first question was often "You all right, kids?"

And now, when Lois got captured, she rarely fought back with any enthusiasm. Instead, whenever a gun was drawn or a villain's trap was sprung, Jimmy threw some punches and tried to resist but Lois just responded with a resigned look that said she'd been in such situations before and knew the drill: get tied up and wait for Superman. Resignation was her go-to response to adversity. When a time machine sent the staff of the *Daily Planet* back to prehistoric times, Lois quickly gave up hope and declared, "Well, let's face it, we're cave people. That's the way it's gonna be."

Whenever difficulties arose while Lois covered a story, her first move was to contact Clark and get him to come sort it out. On one of the rare occasions when their plan actually came together, Lois and Jimmy captured a bad guy but left him tied up in order to go find Clark and figure out where to go from there. In the meantime, one of the bad guy's associates learned that he'd been compromised and took care of the problem, so Lois, Jimmy, and Clark returned to find a dead body. In another episode, Jimmy got arrested in a small town with an Old West feel, and instead of handling the situation herself, Lois called Clark to come deal with the tough local sheriff. Lois started a lot of big adventures, but she was rarely the one who finished them.

As the seasons went on, Lois's role lessened. Jimmy had become popular with the program's young audience, so he moved into the main sidekick role and got a lot of spotlight episodes. Perry White had a fair number of spotlight episodes as well. Lois's diminished role was reflected in the credits; whereas Coates and Reeves had shared top billing in the first season, the credits for the second season listed Reeves as the sole star, with Neill at the top of the list of the featured cast. By the third season, Neill had dropped down to second on the list, behind Jack Larson's Jimmy Olsen, where she stayed for the duration of the series.

The focus on male characters may have been a reflection of the predominantly male writing staff. Only 5 of the series' 104 episodes featured female writers, and two of those were cowritten with men. Doris Gilbert was credited on one first-season episode, while Peggy Chantler worked on four episodes over the rest of the series' run.

The show was overwhelmingly male on all levels behind the scenes; a cast and crew photo from the middle of the program's run showed forty-eight men and only five women.

Lois's sole spotlight episode in later years was season four's "The Wedding of Superman." The episode started in an unusual way, with Lois delivering an opening preamble straight to the camera: "I'm Lois Lane. I'm a reporter on the Metropolis *Daily Planet*. This is my own story. To me it's a pretty important story, but certain men don't always agree with me." This important story began with Lois bursting into Perry White's office, where he was meeting with Superman and Inspector Henderson about a current crime spree. Lois demanded help with the thousands of letters that were pouring into the office and, thinking they were about the crime problem, the men were keen to offer assistance. But when Lois revealed she had taken over the lovelorn column for the week and was overwhelmed with heartbreak-laden letters, the men just laughed at her and Lois left the office in tears.

There were so many letters that Lois took them home with her to keep reading, even though they depressed her and made her think, "Where was the man of my dreams?" The next day, she woke up to a surprise delivery of flowers from Superman and a note that promised a date when the crime spree was solved. Much cheered, Lois set out to get to the bottom of the crime spree, and did so in record time. By that afternoon, not only had Lois booked a date with Superman, but he then proposed to her and she gladly accepted.

Just as Lois and Superman were about to say their vows, Lois's alarm clock went off and she woke up. She'd fallen asleep reading the lovelorn letters, and dreamed the flowers and the proposal. When Lois realized that she wasn't going to marry Superman, she burst into tears. Jimmy stopped by to drop off some flowers that had come for her at the office, but Lois wouldn't even touch them and tearfully said, "G-Give them to someone else, take them to a hospital, anything. Don't give them to me." When she was asked why, she turned to camera and, holding back sobs as the melodramatic score crescendoed, answered, "I just couldn't stand to know who sent them."

And that's how the episode ended, with a heartbroken Lois snapped back to her loveless reality.

It was an odd episode, to say the least. Lois's romantic interest in Superman had never been much of a factor on the program before; on the rare occasions it did come up, it only seemed to be a casual crush at most. She never seemed concerned about her love life in general.* Yet when Lois finally got a spotlight episode, it immediately went to romance and heartbreak. The characterization stuck; later in the series, Superman pretended to marry a female police officer as part of a plan to catch a villain, and Lois couldn't even be happy that she got an exclusive front page story about it because she was so distraught that Superman had settled down with someone else.

But Neill's Lois wasn't all heartbreak and resignation. In one episode, after she and Jimmy were captured, she cleverly suggested using a chimney vent to send an SOS signal to Superman; in another she wrote an editorial encouraging women to get out the vote and defeat a crooked political candidate. Her occasional victories, combined with the fact that she was a working woman in the 1950s, made her a relatively progressive female character for the time. Nonetheless, she was very much a damsel in distress, who lacked the hard-nosed focus and strength that was the hallmark of Coates's tenure. The series ended in 1958 after six seasons and 104 episodes, though it's been rebroadcast countless times ever since.

---

* In the first season of the show, the producers went out of their way to avoid any hints at romance so as not to offend potential sponsors with hints of sexual goings-on. Later in the run, Reeves and Larson cashed in by appearing in ads for Kellogg's and its breakfast cereals, but Neill wasn't allowed to be involved in case someone got the wrong idea when they saw Lois having breakfast with Clark or Jimmy.

A Real-Life L.L.

From the very dawn of his comic book career, the initials L.L. have followed Superman. In his earliest appearances, Lois Lane was his love interest and Lex Luthor was his archnemesis. In the 1950s, comic book writers would play up this alliterative coincidence, adding Clark Kent's childhood sweetheart, Lana Lang, and his college girlfriend, mermaid Lori Lemaris. Families expanded similarly; Lois's sister was Lucy Lane, Lori's sister was Lenora Lemaris, Lex's sister was Lena Luthor, and when Superman's cousin Kara Zor-El arrived on Earth she chose the alias Linda Lee. There was no deeper meaning to the double initials, but young readers ate it up and regularly pointed out new appearances of double *L*s in the letter columns.

The actor behind TV's Superman, George Reeves, was surrounded by the letters L.L. in his real life as well. Both women who played Lois Lane, Phyllis Coates and Noel Neill, had double *L*s in their actual names, and they were more than just Reeves's costars. Reeves and his girlfriend, Toni Mannix, socialized with both women regularly, and the Loises found themselves in an awkward spot in 1958 when Reeves abruptly left Mannix for a younger woman with a familiar set of initials, Leonore Lemmon.*

---

* Though they were both good friends of Reeves, Coates and Neill weren't friends with each other. In fact, they never even met. It seems that sharing the part of Lois Lane created some professional jealousy between the two of them, and they simply avoided one another.

This new L.L. had a significant role in the history of Superman, but it was one parents would've been keen to keep their kids from reading about; it certainly didn't come up in any of the Super-books' letter columns. Soon after he began dating Lemmon, Reeves was found dead.

The death was quickly ruled a suicide, but questions abounded. Coates and Neill were key players in the narratives that emerged, and remain important elements of the many theories surrounding Reeves's death to this day.

Leonore Lemmon

Phyllis Coates met Toni Mannix during the first season of *Adventures of Superman*, and the glamorous socialite and former showgirl immediately launched into an interrogation of Coates to size her up. Coates later recalled, "She wanted to be sure I had no designs on George." The couple's relationship had an odd dynamic; Mannix was nearly eight years older than Reeves and often quite possessive, but they were happy together.* After Coates passed Mannix's initial shakedown, Mannix cheerily invited her to a spa for a steam bath and massage. The two women soon became good friends, and remained so long after Coates left the show.

By the time Noel Neill took over the role of Lois, Mannix often came by the set with lunch and usually a drink or several for Reeves. Neill soon got to know Mannix, and she also learned the couple's "open secret": Mannix was married. Her husband was Eddie Mannix, an executive at MGM, but both parties had lovers on the side and were comfortable with the arrangement. Reeves and Mannix went about like a regular couple, and even shared a home. It was an unusual situation, but Neill was unfazed by it. To her, they seemed like a normal, happy pair, and she thought that Mannix was "a very great gal."

---

* Considering that Reeves was raised by a domineering, overprotective single mother and Mannix was childless, the fact that Mannix called Reeves "the boy" and he called her "Ma" is perhaps a telling hint at their relationship's more complicated dynamics.

Mannix and Reeves dated for years, until Leonore Lemmon entered the picture in 1958. Lemmon was a New York socialite with a bad temper and a penchant for getting into trouble. She was named as a co-respondent in multiple divorce cases before she was even twenty years old, and neither of her own marriages lasted for long. A fixture on the nightclub scene, she was famously barred from the Stork Club in the early 1940s for punching out another girl, and disbarment from the El Morocco soon followed. She'd even once set a photographer on fire for leaving her out of a picture. She was beloved nonetheless; despite her antics, plenty of other clubs and parties were glad to host her. According to author Nancy Schoenberger, "if you wanted to have a good party, you invited Leonore Lemmon." She drank the other guests under the table, flirted shamelessly, and knew everyone, even gangsters; Lemmon was a regular lunch guest of Frank Costello.

In October 1958, George Reeves was in New York on business and visited the popular club Toots Shor's. Lemmon was there, and the two struck up a conversation and chatted until she had to leave to attend a dinner party. The party turned out to be dull, so Lemmon left with a roast squab and a bottle of wine and showed up at Reeves's room at the Gotham Hotel at two in the morning bearing her gifts. He was immediately smitten.

When Reeves returned to California, he broke things off with Mannix. While she initially took the news calmly, she became heartbroken and distraught soon after. Mannix called Coates on several occasions, begging her to try to "talk some sense into the boy," but Coates elected to stay out of it and let Reeves make his own decisions.

Coates's reluctance to get involved wasn't out of any love for Leonore Lemmon, though. Reeves's new flame moved in with him shortly after their first meeting, and the couple began to throw drunken bashes most nights at their home in Benedict Canyon. The parties were boisterous and loud, and Lemmon was a mean drunk. Before long, both Coates and Neill had fallen out of Reeves's social circle and left him to his new lifestyle with Lemmon's crowd. They still saw him occasionally and he'd happily claim, "She makes me feel like a boy again," but neither woman had much fondness for his new girlfriend.

Despite his friends' opinions, Reeves and Lemmon were soon engaged, and things were looking up for Reeves's career as well. He was planning to direct a science fiction film with Coates as the lead, and he was set to return with Neill for a seventh season of *Adventures of Superman*, in which he'd not only star but also direct. With so much going well in his life, the world was shocked when Reeves died of a gunshot wound early in the morning on June 16, 1959, at the age of forty-five. His death was officially ruled a suicide, but fans have been researching the mysterious circumstances surrounding his death ever since.*

Who Killed George Reeves?

The commonly accepted explanation for Reeves's death was that he was depressed about his career and killed himself. Being typecast as Superman limited his opportunities in Hollywood, and in his final days he'd been reduced to performing in wrestling shows to make money. After drinking too much one night, he put a gun to his head and shot himself in his bedroom while Lemmon entertained guests a floor below him.

In the immediate wake of Reeves's death, neither Coates nor Neill could accept this explanation. Reeves had never seemed depressed to them; he was always warm and kind, and quick to laugh and have fun. He also had a lot of new work ahead of him that he was excited about. When Coates last saw Reeves, shortly before his death, they discussed their upcoming film project; Coates later recalled, "He was very up about that, and he looked wonderful." Neill said of Reeves, "George was never depressed when I worked with him on the series, or when I saw him socially. 'Depression' and George didn't

---

* Some of these theories were presented in the 2006 film *Hollywoodland*, which received scorn from both Coates and Neill. Coates thought that the film did an awful job capturing Reeves's story and objected to the suggestion that Mannix had her fired from *Adventures of Superman* because she was flirtatious with Reeves, while Neill felt that the film's depiction of her friends "made them terrible people."

go together." She ran into Reeves at a wardrobe fitting for the new *Adventures of Superman* season just two days before he died, and she remembered him as happy and looking forward to getting back to work. The great shock and disbelief of Reeves's friends has been one of the key factors fueling decades of speculation that he didn't actually kill himself.

On top of this, the shoddy police investigation left many questions unanswered. Without establishing a solid timeline or questioning anyone, the police ruled the death a suicide after a cursory examination of the scene, despite several odd factors. First, Reeves's body lacked the usual markings of a self-inflicted gunshot, specifically powder burns from the shot. His body was also fairly bruised, and he was found on his bed at an angle that some believe to be inconsistent with the trajectory of the shot. Even more confounding, the spent shell casing from his pistol was found underneath his body. Reeves's pistol had no fingerprints on it and there were additional bullet holes in the floor.

Despite all of these irregularities, Reeves's body was embalmed before any further examinations could be done. His mother was so displeased with the police that she hired a private investigator to look into the matter, but his findings were inconclusive. Subsequent independent investigations have gleaned little from the police files; reports and photos went missing soon after they were filed.

For those who think that Reeves might have been murdered, Toni Mannix is a popular suspect. She became somewhat unhinged after their breakup. Not only did she hound Coates and others with pleas to talk to Reeves, but she also hired someone to telephone Reeves's home repeatedly for days on end. Things got so bad that Reeves filed a police report. Furthermore, in the weeks leading up to his death, Reeves's beloved dog went missing and he was in a car accident after his brake lines were cut; both of these events have been linked to Mannix, though no direct evidence exists.

Her behavior following Reeves's death was suspicious as well. On the morning Reeves died, Coates woke up to a call from a distraught and hysterical Mannix at four thirty in the morning, less than three hours after the fatal shot, telling her, "The boy is dead.

He's been murdered." Oddly, she called the death a murder despite it having been immediately labeled a suicide, and she knew several details about the crime scene. This was likely due to the fact that her husband's job at MGM was as a "fixer"; when an MGM actor was involved in any type of problematic or distasteful activity, Eddie Mannix ensured that it didn't become public knowledge and made people go away if necessary.* Because of this, he had an extensive intelligence network, and many connections with the police.

He also had an unsavory reputation, and some researchers have suggested that a heartbroken Mannix may have asked him to punish Reeves, or that he might have done so of his own volition. No proof for this has even been found, but at the very least Eddie Mannix may have had an influence on the quick and shoddy police investigation, just to keep his wife's name out of the press after her recent antics.

Neither Coates nor Neill has ever pointed a finger at Mannix in any way. When they speak of her, the focus is always on how much she loved Reeves and how dedicated she was to him. Mannix was devastated by Reeves's death, and remained a recluse until she passed away in 1983.

Leonore Lemmon is another popular suspect. Her account of the evening didn't match up with other versions of the story, and she didn't call the police until more than half an hour after Reeves died. Lemmon accusers see this as evidence that she made sure that everyone in the home had his or her story straight before the police were brought in. Despite the fact that everyone the police interviewed was quite drunk, they all adamantly pointed out that Reeves was depressed about his career and thus took his own life, to the point that it almost felt rehearsed.

Furthermore, while Lemmon and Reeves seemed like a happy couple, apparently cracks were beginning to form. Friends later said that Reeves was getting tired of the constant parties and Lemmon's quick temper, while Lemmon was unhappy in Los Angeles and missed

---

* One of Eddie Mannix's most infamous jobs involved ensuring that the death of Jean Harlow's husband Paul Bern in 1932 was ruled a suicide. It was most likely a murder, either by a crazed ex-wife or by Mannix's own people. Bern was gay, and the studio may have eliminated him lest his proclivities reflect poorly on Harlow, their marquee star.

her life in New York. Some have even suggested that Reeves called off their engagement. On the night before he died, Reeves and Lemmon dined at Chasen's, a popular Los Angeles restaurant, and reportedly had a heated argument during their meal, while both were drinking heavily. This has led some to suspect that the argument continued at home, culminating in a drunk and volatile Lemmon shooting Reeves in a fit of passion.

Coates and Neill were never fans of Lemmon. To this day, whenever Noel Neill is interviewed about Reeves's death, a look of disdain comes across her face as soon as Leonore Lemmon is mentioned. Neill certainly thought that Lemmon was bad for Reeves; when asked about the circumstances surrounding his death, she once succinctly declared, "He went with the wrong woman at the wrong time and things happened." Nonetheless, neither woman has leveled any accusations against Lemmon, but neither have they ever stated their acceptance that Reeves committed suicide. Neill's response to the matter is usually "I just don't know what happened," and she has said, "I don't know who killed George Reeves, but it wasn't George Reeves," while Coates has definitively stated that she still suspects foul play but has never elaborated on who she thinks was behind it.*

However, many of Reeves's other friends slowly came around to accepting that he killed himself. While Reeves seemed happy, his "bottom of the barrel" television gig was never what he really wanted; he certainly wasn't living the life he'd envisioned for himself when he booked *Gone with the Wind* as his first acting gig. Having to again don the "monkey suit," Reeves's term for his Superman costume, may have weighed heavily on his mind.

Suicide is not the exclusive domain of the glum and the moody. No one knew what was going on behind Reeves's cheery exterior, and he was self-medicating to a troubling degree. He drank often, starting early in the day, and appears to have spent most of the 1950s numbed by alcohol. On the night he died, his blood alcohol level was

---

* Coates has said that she doesn't think the Mannixes were involved, which may be a hint that she suspects Leonore Lemmon, one of the only other viable suspects in the case. She has never made such a claim directly, though.

0.27 percent, more than three times the legal limit, and he was also on painkillers due to injuries sustained in his recent car accident. With limited career options and a relationship on the rocks, it all might have been too much for Reeves that night.

Reeves's death deeply affected both of the women who played Lois Lane. Neill was devastated, and she soon quit acting for a career in public relations. Coates stayed in the business, but today she tends to avoid the world of superhero fandom and rarely does interviews. As for the real-life L.L., Leonore Lemmon returned to the house in Benedict Canyon only once after the night Reeves died, to collect several thousand dollars worth of traveler's checks, and she flew back to New York soon after. She didn't attend Reeves's funeral, nor did she ever return to Los Angeles. In an interview conducted in 1989, Lemmon remained insistent that Reeves had killed himself. She died soon after the interview, from illnesses caused by decades of alcohol abuse.

3

Sharing the Spotlight

*A*t the end of World War II, with superhero comics at peak popularity, Lois Lane was riding high. She appeared frequently in Superman comics, the radio show, and the animated shorts, and she had become an ace reporter for the *Daily Planet*, with the lovelorn column far behind her. But over the next few years, the superhero comic book industry declined. Wartime hits like Captain America and Captain Marvel petered out and ultimately disappeared, and by the early 1950s DC Comics' superhero line was down to just Superman, Wonder Woman, and Batman and Robin. Horror and crime comics took over the newsstands, though not for long.

The same panic over juvenile delinquency that led to the banning and burning of dirty, violent magazines like *Nights of Horror* targeted the comic book industry as well. The 1954 book *Seduction of the Innocent* by Dr. Fredric Wertham alleged that comic books exposed young people to harmful images of violence, crime, and abnormal sexuality, and comic book publishers were called in to testify before Senator Estes Kefauver's Senate subcommittee hearings on the matter. Facing the threat of external censorship, publishers banded together to create the Comics Code Authority, which imposed a strict set of rules regarding comic book content. Horror and crime comics, the most evil influences according to Dr. Wertham, were eliminated completely, and even a genre as benign as superheroes was put on notice.

DC Comics committed itself fully to the Comics Code Authority. The publisher filled the vacuum left by the removal of horror and crime comics with new superhero comics, revitalizing old properties and creating new ones. All were designed to be as wholesome and innocuous as possible. Thus began the Silver Age of comic books. The universally agreed-upon date of its dawn is October 1956, when DC's *Showcase* #4 brought back the Flash, the first of its old superheroes to be revived.

Mistaken Identity

By this time, both Lois Lane and the Super-books were in new hands. After the departure of Siegel and Shuster, *Action Comics* and *Superman* were written and drawn by a rotating cast of creators throughout the 1950s.* Writers like Alvin Schwartz, Bill Woolfolk, Edmond Hamilton, Jack Schiff, Jerry Coleman, and Batman cocreator Bill Finger took turns penning the stories, while artists like Al Plastino, Wayne Boring, and Win Mortimer brought them to life on the page. New creators soon joined the ranks, including some now-iconic names like writer Otto Binder and artists Curt Swan and Kurt Schaffenberger.

A team approach needed effective management, and by all accounts editor Mort Weisinger ruled the Super-books with an iron fist. Weisinger started in the pulps in the late 1930s, founding a literary agency to represent science fiction authors and later working as a publisher for Standard Magazines' adventure pulp fiction line. He moved to DC Comics in the early 1940s and, after a brief hiatus serving in the war, eventually took over the Superman titles. When Whitney Ellsworth left DC to take over the *Adventures of Superman* television show, Weisinger became the undisputed ruler of the Man of Steel's comic book domain.

---

* By the late 1950s, Siegel occasionally wrote stories for a few ancillary Super-books, including *Superboy*, *Adventure Comics*, and *Superman's Girl Friend Lois Lane*.

Weisinger was more than just an editor; he dictated plots and had a rigid formula for storytelling that was strictly enforced, often to the consternation of his creators. Most of the people who worked for Weisinger hated him, considering him arrogant, abrasive, and tyrannical. He regularly humiliated creators, stole ideas and passed them off as his own, and generally undervalued everyone's contributions to the books. Writer Bill Woolfolk recalled Weisinger telling him that "he considered every writer to be like a lemon that he squeezed until it was dry before throwing it away." Many of his employees burned out and went to work elsewhere. Weisinger also introduced the practice of basing stories on a pre-drawn cover; between hewing to the art and following Weisinger's plot decrees, his writers didn't have a lot of room to explore their own story ideas. There was a sizeable team of creators working on the Super-books, but the comics had one consistent voice for the next two decades: that of Mort Weisinger.

One of Weisinger's major innovations was elevating Superman from a valiant superhero to a genius mastermind. Now he wasn't just stronger than everyone, he was smarter than them too. This often came into play with his secret identity, which evolved from a running joke to an elaborate ruse that Superman expertly maintained, outfoxing suspicion at every turn. Lois was a pivotal player in this evolution, as she shifted from effusively praising the Man of Steel to constantly questioning his identity. She took on an adversarial role that allowed Superman to demonstrate his cleverness as he regularly rebuffed her attempts to prove that Clark Kent was Superman.

Lois suspecting such a link wasn't anything new. In a Siegel and Shuster story from *Superman* #17 in July 1942, she got suspicious when Clark turned in a story about Superman averting a subway train wreck immediately after it happened, even though Clark wasn't there when it occurred. She declared, "Come to think of it, it's mighty peculiar that Clark is never present when **Superman** goes into action. And on more than one occasion, I've noticed a faint resemblance between the features of Clark Kent and **Superman!**" Lois set up a trap to try to force Clark to turn into Superman in her presence, but he used his superspeed to stuff Clark's clothes with rags to make a dummy, rescued Lois as Superman, and then switched back into

Clark's clothes by the time she got to him. After her plan was foiled, the matter was dropped for several years. It was a one-off plotline, and not at all a regular feature of the comics.

However, by the early 1950s, Lois's suspicions about Clark and Superman had become her primary focus. Instead of tracking down new scoops for the *Daily Planet*, she spent most of her time trying to prove that the two men were one and the same. This fixation peaked in 1953, when Lois attempted to learn Superman's secret identity six times in the span of only seven issues and was thwarted with a run of convoluted explanations. When Lois noticed that the supposedly ill Clark had wet hair soon after she saw Superman fly out of the ocean, he put a small hole in the hot water bottle that sat atop his head to disprove her theory. When Clark was unfazed by a bullet to the chest and Lois pounced, he assembled a bulletproof vest at superspeed to explain his survival. When Clark disappeared from the Prankster's trick show just as Superman showed up, Lois thought she finally had him cold, but Superman used his super-ventriloquism to have Clark call out that he'd gotten caught in a pulley and had to go change his ripped trousers.

Despite her constant attempts and Clark's comically thin excuses, Lois could never pin down Superman's secret identity. In *Action Comics* #139, after yet another round of shenanigans in which she thought she'd figured out that Clark was Superman but was proved wrong by a dummy and a lengthy excuse, a downcast Lois remarked, "So that's the explanation! I-I . . . guess I'm not as smart as I thought . . ."

She *was* that smart, of course, but the Super-books were primarily interested in making Superman look good, not Lois. After several of these tight escapes, Superman would look out directly at the reader and wink, breaking the imaginary fourth wall to communicate his relief after getting out of another close call. How Lois felt about being constantly proved wrong was irrelevant to the creative teams and to most readers, as long as Superman came out of things on top. After all, he was the beloved star of the books, adored by legions of young readers and treasured by his creators as their chief moneymaker.

When he was asked why Superman didn't just tell Lois his secret and trust her to keep it, Mort Weisinger explained that Lois was untrustworthy. In reply to a letter in *Action Comics* #248, Weisinger wrote, "Since Lois is impulsive, impetuous and sometimes reckless, Superman feels that she may inadvertently reveal his secret." He echoed this statement two issues later, writing, "If he told her he was really Superman, our impulsive, careless, emotional Lois might unwittingly reveal the secret to outsiders." * The truth was probably much more practical: The secret identity ruse was a popular story line, as evidenced by Weisinger publishing some version of it over and over again. He needed some rationale to placate these curious readers so he could keep telling it. If that meant he had to change the way fans saw Lois, so be it. Characterizing her as reckless and untrustworthy would not only ensure their continued acceptance of these tales but also justify her adversarial role. These newly emphasized traits, and the stories of Superman's primacy they were designed to support, continued even as Lois embarked on a comic book series of her own.

Learning Her Lesson

A growing line of Super-books was a key part of DC's Silver Age expansion. Jimmy Olsen launched a spin-off series in 1954, Superman's long-lost Kryptonian cousin Supergirl was introduced in 1959, and Lois Lane debuted her own series in 1958. The executives at DC weren't at all sold on the idea of Lois Lane headlining her own book when Weisinger pitched it, but he was insistent. He made a point of talking to kids in his neighborhood to find out what they liked in their comic books, and he had a "gut feeling" that a Lois Lane series would do well. Weisinger had a lot of clout at DC, owing to

---

* Weisinger seemed to forget that in a story in *Superman* #78, Lois reluctantly teamed up with Lana Lang, Clark Kent's boyhood sweetheart, who was out to try and prove once and for all that Clark was Superman. When she thought they'd found undisputable evidence, Lana wanted to tell the world, while Lois was adamant that she keep it to herself lest it damage Superman's career. Lois even offered to stop dating Superman so Lana could have him if she promised to destroy the film proving his secret identity.

the continued success of the Superman line, so he was able to launch the series despite the executives' trepidation.

Titled *Superman's Girl Friend Lois Lane*, the book was a top-five comic throughout the 1960s, hitting an average circulation high of more than 550,000 copies per issue in 1965. Its sales were in the same league as *Superman*, and it regularly outsold successful titles like *Batman, Justice League of America, Superman's Pal Jimmy Olsen*, and even *Action Comics*.

On top of being a bestseller, *Superman's Girl Friend Lois Lane* was also an achievement for female representation in comics. When the book debuted in March 1958, only 18 percent of the comics released that month had a female lead. Furthermore, romance comics accounted for over 60 percent of the fifty different female-led series published over the course of 1958; almost every publisher in the 1950s had a romance line consisting of several titles. Another 30 percent of the female-led comics were humor series, with a mix of child and adult leads. The series with older characters usually had a romantic element, but humor was the primary focus.*

In the superhero genre, only Wonder Woman and Lois Lane headlined their own books.† While Wonder Woman had a rough time in the Silver Age, she was certainly august company when compared with *First Love Illustrated, Sweetheart Diary*, or *True Bride-to-Be Romances*. In terms of sales, *Superman's Girl Friend Lois Lane* outsold *Wonder Woman* for the next decade, often by nearly triple.

The series had a similar audience to the rest of the Superman line. While readership data for this era is spotty at best, it's possible to use a book's letter column to get a sense of the audience breakdown by tabulating the names of the many letter writers by gender. This information isn't exact; the letters that got published weren't

---

* Two series were westerns, Dell Comics' *Annie Oakley and Tagg* and *Queen of the West, Dale Evans*. Gun-toting female leads were rare indeed, and they weren't long for the world either. Both series were leftovers from when westerns were a hot comic book genre earlier in the decade, and they were canceled in early 1959.

† While several new female characters like Batwoman and Supergirl were introduced within existing male-led superhero titles in the early Silver Age, Lois was the only woman who launched her own solo book.

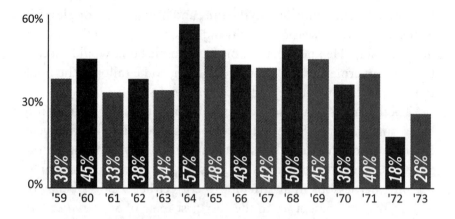

necessarily a perfect reflection of the book's readership. Nonetheless, this data offers a broad-strokes look at who was reading the book.

The chart above shows the percentage of female writers published in the letter column of *Superman's Girl Friend Lois Lane* over the course of its entire run. Assuming the letter column was indicative of the book's readership, it seems clear that more boys than girls read the series; girl writers outnumbered boys only once in fifteen years, despite the book having a female lead. Moreover, for the first five years of *Superman's Girl Friend Lois Lane*, girls accounted for an average of only 38 percent of letter writers.

This percentage is comparable to the numbers found in other, male-led Super-books over the same time period. *Action Comics'* letter column averaged 24 percent female writers, while *Superman's Pal Jimmy Olsen* averaged 27 percent. *Superman's Girl Friend Lois Lane*'s girl letter writers topped them both, but not by a considerable margin. This margin appears even less significant when compared to the numbers of DC's only other female-led superhero title. From 1959 to 1963, girls accounted for 66 percent of *Wonder Woman*'s letter writers, a striking majority.

Since the audience of *Superman's Girl Friend Lois Lane* was comparable in number and gender to those of the other Super-books, it seems likely that there was a great deal of overlap and that readers were there for the one thing that all of these books had in common: Superman. While Lois was ostensibly the main character of her series,

Superman's name came first in the title, and he was a major player in almost every story. Weisinger really did have his finger on the pulse of his readership. He knew that a Lois Lane comic book would succeed because Superman was a guaranteed seller, so he tailored the book to the expectations of the audience he already had.

These readers were used to a curious, impetuous Lois constantly being outsmarted by Superman, so Weisinger continued in that vein. But he introduced a new twist: instead of Lois trying to figure out Superman's identity, the focus in Lois's solo series was on Superman teaching her lessons in an attempt to correct her reckless behavior. In fact, the very first story in the very first issue of *Superman's Girl Friend Lois Lane* was about Superman teaching Lois proper reporting habits. When Lois disguised herself as a French movie star named Lois LaFlamme so that she could get into a reception and interview a foreign ambassador, Superman was not impressed. He thought, "I'll have to teach her a lesson for using such tactics to get a story!" The ambassador soon fell in love with the disguised Lois, then challenged Superman to a duel with pistols when he saw her talking to him. Superman agreed, but the ambassador's shot ricocheted off Superman's chest and straight back at him, killing him instantly. A weeping Lois cried out, "My impersonation of LaFlamme caused the count's death! Oh dear me—how stupid I was to try a hoax like that! I'll never do it again!" The real hoax was on Lois: the ambassador was actually Jimmy Olsen in disguise, and he was fine. The duel was an elaborate ruse set up by Superman.

Similar lessons followed at a relentless pace. When Clark and Lois were trapped in a prehistoric land, Superman secretly helped a caveman win Lois as his wife, despite her strong objections to the marriage, because Lois had called Clark a "timid, weak-muscled jellyfish" earlier in the story. When an experimental youth ray slowly de-aged Lois, Superman let her turn all the way back to a baby instead of immediately helping her, to teach her not to fool around with untested technology. When Lois joined the army and led her troops on a long march to try to whip them into shape, Superman spiraled through the air to create a tornado to carry Lois off so that she'd learn not to be so hard on her soldiers, including a newly enlisted Clark Kent. The lessons were often half condescension and half revenge.

As in the case of Ambassador Jimmy Olsen, the other men in Lois's life also took part in the lessons, always doing so to help out Superman. After Lois pretended to feel faint so that she could sneak into an experimental space rocket, Superman came up with a plan to make Lois think she'd been in space for fifty years. When he ran the idea by Perry White, the editor said, "What an idea! The staff will be delighted to co-operate, **Superman!**" He donned old-age makeup to help sell the ruse, as did Batman and Robin.

Jimmy Olsen even masterminded his own plan to teach Lois a lesson when he noticed how often she called on Superman. He thought, "Gosh, I wish I could save **Superman** from her romantic scheming!" and tried to marry her off to Clark to get her out of Superman's hair. The whole scheme went sideways, and ultimately left Lois heartbroken.

When Superman turned his corrective attention to another woman, Lois still got pulled in. Superman kept his younger cousin Supergirl hidden in an orphanage under an alias so that she could be his secret weapon. She was so lonely there that she tried to get Superman and Lois together in the hope that they'd adopt her. She worked hard to set up the perfect date for the duo, but it all ended terribly with Lois in tears. Superman, on the other hand, knew he was being set up the entire time; he played along with Supergirl's plans to teach her a lesson about interfering with his love life.

The Man of Steel was fully committed to the theory that the ends justified the means. Even when Superman tried to do something nice for Lois, he was fine with hurting her feelings in the process. In the second issue of *Superman's Girl Friend Lois Lane*, Lois was sad because Clark, Jimmy, and Perry all got to play themselves in a movie about Superman, but the director thought that Lois wasn't a good enough actor to play herself and made her the prop girl. Superman sabotaged Lois's work repeatedly, ruining the filming, and then told her that he never wanted to see her again, leaving her weeping. It was, yet again, all a ruse; Superman had filmed everything in order to show the director Lois's range of emotions and get her the part. When the footage showed her sobbing, a tone-deaf Superman proudly exclaimed, "Finally, her expression of grief when I broke up with her . . . utter **heartbreak!**"

Superman always thought that he was acting in Lois's best interests, and sometimes he was so pleased with the results that he didn't bother to tell Lois that she'd been the target of another one of his tricks. Superman's most elaborate and longest-running lesson occurred in *Superman's Girl Friend Lois Lane* #16 from April 1960.* Superman brought a box of artifacts he'd collected in space to the *Daily Planet* offices, and gave Lois strict instructions not to touch them. Ever curious, Lois touched them all, and as a result her eyes began to emit Kryptonite radiation. She tried to cover up her Kryptonite vision with a blindfold and dark glasses, but eventually she laid eyes on Superman and blasted him with the green rays, causing him great pain. Superman exploded at her, yelling, "You little idiot! I warned you to keep **hands off!** Now you're a menace to my life! Go far away! Get lost!!"

A despondent Lois immediately went home and packed her bags, and as she looked out her window across Metropolis one last time, her Kryptonite vision happened to catch Superman as he was flying by. He laid into Lois again, shouting, "Great Scott! Are **you** still here?? What do you want to do, destroy me? Get out of town before you **kill** me!" Wanting to stay as far away from Superman as possible so she wouldn't hurt him again, Lois moved all the way to Nome, Alaska, where she taught English in an Inuit community. She cried the entire time she was up North, until weeks later when Clark and Jimmy showed up in a helicopter with an antidote that Superman created for her Kryptonite vision. She drank it and was cured, and returned to Metropolis thinking, "I can hardly wait to personally thank the man who cured me, the dynamic man I love . . . **Superman!**"

---

* This was a rough issue for Lois all around. In an earlier story, Superman gave Lois a signal watch so that she could contact him whenever trouble arose, but when she used the watch for minor problems he lost his temper and screamed at her, calling her a "**PEST!!**" in front of a laughing crowd. Lois was so embarrassed and hurt that she refused to use the watch when gangsters kidnapped her later in the story, and she was almost killed as a result.

In a lengthy internal monologue that took up most of the last page of the story, Clark revealed to the reader what had actually happened. Superman brought the space artifacts to the *Daily Planet* because he knew that Lois would touch them and he "wanted to teach her that reckless curiosity is dangerous." He also knew that the artifacts would make Lois's eyes emit green rays, but Clark chuckled to himself, "The biggest laugh of all is that Lois **never** did have **Kryptonite vision!** Those green rays emerging from her eyes were completely **harmless!** I only pretended that they made me suffer whenever she looked at me!" He had the antidote all along, and sent it to her when he figured that she'd learned her lesson.

These asides to the reader were a common feature of Superman's lessons for Lois. Much like his secret identity escapes, many stories ended with Superman breaking the fourth wall and winking at the reader as he explained his clever machinations with a thought bubble. Only the reader was privy to his internal monologue; Lois remained in the dark. In one issue, as Lois wondered how she'd fouled up a possible wedding with Superman, Clark winked at the reader, pointed his thumb back at a flummoxed Lois, and thought, "I'm afraid Lois will always be confused!" In another, after a day of tricking Lois into thinking she had magic powers, Lois rhapsodized about her adventures while Clark thought, "Lois will never know **whose** magic was at work!"

Where Superman's earlier winks came from a sense of relief at evading detection, his winking in *Superman's Girl Friend Lois Lane* had a different connotation. Because Superman was the instigator of these lessons and not the target, the gesture was celebratory; he had successfully accomplished what he had set out to do, and informed the reader how he did so. Moreover, by winking at the reader and revealing the details that Lois didn't know, he was bringing the reader in on his plan. Instead of being on the side of Lois, the series' supposed protagonist, the readers became coconspirators with Superman in his many lessons.

The skewed dynamic created by Superman breaking the fourth wall was well demonstrated in *Superman's Girl Friend Lois Lane* #6. As Lois celebrated getting a front page scoop without Superman's help, Clark winked at the reader and "complimented" her acting job in getting the story. To Lois, Clark was paying her a sincere compliment, but the readers had access to Superman's thoughts throughout the story and knew that he was involved in her scoop, so the compliment with the wink read as sarcasm. Similarly, in a later issue, when Jimmy remarked that all of Lois's stories were about Superman, she recounted three scoops she got without Superman's assistance, but Clark reflected on how Superman was secretly involved with each one. At the story's end, Lois declared, "If you don't believe me, **Superman** will tell you I did it all without his help!" as Clark winked at the readers with whom he shared the real truth.*

Through these asides, the reader saw the world through Superman's eyes; the stories in the early years of *Superman's Girl Friend Lois Lane* were about Lois, but many were told from Superman's perspective. Lois's experiences were either trumped by Superman's actions or set into motion by him in the first place. A book that could have presented a rare female perspective instead had that female perspective constantly overridden.

Some of Superman's final-panel asides even hinted that this was more than accidental or careless sexism. In one issue, after Lois refused to listen to Superman, Clark scratched his head and thought, "Women! Even a **Superman** can't understand them!" In another, Superman thought, "But it'll have to remain Clark's secret and mine . . . because we **boys** have to stick together!" While "we boys" in this case can be read as a reference to Clark and Superman, it can also be taken as a reference to the series' majority male readership. After several issues of Superman explaining everything at the end of each story, and years of similar conceits in the other Super-books, readers were trained to be brought in as coconspirators in the final panel. Complaining about women and talking about boys sticking together sent a clear message about who those coconspirators really were.

---

* Jimmy's comments about Lois's scoops came about because Perry threw her a surprise party at the *Daily Planet* offices to celebrate the anniversary of her first day on the job. The story ended with Lois cleaning up all of the dishes from her own party.

3a

Corporal Punishment

After the Super-books spent almost a decade casting Lois Lane in an adversarial role, it wasn't surprising that their readers began to build up some resentment for the character. Superman was the star of the comics, and thus the character that fans most identified with, but he was also an authority figure, someone his young readers looked up to and respected. By trying to find out Superman's secret identity and constantly frustrating him with her impetuous shenanigans, Lois was antagonizing the audience's hero, and they were not pleased with her disrespect.

Some fans were even moved to voice their indignation to the publisher. The letter column of *Superman's Girl Friend Lois Lane* was uneventful most of the time. Fans suggested plotlines, pointed out errors, asked random questions about Lois and the comic, and tried to come up with ways that Superman could reveal his secret identity to Lois without that reckless Lois spilling the beans to the world. But a spirited subsection of "Letters to Lois" involved readers expressing their frustrations with the titular character.

In the book's very first letter column, in *Superman's Girl Friend Lois Lane* #5, Thomas Emory listed his many problems with Lois and concluded, "If you ask me, Lois is a big headache for the MAN OF STEEL. Why doesn't she simmer down?" Mort Weisinger responded, "If she did, Tommy, you probably wouldn't enjoy the magazine!" Stories are fueled by conflict, and Lois pestering

Superman was the primary plot for this era, even in her own comic book.

A few issues later, a reader asked why Lois kept trying to prove that Clark is Superman when he'd proved so many times that he wasn't, and Weisinger's reply underlined his commitment to keeping Lois in an adversarial role. In a moment of honesty, he wrote, "What would our writers do for plots if we eliminated this angle for keeps?" Lois had a specific role within the Superman universe, and launching her own series didn't change that. She was intentionally written as a pest who bothered Superman, but Weisinger's treatment of Lois created an audience that wasn't just hostile toward Lois; they wanted justice.

A Lesson She Won't Forget

Weisinger always made a point of talking to his young readers and tried to target his books at what they wanted to see, which created an escalating cycle of reprisals for Lois. Having Lois pester Superman about his identity turned the audience against her, engaging the readers but resulting in demands for Superman to straighten her out. More pestering followed, along with lessons to teach Lois the error of her ways, which only reinforced the image of Lois as a constant annoyance for Superman and amplified calls for retribution. Weisinger claimed that his comics were giving the kids what they wanted, but what they wanted was a direct result of how he presented the characters in the first place. He didn't get feedback so much as an echo chamber.

All of this outrage toward Lois culminated in a series of missives that ran in the letter column for more than a year. The first clarion call came in *Superman's Girl Friend Lois Lane* #21 in November 1960. The letter read:

> Dear Editor: Lois Lane is constantly, to put it bluntly, messing up things for SUPERMAN. I love Lois, but I think she needs to be taught a lesson she won't forget for a while. The next time Lois fouls up SUPERMAN's plans, why doesn't he bend her over his knee and give her a super-spanking? I'm aware that

Lois was paddled by a robot in "Three Nights in the Fortress of Solitude," but why doesn't SUPERMAN give her the real thing (not harming her, of course) but hard enough so she'll find it difficult to sit down for a time. I think that would give her time to think about mending her ways.

F. Twill, Falmouth, Mass.

The story F. Twill mentioned was from *Superman's Girl Friend* #14. Lois had arranged to stay in Superman's secret arctic hideout, the Fortress of Solitude, for three days, where she would prove she could survive in his dangerous home and thus convince Superman that they could live there together as husband and wife. After tumbling out of a Kryptonian antigravity bed, Lois crashed into a Superman robot that became accidentally activated. Its arm moved up and down seemingly mindlessly as it struck Lois on the rear end repeatedly. When Superman stopped by the next morning, he found Lois eating breakfast standing up as she thought, "I couldn't sit down all night, after what that robot did to me!"

It turned out that Superman was wise to Lois the whole time, and he'd arranged for various things to go wrong to teach her a lesson about trying to marry him. The robot wasn't activated by accident at all; Superman did so from afar, thinking, "My X-ray impulses are guiding the robot so that she gets a well-deserved spanking! I'll see that the **fortress** proves to be the **last** 'home' in the world she would want!" Ultimately, Lois left the Fortress of Solitude early and failed to prove her point to Superman.

Punishment by robotic proxy wasn't enough for F. Twill, but Weisinger wasn't thrilled with the idea of a more direct spanking, replying, "SUPERMAN is too much of a gentleman to strike a lady." He also pointed out an early *Superman's Girl Friend Lois Lane* story where Lois had turned into a baby and Superman had spanked her, perhaps in hopes that mentioning another example of corporal punishment might assuage the young readers who demanded harsh recompense. But they were undeterred.

Three issues later, another reader was demanding a spanking, and he brought along some friends to help his case:

Dear Editor: I represent the "North Shore Superman Fan Club."
By a vote of 27 boys and 22 girls against 2 girls we want to
protest against your answers to a request that Lois Lane get a
super-spanking in No. 21 of LOIS LANE comics. We like Lois,
but she is an awful pest at times. So please have SUPERMAN
teach her a much-needed lesson and give her a good hard spanking. Please do not refuse our request.

                                   Danny Rining, Winnetka, Ill.

A vote of forty-nine to two is an overwhelming majority, particularly from a group who were likely spanked themselves and knew
how unpleasant it could be. Spanking children was still fairly commonplace in the early 1960s, and many schools had corporal punishment. Whether or not to spank a child continues to be a topic of
debate even today, but the fact remains that a spanking, super or
otherwise, is a punishment for children.

That readers wanted Lois to receive such a punishment speaks
volumes about how they saw the character. Lois was a grown woman,
with a job and an apartment and all the accoutrements of adult life,
but she got none of the respect that children usually afforded to their
elders. They saw Superman as the adult, authority figure, while Lois
was on their level. Her behavior was not inherently negative; curiosity, persistence, and impetuousness could be portrayed any number
of ways. But the comics framed them as character flaws, a depiction
reinforced by the fact that Superman frequently attempted to correct
them. Superman treated her like a misbehaving child, so that's how
young readers saw her.

Weisinger tried to remind readers that Lois was a grown woman:
"Sorry, but SUPERMAN is a gentleman through and through, and
would never inflict bodily punishment on a lady, Lois in particular."
He also pointed out that Superman preferred to teach Lois lessons
with his ingenuity, but by this point he had warmed to the idea that
Lois's actions merited further retribution. He told readers that Superman would come up with a more fitting response and would "mete
out a punishment which fits her crime."

His response didn't dissuade readers in the slightest. In *Superman's Girl Friend Lois Lane* #26 in July 1961, another pro-spanking letter appeared:

> Dear Editor: A number of readers have requested that Lois Lane get a good spanking from SUPERMAN because of the way she is always trying to pry into his private life and guess the secret of his identity. I agree. She should be treated like any spoiled child who raids the cookie jar too often.
>
> Sharon Bush, Mt. Clemens, Mich.

Sharon stated outright what had been merely implied in the first two pro-spanking letters: Lois Lane acted like a child, and she should be punished as such. What's more, Weisinger didn't try to dissuade her. He abandoned his tack that Superman was a gentleman who would never hit a lady, replying instead, "If the Man of Steel ever spanked Lois, she'd go right through the time barrier from the force of the very first stroke." It was no longer a moral argument against spanking a grown woman but instead a physics problem. Superman was just too powerful to give Lois the spanking that she deserved.

Weisinger told Sharon to look for an upcoming story, "The Punishment of Lois Lane," so that she could "see how SUPERMAN teaches her a lesson she'll never forget!" That story never appeared, and pro-spanking letters kept pouring in. The next came in the following issue:

> Dear Editor: Everybody keeps asking for a story in which Lois gets a super-spanking. You keep saving Lois from a well-deserved thrashing by saying SUPERMAN is a gentleman and would never hit a lady. Well, I KNOW he's a gentleman. But what about a story in which SUPERMAN meets up with Red Kryptonite. The effect is that it makes him forget his manners and he gives Lois a super-spanking. Later, when he recovers, he apologizes to Lois and she forgives him. So that way Lois will

have received her punishment and no one can accuse SUPER-
MAN of not being a gentleman.

Betty Makohan, Pacoima, Calif.

In the Weisinger era, a wide array of Kryptonite variants made
their way into the Super-books. While the classic green Kryptonite
robbed Superman of his powers, red Kryptonite was a wild card.
It always had a peculiar effect on the Man of Steel that lasted for
twenty-four hours; some of these effects included Superman turning
into a half-man, half-ant creature, Superman growing long hair and
a lengthy beard, and Superman's face lighting up like a mood ring
that reflected his emotions. Superman forgetting his manners would
have been one of the less bizarre effects of red Kryptonite.

Betty's assumption that Lois would forgive Superman for assault-
ing her demonstrates the degree to which readers had internalized
Superman's treatment of Lois. These young fans read years of stories
in which Superman chastised Lois, and each story ended with Lois
loving Superman more and even appreciating his correction. That
Lois would forgive Superman for physical abuse was a given; he'd
already been emotionally abusing her for a decade. Young readers didn't question this skewed power dynamic because they'd been
inured to it.

Weisinger tacitly agreed that Lois deserved a super-spanking but
presented Betty with a publishing problem. He wrote, "But how could
we keep producing further Lois Lane stories when we'd be unable
to show her sitting down for at least two months?" His answer was
a halfhearted punt, perhaps indicative of a growing frustration with
these letters.

The final pro-spanking missive was printed in *Superman's Girl
Friend Lois Lane* #30 in January 1962. It put forth further work-
arounds to Weisinger's anti-spanking excuses:

Dear Editor: Although I am a great fan of Lois Lane's, I dis-
agree with you for not having SUPERMAN teach her a lesson
for her many impetuous tricks by giving her a spanking. You
often state that SUPERMAN is a gentleman and would not

hurt Lois. Well, my father is every inch a gentleman and he has spanked me several times for being far less mischievous than Lois is. Even if SUPERMAN were to use all his ingenuity to punish Lois, it can never be as effective as a good sound spanking. Her problem of sitting down after the punishment can be solved with the use of a soft pillow under her. Please do not refuse my request, for I know many readers like myself would like to see the Man of Steel turn Lois over on his knee and give her the good, old-fashioned spanking she deserves!

Larraine Lertura, Bronx, N. Y.

By this point, Weisinger was done listening to the spanking arguments. He replied, "Your request that Lois Lane receive corporal punishment comes a bit too late," and went full circle, telling Larraine to refer to Lois's robot spanking in "Three Nights in the Fortress of Solitude." That spanking would have to suffice. Weisinger didn't print any more pro-spanking letters after this issue.

Despite his dismissive responses at the end of this chain of letters, Weisinger's answers ultimately reinforced the idea that Lois deserved to be physically punished for her behavior. It is an odd institution indeed that inspires such a strong desire for vengeance in children and then loses an argument with said children about whether this vengeance is deserved. The writers and artists behind Lois's stories had turned her into such a persistent bother that the readers' reaction was beyond their ability to control, except by stopping the conversation entirely. The juvenile chorus of Weisinger's echo chamber had turned wholly against Lois.

4

Romantic Rivals

*A*nother frequent plotline in *Superman's Girl Friend Lois Lane*, second only to Superman's lessons, was Lois's infatuation with Superman. Ads for the series' debut listed her occupation, hair color, age, and weight, and closed with "**AMBITION:** To become **Mrs. Superman**. (But the MAN of STEEL has other plans!)" Marrying Superman was Lois's goal from the very start.*

After *Superman's Girl Friend Lois Lane* #1 began with an elaborate lesson from Superman, it's fitting that the issue's second story began with Lois thinking, "If I could only find a way to win **Superman's** love and become **Mrs. Superman!** . . . (sigh!)." She then heard the adage "The way to a man's heart is through his stomach," so she took a job at a local diner, convincing Perry White that it would make a good human interest story. Superman popped by on her first day to try her Super-Steak, but he inadvertently burned the meat to a crisp in the oven when he used an intense beam of his X-ray vision to fix a cracked subway rail from afar. Superman had to leave before Lois could broil another steak, but he came back the next day to

---

* Lois married Clark in the *Superman* daily newspaper strip in 1949, and the two remained wed for a couple of years without Lois ever realizing that Clark was Superman. In the end, the writers got bored with the story and one day Clark woke up to realize that his marriage to Lois was all a dream.

try her Super Pancakes. Unfortunately, news got out that Superman frequented the diner, and the restaurant was packed; by the time Lois got to Superman, she was all out of batter.

The next day, Lois tried a Super-Sundae, but just as Superman was about to dig into the dish, he saw that a huge icicle had broken off a high wire a few blocks away and was about to impale some pedestrians. Thinking quickly, Superman grabbed a plate and rubbed it furiously to create super-friction, then threw the red hot plate at the icicle, melting it instantly. But the super-friction also melted the sundae, and Superman had to again take off before Lois could prepare another one. On her last day, Lois served alphabet soup and Superman stopped by for a bowl. He had to leave mid-meal when a volcano erupted, and Lois thought she'd failed in her quest to win his heart with her cooking, but the noodles remaining in the bowl read, "I love you." A frazzled Lois wasn't sure if it was intentional or an accident, and that night she dreamt that Superman had left another message in the soup that read, "If only you could cook."

Failed plans and mixed messages from the Man of Steel were the typical fruits of Lois's romantic endeavors. The dictates of the genre meant that romantic limbo had to be maintained so as not to lose a rich story line, so Superman knew about her feelings for him but never gave her a straight answer. This left Lois constantly confused, but still wholly dedicated to pursuing Superman above all else.

Such romantic obsession was common for most female comic book characters in the Silver Age. The majority of female-led comics were romances, in which marriage was always the goal. The Comics Code Authority, firmly committed to bolstering dominant cultural norms in an attempt to remain as unobjectionable as possible, was pro-marriage as well. One of its rules stated, "The treatment of love-romance stories shall emphasize the value of the home and the sanctity of marriage." Even Wonder Woman, the fierce feminist heroine of the Golden Age, wished that she could give up crime fighting so she could settle down with her beau, Steve Trevor.

Silver Age superhero comics were products of a postatomic culture that embraced space exploration and scientific advancement, and Lois continued the science fiction trend. Her romantic adventures were laden with spacemen, time travel, and all manner of scientific experiments gone awry, but at the heart of them all was Lois's fixation on marriage and settling down to start a family. Lois's attempts to become a wife may have taken her through locales ranging from laboratories to deep space, but at the end of the day, as Mort Weisinger wrote in the *Superman's Girl Friend Lois Lane* letter column, "Superman believes that a wife's place is in the home."

Keeping Up Appearances

Lois had always been madly in love with Superman, dating back to her earliest appearances, and in *Superman* #58 in May 1949, she saw a psychologist about her obsession. His remedy was to try to transfer her affections to Clark, but ultimately Lois realized that what was most important to her was her job. She declared to Clark, "Newspaper reporting is my **first** love . . . **Superman** was my **second** . . . but **you're** only **third!**"

That had changed by the time *Superman's Girl Friend Lois Lane* debuted nearly a decade later. Although she still loved reporting, wedded bliss was now her primary goal. She was literally defined by her romantic relationship with Superman in the title of her own series, after all.

This transition from career woman to would-be wife necessitated some changes to the way Lois was presented. Lois took pride in her appearance in both eras, but there were different connotations. In the 1940s, Lois was a fashionista. She paid $150 for a designer dress in 1943, the equivalent of nearly $2,000 today, and she wore an impressive selection of dresses and skirt suits throughout the Golden Age.* However, hats were Lois's true sartorial obsession. She had a new hat in each story she appeared in; tall or short, brimmed or not, ornately curved or sharply angled, Lois had the perfect hat for every occasion. Lois was so into her hats that she had Superman move a mountain in *Action Comics* #159 to rescue a new hat that

---

* Lois later saw a knockoff of her expensive dress on sale for $7.50, and she ended up writing an exposé about the designer imitation racket.

had blown into a crevasse. In a later story, Superman saw through Lois's scheme to fake her own death when he noticed that the hat found at the explosion was three years old. He realized, "I knew Lois never wore **old** hats . . . so it **had** to be a trick!"

Lois's Golden Age fashion was reminiscent of the style of fictional female reporters like Torchy Blane and Ellen Garfield. Her outfits were aspirational; even when Lois was still a sob sister stuck at the lovelorn column, she dressed like an ace reporter, fully prepared to make the leap to the front page.

By the Silver Age, Lois's relationship to her appearance had become preventative: instead of enticing Superman with new outfits, she spent far more time avoiding Superman when her appearance was drastically altered. In *Superman's Girl Friend Lois Lane #5*, Lois was accidentally exposed to an experimental growth ray while researching the machine in a story titled "The Fattest Girl in Metropolis." By the next morning, Lois's weight had doubled, and she had to borrow some clothes from her overweight neighbor so she could go to work.* As Lois got dressed, she thought, "What if **Superman**, the man I love, saw me now? I must **avoid** him at all costs!" When her added weight bent the tires on a small car, she even let Superman assume she was someone else when he flew her and the car to a garage.

Similar situations ensued. When Lois was hypnotized into believing that her head had turned into that of a cat, she went to a welder and encapsulated her head in a lead box so that Superman couldn't use his X-ray vision to see through it. She then quit her job and moved away, to lessen the chance of Superman ever seeing her. In another issue, Lois was researching an electronic brain bank and accidentally downloaded the accumulated knowledge of several scientists and mathematicians into her own mind. Her increased brain size resulted in her having a bald, bulbous head, which she covered with a variety of hats and turbans lest Superman see it.†

---

* In an odd bit of emphasis, Lois's neighbor declared, "Of course you can borrow one of my dresses. I buy them at the **fat girl's shoppe!**"

† When her head returned to normal, Lois clutched a picture of Superman to her heart as she proclaimed, "Any girl would prefer her own pretty face to a having a super-brain . . . if she's **really smart!**"

Lois's concerns about her appearance were shared by the Super-books' editorial staff. When several fans wrote to suggest that Lois get a new haircut, Weisinger put together a contest to determine her new look in *Giant Lois Lane Annual* #1 in 1962.* He went all out, consulting with the editors of *Young Beauty & Hair Style* magazine to come up with six new styles that were then illustrated by Kurt Schaffenberger. Weisinger had held a similar contest a year earlier in *Action Comics*, allowing readers to choose a new hairstyle for Super-girl's alias, Linda Lee; the "campus cuddle-bun" won, and replaced her usual pigtails. Oddly enough, Superman and Jimmy Olsen were never subjected to a plebiscite about their appearance.

Lois's hairstyle contest attracted more than twenty-two thousand votes, and the ponytail did best among the new styles, outshining options like the bouffant, the pinwheel band, and the ruffle cut. But the ponytail was still nearly two thousand votes behind the winner, as readers decided that Lois should keep her original haircut. Apparently many voters were as anxious about Lois's look being altered as she was.

The numerous stories in which Lois hid unsightly physical altera-tions were meant to be silly and comical; an ad for "The Fattest Girl in Metropolis" called it "A TON of Laughs," while the brain bank story included a scene in which Lois had to stick her head in the sand like an ostrich. At the same time, the over-the-top lengths that Lois went to demonstrated her earnest commitment to landing Superman.

Or any man, for that matter. By the time *Superman's Girl Friend Lois Lane* launched, Lois was keen for marriage however she could get it. Throughout the 1950s, Lois had used other heroes to try to make Superman jealous. Lois kissed Cosmic Man, feigned interest in Mental Man, and even agreed to marry Futureman, but did so only to get a rise out of Superman. By the early 1960s, Lois had moved

---

* Weisinger wasn't the first editor to be concerned with Lois's appearance. In 1941, Whitney Ellsworth took issue with the way Joe Shuster shaded her body. He thought that his art made Lois look pregnant, and in a letter to Jerry Siegel he suggested that Shuster "arrange for her to have an abortion or the baby and get it over with so that her figure can return to something a little more like the tasty dish she is supposed to be. She is much too stocky and much, MUCH too unpleasantly sexy."

on from subpar superheroes to a more impressive class of men, and was willing to marry them since Superman refused to seal the deal.

Lois regularly traveled back in time, for myriad fantastical reasons, and almost wed heroic figures like Achilles, Robin Hood, and Leonardo da Vinci before she was transported back to the present.* In *Superman's Girl Friend Lois Lane* #18, a handsome alien named Astounding Man showed up out of nowhere in his flying saucer and declared, "Lois Lane of Earth! The time has come for us to meet! I love you! Please marry me!" She agreed to visit Roxnon, his home planet, and saw his massive shrine to her, which included a video library with footage of Lois at the beach and modeling in a fashion show. After Lois watched Astounding Man defeat a platoon of foes in gladiatorial combat, she agreed to marry her interstellar stalker. However, Lois had second thoughts when she found out that her fiancé was actually a robot controlled by an old, bald alien. She slyly evaded the marriage by commissioning a Lois Lane robot that was controlled by a "love-starved old lady," and returned to Earth. Lois remained single, but at least someone else got her long-awaited happy ending.

In the end, Lois always returned to pining for Superman, though she was not unaware that her antics in trying to nab him were over the top. In one story, after bleaching her hair blonde and manufacturing an alias to go undercover, Lois got amnesia and thought that she was her fake alter ego, reporter Sheila Dexter. Superman took her to his Fortress of Solitude to refresh her memory, and when she saw rooms dedicated to girls like Lois Lane, Lana Lang, and Lori Lemaris, she declared, "What a fickle heartbreaker this **Superman** is! Why, he almost has as many girls as a sultan has wives in a harem!" When Superman tried to jog her memory with a kiss, she slapped him across the face.

Back at the *Daily Planet*, Sheila reviewed old articles that featured Lois, and said, "The way she **always** chases after **Superman** is

---

* Anyone familiar with Greek mythology will know that it was probably for the best that Lois returned to the present before she could marry Achilles; that marriage would've been destined for an unhappy ending. Certain histories of da Vinci suggest that Lois may have experienced similar difficulties with him as well.

. . . pathetic! [. . .] That girl has no pride!" Clark and the gang kept trying to convince her that she was Lois, but Sheila held firm and insisted, "I'm sure glad I'm **not** that silly drip!" Sheila had all of Lois's faculties, just none of her memories, and as an outsider looking in she thought that Lois's behavior was ludicrous. Nonetheless, as soon as Lois's memory returned, all of Sheila's critiques were instantly forgotten.

Lois still occasionally tried to get help for her Superman obsession, though that only ended up further entrenching it. Her sister, Lucy, had her hypnotized into feeling nothing for Superman, but it didn't last. At the end of the story, Lois pulled her Superman photos out of the trash and berated her sister: "How dare you throw them out, Lucy? That's the man I love, and I'll never give up till I marry him!" In another story, Lois fainted when she saw another woman kiss Superman, and a doctor again suggested that she try to pursue a normal guy like Clark. When that plan didn't turn out well, Lois returned to the doctor's office, smashed his diploma over his head, and proclaimed, "I'm mad about **Superman**, and I'm going to **stay** mad about him! And if you think I'm crazy for loving him, **you** should get **your** brains examined!"

Because every story ended with a return to the status quo, Lois was perpetually frustrated. Superman and Lois couldn't get married, and Lois couldn't settle down with someone else; the romantic tensions were too useful as story fodder. Instead, DC Comics embraced the ridiculousness of the situation, and Lois's romantic hijinks got even broader with the appearance of a rival for Superman's affection.

Lana Lang, That Brazen Hussy

Superboy was the catalyst for the lawsuit that ended Jerry Siegel and Joe Shuster's relationship with DC Comics, but DC's decision to fight for the character ultimately paid off handsomely for the publisher. By the late 1940s, Superman's teenage adventures were appearing in *Adventure Comics* and *Superboy*, two of the few superhero series that survived into the 1950s. When he wasn't flying around in his cape and tights, young Clark Kent attended Smallville High alongside a curious redhead named Lana Lang. Introduced in *Superboy* #10 in October 1950, Lana was Clark's next-door neighbor and took on a Lois Lane–like role. She had romantic feelings for Superboy, was disinterested in Clark, and spent a lot of her time trying to find out Superboy's secret identity.

A teenage Lois actually met Lana and Superboy in *Adventure Comics* #261, when the two girls shared a bunk at Camp Hiawatha one summer. Lois was taken aback by Lana's zeal for finding Superboy's secret identity and surreptitiously jinxed her efforts,* but the girls were united in outrage when they realized that Superboy had invited both of them to the big dance. They embraced while Lana cried, "He . . . he trampled on our hearts without any feelings! . . . Sob! Just wait'll that **super two-timer** shows up again!" When Superboy stopped by later, Lois hit him with a tennis racket while Lana smashed a framed photo over his head.

Their unity was short-lived. Several months later, Lana visited a scientist's lab with her father and caught a glimpse of Superboy's future in a time machine. Superman was kissing Lois at the *Daily Planet* offices, and a furious Lana exclaimed, "So that's the hussy who will be **Superboy's** sweetheart when he grows up to be **Superman!**" Lana pieced together who her rival was and set out to visit teenage Lois to prevent her from becoming a reporter, in hopes that it would keep her from ever meeting Superman. Lana tried to sabotage Lois's composition so she wouldn't make the school newspaper, attempted to trick her into becoming a scientist, and even bribed a local artist to tweak Lois's sculpture so that she'd win a scholarship to an art school. It was all to no avail; the future remained the same.

A grown-up Lana made occasional appearances in *Action Comics* and *Superman* in the late 1950s, but *Superman's Girl Friend Lois Lane* became her primary vehicle. She first guest-starred in the seventh issue of the series, and appeared more often as the book went on. By *Superman's Girl Friend Lois Lane* #64, she'd even made it

---

* After foiling one of Lana's plans to find Superboy's identity, Lois thought to herself, "I'll keep stopping her if she tries again to betray **Superboy!** Hmff . . . I would never stoop that low myself!" and the narration read, "Oh, Lois! If you could only look into the future!"

into the letter column, the title of which was changed to "Letters to Lois and Lana." While the classic love triangle had been Superman, Lois, and Clark, now it was Superman, Lois, and Lana.

The camaraderie the girls had shared at Camp Hiawatha was long gone. Lana's first appearance was relatively innocuous; she pretended to be terrible to Lois as part of one of Superman's plans in which everyone acted horribly toward Lois in order to ultimately do something nice for her.* But Lana's second appearance came in the story about the youth ray that turned Lois into a baby; when Superman took her to Lana's house so that Lana could look after her, an infantile Lois pitched blocks at Superman and Lana's heads while they sat on the couch together.

By Lana's third appearance, in *Superman's Girl Friend Lois Lane* #11, the game was afoot. Lana wrote a novel, and Lois went out of her way to help her publicize the book, donning a leopard skin dress and pretending to be a jungle girl in the wilds of Africa, just like Lana's heroine. Superman was impressed, telling Lois, "You did this—for the girl you consider your rival? Lois, you're a good-hearted person!" Lois smiled and revealed her secret plan to the reader: "That's why I did it—to make **Superman** realize I have such good qualities that he'll learn to love me!"

In the following issue, Lois learned about a formula that would make her superstrong and invulnerable to harm. She was going to use it to convince Superman she'd be safe from his enemies and thus he could marry her, but when she mentioned the formula to Lana, she stole it and set out to do the same thing. Lois was irate but quickly came up with a plan. She tricked Lana into spending weeks using her new strength in charity drives to impress Superman. After ten superstrength appearances a day, pulling freight trains and holding teams of horses at bay, Lana suddenly locked herself away. When Superman and Lois found her, a newly buff Lana leapt at Lois and

---

* Superman had given Lois a ring that he later learned was made of a dangerous alien metal. He knew he would hurt Lois's feelings if he asked for it back, so instead he had Lana ruin all of Lois's romantic plans with Superman while he pretended to not notice Lana's interference. In the end, a fed-up Lois was so mad at Superman that she took off the ring and threw it away in disgust.

yelled, "That scheming hussy egged me on to do hundreds of things that require exercise! She knew I'd develop **huge, powerful muscles** so I'd become ugly-looking!"

Superman concocted an antidote that restored Lana's figure at the expense of her superstrength, and the issue even ended with Lois and Lana shaking hands as Lois said, "It's nice to remain friends!" She then quickly corrected herself, perfectly encapsulating their relationship in the process: "Or rather . . . friendly **rivals!** . . . Just shake hands and come out fighting!"

Another battle erupted when both women got superpowers. Instead of fighting crime and doing good they immediately agreed upon a contest to prove who would be the best wife for Superman. Lana declared, "We'll be perfect ladies while fighting to get our man," but their friendly facade quickly deteriorated. The contest ended with the two super-powered women brawling in midair and screaming: "**Superman** will marry **me!**" "No . . . **me!**"

More confrontations followed that ludicrous display, as did some nasty plans. In one issue, Lana used a Kryptonian weapon to send Lois to the Phantom Zone, a ghostly realm where she would be hidden from Superman forever. In another issue, Lois framed Lana for murder, going out of her way to do so in a state with the death penalty.* Their rivalry continued even when Lois and Lana were separated by centuries. When Lois journeyed to the past, there was often a redheaded woman there solely to vex her, who not coincidentally looked exactly like Lana. In one story, that woman actually *was* Lana; she had secretly traveled back to ancient Greece with Lois, pretended to be a local, and tried to convince Lois to marry Achilles and stay in Athens so that she could return to Metropolis and have Superman all to herself.

Superman was at the very core of their rivalry, but he refused to marry either woman. He wouldn't even pick a favorite; when asked

---

* Both women were under an evil influence at the time of their respective nefarious schemes, but given their relationship it seems unlikely that the evil influence had to push either woman very far. After Lois was freed, Lana promised to never send her to the Phantom Zone again and Lois replied, "Possibly because I may send you there **first!**—Ha-ha! I'm only joking!" but then Lois thought to herself, "I hope!"

who he preferred, he only answered in initials: "L.L." In *Superman's Girl Friend Lois Lane* #31, Lana finally had enough. She met a nice astronaut and decided to move on, and was soon engaged. When Lois saw how happy Lana was, she ruminated, "If I could stop carrying the torch for **Superman**, maybe I, too, could fall in love with somebody else, and have a home and children . . ." Lana set Lois up with a few of her fiancé's bachelor friends, but Lois couldn't forget about Superman. The night before Lana's wedding, both women showed up at Clark's apartment; Lois was a wreck because she couldn't forget Superman no matter how hard she tried, and Lana called off her wedding because she was still in love with Superman. Lana said that longing for Superman was "agony" and Lois agreed, but she declared, "I'd rather go on hoping! Maybe someday **Superman** will marry one of us!"

The women's mutual mania was intense, even by the romance-obsessed standards of the Silver Age. Over at Archie Comics, small-town teenagers Betty and Veronica were also romantic rivals with their own series. The title, *Archie's Girls Betty and Veronica*, was reminiscent of *Superman's Girl Friend Lois Lane*, but the similarities ended there. While Betty and Veronica fought over boys, it was never about the boy himself but rather about wanting to take what the other girl had. Veronica never won Archie so much as she beat Betty by taking Archie from her.

In this era, the wealthy and confident brunette Veronica Lodge often came out on top over the sweet and unlucky blonde Betty Cooper, but no matter the victor, Archie was hardly much of a prize. The awe and respect Superman received from Lois and Lana was nowhere to be seen for Archie. When Betty got some money and used it to take Archie wherever he wanted, after nights of boxing, a wrestling match, and a lecture on fishing, Betty was so bored that she gave Archie back to Veronica. In another story, Veronica paid a doctor to tell Archie he needed to go away for a few days and rest because she wanted to see another boy and Archie "keeps cramping my style."

Archie was merely a pawn in a game, and both girls were willing to sacrifice his well-being to keep him from the other. Betty disrupted Veronica's date with Archie by convincing the gullible and extremely jealous Big Moose that Veronica was his girl; when Big Moose found Archie with Veronica, the muscle-bound behemoth beat him soundly. Similarly, when Archie told Veronica that he had a date with Betty, Veronica launched a campaign to knock some sense into him. Before he left her house, he'd sat on her knitting needles and took a hard fall off the front stoop. Once his date began, a Lodge messenger ran by and knocked Archie into a garbage can, a Lodge truck splashed him with mud, and a bundle of Lodge newspapers collided with his head. A battered and bruised Archie concluded that the only sensible thing to do was invite Veronica along on their date.

Archie's Girls Betty and Veronica reflected the Silver Age's romantic fixation, but it was always in the context of the girls' competitive friendship. The teens' obsession with winning was hardly progressive, a symptom of a culture that fostered competition among women rather than cooperation, but at least their lives didn't revolve around a man. Lois and Lana, two grown women, were completely obsessed with Superman.*

So too were Lois and Lana's readers, and the characters' competition to win Superman led to fans taking sides in the letter column. There was a definite Team Lois and Team Lana dynamic, but it wasn't based on how the readers felt about each woman in and of herself. Instead, it centered on who the readers thought would make a better wife for Superman. Fitness for the Man of Steel was the sole measure of each woman's worth.

Weisinger's depiction of Lois as an impulsive pest resulted in many readers leaping at the chance to back a new love interest for Superman; every letter in support of Lana was little more than Lois-bashing. In *Superman's Girl Friend Lois Lane* #34, Stanley Chan's letter began:

---

* Betty and Veronica were also less anxious about their appearance than Lois and Lana. When Veronica attempted a teased hairdo in *Archie's Girls Betty and Veronica* #85, everyone hated it but Veronica refused to change it; her pride was more important than her vanity, and she'd rather look foolish and turn off the boys than admit she was wrong. Several issues later, Betty and Veronica learned that a 1920s vaudevillian style was all the rage in Paris, so they dressed accordingly at school the next day. Everyone laughed at them, including Archie, but by the end of the story, all of the other girls at school were dressed in the very same style.

Dear Editor: In my opinion, Lois Lane is nothing but a snoopy identity-seeker, a foolishly impetuous reporter who will almost stoop to any means just to get a story. It burns me up the way Lois practically uses SUPERMAN for 'her special flunky,' making him save her life every time she recklessly gets into a tough spot."

Stanley continued on in this manner for a while before concluding, "Lana is warm, charming, beautiful and sincere. Personally, I think Lana would make a better wife for Superman than Lois Lane." Joe Pedicino took a similar tack four issues later when he wrote, "Dear Editor: I think Lana Lang would make a much better wife for SUPERMAN than Lois Lane for the following reasons," and proceeded to list the many ways Lana was superior to Lois, including her looks and her less inquisitive nature.

In one story, Superman temporarily lost his superpowers, and one woman declared that she was no longer interested in him while the other pledged her undying love no matter the circumstances. The comic didn't reveal which woman expressed which sentiment, but DC's offices were inundated with hundreds of letters from kids who were sure they knew which woman had spurned Superman. The responses filled two letter columns, with fierce arguments on both sides.*

It was an odd debate, because Lois and Lana were in fact practically identical. Both were equally culpable when it came to bizarre antics, both were drawn in the same way apart from their hair, and Lana was even a journalist just like Lois. The differences were minuscule, yet the fan reaction was rabid.

Before long, Team Lana and Team Lois stopped focusing on the characters and turned their sniping toward real-world targets. In *Superman's Girl Friend Lois Lane* #43, the pro-Lois Terry Matalon began his letter by declaring, "Dear Editor: I'm thoroughly disgusted

---

* The printed letters were slightly more pro-Lana than pro-Lois. Readers mentioned Lois's penchant for falling in love with other strong men as their main evidence for why she'd spurn a depowered Superman.

with your partisan group of readers, the 'Lana Lang Lovers.'" A few issues later, the pro-Lana Tom Schweizer complained about an anti-Lana conspiracy when he wrote, "Dear Editor: I can prove you are anti-Lana Lang and strictly prejudiced in favour of Lois Lane!" Both sides were passionate in their hatred not only of the other character but also of the other character's supporters, and the writers, artists, and editors who were so obviously dead set against their preferred L.L. There was no satisfying these rabid factions; when the letter column changed its name to include Lana, Linda Fried wrote in: "But it reads 'To Lois and Lana,' not 'To Lana and Lois.' To me, that is just as good as saying, 'We hate Lana.'"

The big winner in this competition was Superman. Fans were so busy tearing down the female characters that they failed to notice what an inconsiderate heel Superman was for stringing both women along. The Man of Steel also overcame the combined might of Lois and Lana on the rare occasions when they set aside their differences and worked together.

When the duo threw a party for Superman in *Action Comics* #309, they also asked Clark to come as part of a secret plan to prove that he was Superman. They invited all of Superman's friends so no one could cover for him, and had electronic sensors to tell if Superman was using one of his robots as a double, yet Clark and Superman mingled throughout the party without setting the device off. The women were flummoxed, but they forgot that they were dealing with a nigh-omniscient superhero. Superman had overheard their plan and called in a favor owed to him by President Kennedy, and the president gladly disguised himself as Clark Kent to help Superman preserve his identity.* With the two most powerful men in the world working in concert against them, Lois and Lana never stood a chance.

---

* In an awkward turn of events, this comic came out a few weeks after President Kennedy was assassinated, and DC was powerless to stop its release because the book was printed and in the process of being shipped out by their distributors when the news broke. DC got a lot of irate letters but explained the situation a few issues later, and the company refused to print extra copies of the issue when it immediately became a collector's item, thinking that it was in bad taste to profit off the death of the president.

4a

Cry for Help

Lois weeping in sadness or shame was beyond commonplace in *Superman's Girl Friend Lois Lane*; it was practically a staple of the book. Each of the series' first ten issues featured at least one scene in which Lois was in tears, as did forty-one of the first fifty issues, almost always because of Superman. The tears were exquisitely rendered by Kurt Schaffenberger, the series' primary artist. His expressive style always communicated the emotion of a scene, capturing the agony of each tear that Lois shed.

Superman's lessons were a regular cause of Lois's tears. She wept at the end of her first lesson in the first story of *Superman's Girl Friend Lois Lane*, thinking that she'd caused the death of an ambassador, and cried at some point during most of the lessons that followed. When Lois had to leave Metropolis because of her Kryptonite vision, she wept throughout the entire journey there and continued weeping until Clark and Jimmy finally showed up with the antidote weeks later.

Her romantic travails often reduced her to tears as well, again starting from the very beginning of her series. In the second story of *Superman's Girl Friend Lois Lane* #1, Lois burst into tears when her alphabet soup failed to capture the heart of the Man of Steel, and she sobbed into her apron as he flew off. Reminders of her romantic situation also set her off; in a later issue, when Lois learned about someone else's happy marriage, her only response was to cry and wonder, "W-Will that glorious day ever c-come for **me**???"

Lois didn't even have to be confronted with romantic failure before dissolving into tears; just the anticipation of it was enough. Once she noticed her Kryptonite vision, before Superman was at all aware that she'd gained this affliction, she sobbed on her sister's shoulder, crying out, "**WHY?!!** Why did I ever defy **Superman** and surrender to that reckless impulse? Oh, what a terrible fool I am!" Similarly, when Lois believed she had the head of a cat, she thought, "I knew that though **Superman** would try not to show it, he'd be repelled by my face," and she wept as she imagined Superman moving on without her. Her fear of disappointing Superman kept her constantly distraught.

Imaginary Stories

Lois's tears continued even when Mort Weisinger gave her what she wanted most. While Superman could never settle down with Lois or Lana for good, Weisinger concocted a way to have his cake and eat it too by telling "imaginary stories." These what-if tales satisfied the readers' desire to see Superman settle down with a wife and children without permanently altering the status quo.

In the first imaginary story, from *Superman's Girl Friend Lois Lane* #19 in August 1960, Clark proposed to Lois. When she replied that she couldn't marry him because she was in love with Superman, he burst out of his suit and tie to reveal his Superman costume underneath. An overjoyed Lois immediately accepted his proposal, and soon they were wed and living in the suburbs.

But tears soon followed. Her neighbors were unimpressed with Clark and refused to invite the couple to local events. Lois burned to tell them Clark was actually Superman, but she held it in and instead sobbed when she returned home, telling Superman, "Those witches practically came right out and told me I married a creep!" Superman soothed her pain with a super-kiss,* but before long

---

* In the Silver Age, super-kisses were Superman's go-to tactic when a regular kiss just wouldn't do. If Lois was upset or angry, Superman would plant one on her to placate her and buoy her spirits.

Lois was crying again, sad that she couldn't tell her sister that she'd actually married Superman. Angry tears came next when an actress kissed Superman right in front of Lois; the actress didn't know that he was married and Superman couldn't tell her, but the Man of Steel still got quite an earful when he came home. The story ended with a caption that read, "After Lois simmers down . . ." as a distraught Lois told Superman, "I'm so unhappy! Won't people **ever** know we're married?"

This imaginary marriage continued in the following issue, and wedded bliss remained elusive for Lois. The couple decided to adopt Supergirl, who was living in a local orphanage as Linda Lee. The headmistress wasn't keen on sending Linda to a family without a stay-at-home mom, so Lois quit her job at the *Daily Planet* immediately. Superman and Supergirl took off on superhero adventures so often that Lois was home by herself most of the time, and without a job she was bored out of her mind. Her only companions were duplicate robots of Clark and Linda built by Superman so that the neighbors wouldn't be suspicious of their absence. She was fixing the Linda robot one day, pounding in a loose screw in her rear end with a hairbrush, when someone from the orphanage stopped by for a surprise inspection and thought that Lois was spanking Linda. Linda was taken back to the orphanage, and the story again ended with Lois in tears as she said to Superman, "I'm sorry our adoption of **Supergirl** had an unhappy ending, dear! Will I ever be able to make it up to you?"

Things didn't improve from there. In a new imaginary story a few issues later, Lois and Clark had young twins, but Lois was more concerned that Lana had taken her job at the *Daily Planet* and was using it to make time with Superman. Lois tried to get her job back, but Perry refused her because "a married woman's place is **in the home!**" Other papers said no because they had "a policy of never hiring married women!" So a frustrated Lois stayed home, and the story ended with Lois in tears.

Sick of the world not knowing she was married to Superman, Lois convinced him to share the news in a fourth imaginary story. Chaos ensued. Lois was shot at, then attacked by her own protective robots, and eventually space monsters destroyed their home. The story ended with Lois in tears.

Weisinger mixed it up a bit after that. In one what-if story, *Lana* married Superman; the story began with Lois in tears and ended with Lana in tears. In another, Lois married Lex Luthor, and the story ended with Lois in tears. They returned to the old formula in *Superman's Girl Friend Lois Lane* #51, with Lois marrying Superman, and this time the story didn't end with either woman in tears. However, this was because both women were dead. A side effect of a super-serum Lois took to protect herself from Superman's enemies ended up killing her, and when Superman later married Lana, she ended up sacrificing herself to save Superman from a gold Kryptonite meteor that would have stripped him of his powers.

The imaginary stories in *Superman's Girl Friend Lois Lane* put the blame for any marital strife squarely on Lois. Her vanity was why she was so unhappy with the world not knowing she was married to Superman, she was the one who fouled up Supergirl's adoption, and her jealousy of Lana was why she hated being at home with her twins. The problem was never with the institution of marriage itself, which the Comics Code Authority was sworn to uphold.

Nonetheless, the stories shattered the myth that marriage was complete joy for everyone involved. In nonimaginary stories, marriage was just a dream that was romanticized by both Lois and the readers who were so hungry to see her wed. In practice, marriage for Lois was terrible, and each successive development, from quitting her job to having kids, only made things worse for her. The aim of each story was to present another wacky adventure for Lois, but between the lines was a critique, however unintentional, of marriage as the ultimate panacea.

Tracking Her Tears

The gender dynamics at the core of *Superman's Girl Friend Lois Lane* can be uncomfortable for modern audiences, and it's easy to dismiss the series out of hand as a sad relic from a bygone era. However, hidden in the midst of Lois's tears was a subversive subtext.

Lois's crying showed her unhappiness, and these tears exposed the harsh aggravations of the limiting world of the 1950s.

Not that this subversion was intentional on the part of the writers or artists; the Superman team wasn't trying to challenge the status quo or make a statement about society's gender roles. In fact, they aimed to do the exact opposite. They crafted stories based on whatever zany cover ideas Weisinger came up with while trying to keep their content in compliance with the Comics Code Authority so that no one could possibly find their books objectionable. The comic book industry wasn't yet on firm ground, and no one wanted to upset the balance.

So *Superman's Girl Friend Lois Lane* entirely embodied the values of the time. It was written, illustrated, and edited by men who had no interest in questioning the societal norms of the day. They crafted simple stories that were subconsciously informed by their own experiences of the world as men in midcentury America. The series was the quintessential Silver Age comic, perfectly encapsulating the gender dynamics, campiness, and strict adherence to dominant values that characterized the Comics Code years.

Thus, *Superman's Girl Friend Lois Lane* inadvertently served as a mirror for readers, reflecting the world they lived in back at them through the hyperreality of superhero comics, all via the lens of one female character. The myth of this era was that being different was bad and that submitting to the rules and ideals of those in authority would lead one to happiness. But that certainly wasn't the case with Lois. She was never happier than when she came up with a new plan to get a story, and never more despondent than when she was shown the "error" of her ways. Lois was trapped in a very small box; whenever she was curious, or came up with a clever way to get a story, or behaved in a way other than how the men in her life wanted her to, patriarchy in blue tights showed up to correct her behavior. She cried because it was all she could do to show that her lot in life was deeply unsatisfying, and that she was stuck in a system she clearly hated.

This is a very modern reading of an old comic, a reclamation of an otherwise troubling era for Lois Lane, but some female readers at the time also questioned Lois's treatment in the series and expressed their frustration in the book's letter column. "Blissful Betty" asked Weisinger, "Don't you think it's time Lois Lane gave SUPERMAN the air and got herself a new boyfriend, one who appreciates her?" But Weisinger just told her to "see what happens in the next issue." Judith Stevens was particularly incensed and wrote, "I think it's awful the way you insult women, and particularly the way you heap abuse upon Lois. You're always saying she's snoopy, inquisitive, curious, a pest, and can't keep a secret. Well, men aren't angels, either!" Weisinger's only reply was that she'd taken things out of context.

Lynda Leigh got right to the point and demanded, "Dear Editor: Why do you persist in making Lois Lane look so stupid?" Lynda also suggested some ways that Lois could easily figure out that Clark was Superman, but Weisinger replied that she'd already tried them all and Superman had outwitted her. Karen Ruck wanted Weisinger to turn the tables on Superman, writing, "I am sick and tired of the way Superman is teaching Lois and Lana lessons all the time for being inquisitive or for being too reckless. How about a story in which Lois and Lana teach the Man of Steel a thing or two?" Weisinger pointed her to an older story called "Lois Lane's Revenge on Superman," in which Lois actually helped Superman and got absolutely no revenge on him whatsoever.

It's not a surprise that the girls who read *Superman's Girl Friend Lois Lane* in the 1950s and saw her despair with the patriarchal systems of the time were the same generation who grew up to protest these systems in the late 1960s as the women's liberation movement emerged. It wasn't just Lois, of course. It was every book, magazine, and TV show that reflected these values back at them, as well as their own lived experiences chafing under limiting expectations. Lois's travails were symptomatic of the broader plight of American women as depicted in the popular culture of the time, and in some small way they helped pave the way for future change.

5

Lois Lane's Brief Feminist Revolution

To say that Mort Weisinger was fired from the Super-books would be an overstatement, but the people in charge made it very clear that they wouldn't be sad to see him go. Through a series of mergers in the late 1960s, DC Comics became a subsidiary of Warner Communications, and the new owners began to rearrange the top brass at the publisher. Weisinger was gunning for the role of editor in chief, but despite his lengthy and profitable editing record, he eventually lost out to Carmine Infantino, an artist who had recently been promoted to DC's art director. Weisinger increasingly found himself on the losing side of big decisions, such as DC's hiring of superstar artist Jack Kirby away from Marvel Comics. Kirby took over one of Weisinger's titles, *Superman's Pal Jimmy Olsen*, after Weisinger had already lost *Superboy* in a previous editorial shake-up. Seeing the writing on the wall, Weisinger retired in 1970 at the age of fifty-five, ending a career at DC that had spanned nearly three decades.

Weisinger had been on the outs at DC in part because the past few years had seen some radical changes in the superhero business. Marvel moved to the forefront of the genre over the course of the 1960s with new characters like the Fantastic Four, Spider-Man, and the Hulk. The publisher's comics went over particularly well with older readers, teenage and up, because they eschewed the innocuous frivolity of DC's post–Comics Code offerings and instead presented flawed, human characters in actual American cities. Their comics were half superhero adventures and half real-life angst; while costumed superheroes were the stars of DC's comics, their mundane alter egos were at the core of Marvel's books. Peter Parker spent as much time managing his schooling, family issues, part-time jobs, and chaotic love life as he did web-slinging around New York City as Spider-Man, while the *Incredible Hulk* series was as concerned with Bruce Banner's anger issues and their repercussions in his life as it was with his other half busting up bad guys.

Marvel also appealed to a more sophisticated demographic by allowing its stories to address real-world issues. The discrimination faced by the mutant X-Men was a clear commentary on the civil rights movement, while *The Amazing Spider-Man* tackled a host of teen issues, including drug abuse. In 1966, *Esquire* magazine polled college students about their favorite revolutionary icons, and Spider-Man and the Hulk were at the top of the list with Che Guevara and Bob Dylan.

Marvel had completely changed the game, and DC had to play catch-up. Old-school editors like Mort Weisinger found themselves out of favor and were replaced, while new editors and creators tried bold new story lines, with mixed results. Wonder Woman gave up her superpowers for mod fashions and the life of a normal American woman, but feminists decried the change and her tiara and bullet-deflecting bracelets soon returned. *Green Lantern/Green Arrow* addressed racism and drug abuse head-on to much critical acclaim, but sales didn't follow. Even the addition of Jack Kirby and the launch of his interstellar Fourth World epic failed to pay off for DC; today, they are heralded as some of the best comics of all time, but DC canceled them after just three years due to low sales.

This period of experimentation, moving beyond the strict limitations of the Comics Code Authority, marked the beginning of what is known as the Bronze Age of comics. For *Superman's Girl Friend Lois Lane*, this meant a new series editor in E. Nelson Bridwell and some direct attempts at relevancy. As with most of the other series at DC, the changes were hit and miss and didn't translate into much success on the newsstands, but they helped redefine Lois for a new generation and moved her beyond her Silver Age woes.

Diversifying the Super-World

In many ways, the history of Lois Lane is the history of American women, but there are obvious limits to how broadly that statement applies. Specifically, Lois Lane is white, and while her experiences reflect certain cultural trends, they don't represent the experiences of all women. Lois was never moved to an internment camp, didn't lose her ancestral land, and could eat at any lunch counter. Her stories presented a white-focused version of the world, and not just because of her own racial background.

For thirty years, the Super-books had been startlingly white. Lois and Clark were always out and about Metropolis chasing stories, and frequently journeyed throughout the United States, but rarely did they ever come across people of color, even in passing. When they did, it was usually a harsh stereotype. Black characters were witch doctors in grass skirts, Middle Eastern characters were opulent sultans, and Indian characters were mystic seers. On the streets of Metropolis, it was wall-to-wall white people, and Lois and Clark sat out the vast majority of the civil rights movement.

E. Nelson Bridwell set out to change that. Before he took over *Superman's Girl Friend Lois Lane*, Bridwell was a freelance writer at several comics publishers and then an assistant editor on a few Super-books. His work at DC is best known for his focus on continuity; Bridwell used his encyclopedic knowledge of comics to unify what had been disparate comic book series into one interconnected universe.*

---

* Bridwell had another claim to fame from his time writing for *MAD Magazine*, where he coined a now-iconic joke. In a 1958 send-up of *The Lone Ranger*, the title character and his Native American companion, Tonto, were surrounded by a group of angry Native Americans, and the Lone Ranger declared, "Well, Tonto, ol' kimosavee, it looks like we're finished!" to which Tonto replied, "What do you mean . . . WE?"

Bridwell brought his focus on creating a cohesive setting to Lois Lane's world, expanding and diversifying the range of people Lois encountered in an attempt to better reflect reality. *Superman's Girl Friend Lois Lane* #110 from May 1971 is indicative of the types of stories he tried to tell, and the problems therein. The cover showed Lois, dressed in Native American clothing, protecting a baby from an angry mob as Superman called out, "Lois—you must give up that Indian papoose **now**—for **your own safety!**"

The first page inside the book was no better. The issue began in dramatic fashion, with a full page spread of Lois and a group of Native Americans armed with dynamite standing atop a dam. The leader declared, "Go back, Lois Lane! This is the **red man's** last charge to fight for his own land! . . . We do not want a white woman to fight **our** battle!" and Lois replied, "You're wrong, **Johnny Lone Eagle! Your** fight is **mine!** No matter what the cost, I'm staying—till the **end!**"

The writer of this cringe-worthy dialogue was Robert Kanigher, a fifty-five-year-old man who smoked a pipe and had been writing comics since the early 1940s; he was hardly hip to the times. Many of his Lois Lane stories engaged in racial stereotypes along with a big dose of the white savior cliché. These early attempts at racial understanding were hackneyed at best, though well intentioned.

After the explosive first page, the story went back in time to explain its dramatic beginning. Lois and Clark were in Santa Fe, New Mexico, where a group of Pueblo natives clashed with the white population over a new dam that would impede the Pueblos' sacred river and flood their land. Lois went with the Pueblos to get their side of the story, and the stereotypes were rampant: flashbacks to buffalo roaming the plains, dances around the fire. Lois even sent in her story via smoke signal. Even so, the story did present the Pueblos' point of view, from their warranted distrust of white people to their desire to fight for their land and their heritage. Furthermore, Lois sided with them wholly, and the white dam-builders became the story's villains. Ultimately, Superman solved the problem before it escalated to serious violence, moving the dam to a different river.

But Lois's troubles were just beginning. When a Pueblo woman died of heartbreak after learning her husband was missing in action in Vietnam, she made Lois swear to raise her baby for her. Lois and the baby, Little Moon, returned to Metropolis, where they were met with disgust and public outcry at a white woman raising a Native American baby. In the end, Little Moon's father returned to America after escaping a Vietcong prison, and Lois returned Little Moon to him. The issue concluded in a mixed fashion; it was overly congratulatory toward Lois, who was named Metropolis's Foster Mother of the Year, but in the last panel Lois addressed critics of interracial adoption directly: "It's **you** who are **blind! My heart** and **Little Moon's** are the **same color!**"

In other issues, Lois interacted with more people of color, including members of Metropolis's Latino community, but the most infamous issue of the entire series centered on Lois's attempts to reach out to the city's African American citizens. The story in *Superman's Girl Friend Lois Lane* #106 was called "I Am Curious (Black)!" and the title alone came with a host of problems. It was an obvious reference to the Swedish left-wing art film *I Am Curious (Yellow)*, which did quite well in America, not because of its many direct discussions of Swedish class and gender divisions but because it was one of the first movies screened in American theaters that featured full frontal nudity and sex. Massachusetts banned the film, deeming it pornographic, and subsequent legal challenges made it all the way to the Supreme Court, garnering further press for the film. This was an odd and rather inappropriate source for the title of a story in a comic book aimed at children, but it was also the least bizarre part of the issue.*

The cover of the issue showed Superman putting Lois in a "body mold" machine and flipping the switch. When Lois emerged from the machine, her skin was darker, her hair had turned into an Afro, and she declared, "It's **important** that I live the next **24 hours** as a **black woman!**" Lois was about to take blackface to a new level.

The story began with Lois at the *Daily Planet* offices, telling Clark that she was going to get "the inside **story** of **Metropolis' Little**

---

* There are no obvious connections between the film and the comic, except perhaps an attempt to challenge social norms. *I Am Curious (Yellow)* did feature a brief interview with Martin Luther King Jr., but those tenuous links are all there are.

Africa!" a story she was sure would net her a Pulitzer for "telling it like it is!" However, when Lois arrived in the city's African American district, no one would talk to her. People turned away and slammed doors in her face, and Lois stumbled onto an impromptu street meeting in which a young black man exhorted the crowd to stay away from Lois because "Never forget . . . **she's whitey!**" and "That's why she's our **enemy!**"

A frustrated Lois turned to Superman, who took her to the Fortress of Solitude to use his "transmoflux pack"–powered "plastimold" to change her into a black woman for a day. When Lois returned to Metropolis, clothed in a colorful dashiki and a bright pink head wrap, she was surprised to find out that black people were treated differently from white people. Her usual cabdriver drove right past her, and people stared at her on the subway. Once Lois arrived in Little Africa, she met a woman who invited her into her apartment for tea and saw that her host had to deal with trash fires, falling plaster, and rats. Nonetheless, the woman asked how she could help Lois, and a touched and tearful Lois thought, "She lives in misery . . . yet asks if she can help **me!**"

Later in the day, Lois met Dave Stevens, the young man who had harangued her during her first visit. The duo ran into an alley to stop a pair of gangsters, one white and one black, from selling drugs to kids, and Dave was shot. Superman rushed them both to a hospital; Dave was desperately in need of blood, and Lois was the same blood type and donated her blood to keep him alive. By the time Dave woke up, Lois's blackness had faded away.* Because of their vitriolic first encounter, Lois was nervous to visit Dave, and Superman wasn't particularly encouraging when he said, "If he **still** hates you . . . with your blood in his veins . . . there may **never** be peace in this world!" But she went in, and in a wordless series of panels, Dave went from shocked to beaming happily, and the story ended with a close-up shot of Lois and Dave shaking hands.

---

* Before her blackness disappeared, Lois said to Superman, "Suppose I couldn't change back? Would you **marry** me? Even if I'm black? An **outsider** in a **white man's world?**" While Superman made his usual excuses for not marrying Lois, she wasn't having any of it.

Again, everyone had the best of intentions. The story promoted understanding and acceptance between races as Lois learned about the black experience of 1970s America, but the execution was painfully flawed. Having Lois change the color of her skin and impersonate an African American carried with it the harmful legacy of blackface, however unintentionally. For over a century, white people had painted their faces black and performed offensive and degrading caricatures of black culture in minstrel shows.* The civil rights movement led to the end of most of these performances, but the legacy remained; a white person pretending to be black, no matter the circumstances, was and continues to be distasteful.

The moral of the story was also somewhat muddled. Lois didn't actually learn any sort of lesson; she found out about Little Africa and what life was like for the black citizens of Metropolis, but she never understood why they ignored her when she was white, nor did she see anything wrong with pretending to be black. The story's lesson wasn't about white people recognizing their prejudices and learning to accept black people, and Lois didn't acknowledge that she was part of a larger problem at all. In fact, when Dave called her "our enemy," Lois thought, "He's **wrong** about **me** . . . but **right** about so many others!" To Lois, she was already accepting of black people. They just weren't accepting of her.

Thus, the story's real lesson was learned by Dave Stevens, who realized that not all white people were the same. It was Dave who was presented as the prejudiced one, not the privileged, tone-deaf Lois, who thought she could swoop into Little Africa and pick up a Pulitzer on her way out. It's possible to read a subtle critique of Lois between the lines of the story, but it was never directly acknowledged. Instead, a black man learned that he should be nicer to white people.

The story suffers further when compared to DC Comics' most well-known Bronze Age discussion of race, *Green Lantern / Green Arrow* #76 from April 1970. The liberal Green Arrow took his intergalactic

---

* Oddly enough, a Kodak advertisement on the inside cover of *Action Comics* #103 in December 1946 showed a young man in blackface and a minstrel outfit, seemingly as part of a high school play.

police officer pal Green Lantern to visit a rundown tenement, where an elderly black man approached Green Lantern. In a now-famous speech, the man said, "I been readin' about you . . . how you work for the **blue skins** . . . and how on a planet someplace you helped out the **orange skins** . . . and you done considerable for the **purple skins!** Only there's **skins** you never bothered with—the **black** skins! I want to know . . . **how come?!** Answer me **that**, Mr. **Green Lantern!**" A chastised Green Lantern could only look down in shame and murmur, "I . . . can't . . ." The story was an indictment not just of Green Lantern but of the superhero genre as a whole, which spent the Silver Age telling stories about aliens and bizarre creatures while completely ignoring the civil rights movement. It was a stirring critique of the industry's willful ignorance aimed squarely at a white hero, who immediately saw the folly of his misplaced priorities. Meanwhile, Lois was showing Dave how great white people can be if you just give them a chance.

While the message of *Superman's Girl Friend Lois Lane* #106 wasn't particularly enlightening, a Super-book that explored black characters at all was a long-overdue change of pace. The story show-cased the everyday racism faced by African Americans, the justified anger that this treatment caused, and the dangerous conditions in black neighborhoods to which the rest of the city turned a blind eye. Moreover, it portrayed a variety of African American characters, from social reformers to homemakers to teachers, doctors, and nurses.

Even better, after their awkward first adventure, Dave Stevens became a regular presence in Lois's stories for years to come, along with several other African American characters. Lois visited Dave at his local newspaper, the *Black Beacon*, and participated in a peaceful protest against the construction of office buildings in Little Africa, siding with residents who thought that schools and low-income hous-ing would better serve the community.* She convinced Dave to take his crusade against inequality to a larger audience and got him a

---

* The protest had another awkward instance of Lois setting black people straight about their own prejudices. When a black woman saw Lois and declared, "We don't need whitey to fight **our** battles," Lois replied, "Funny—I thought I was just another human being! If **you** don't believe that we're all sisters under the skin—then **hate** has already **won** the **battle!**" The black woman then welcomed Lois warmly, clearly moved by the righteous passion of Little Africa's alabaster champion.

regular column in the *Daily Planet*, which led to him and his girl-friend, Tina Ames, becoming a fixture at Lois's office.

In the same issue, Dave and Tina showed Lois a display they'd created to teach children about black history. The double-page spread showcased African American heroes with art and a brief description. One side profiled well-known figures like George Washington Carver, Thurgood Marshall, and Harriet Tubman, while the other was dedicated to lesser known heroes like Benjamin O. Davis, the first African American general in the US army, and Daniel Hale Williams, who performed one of the world's first successful heart surgeries in the early 1890s. Altogether, the spread discussed eighteen different notable African Americans and their important contributions.

A few issues later, Lois met a young black woman named Julie Spence when she attacked a pair of thugs who had just mugged Lois. The two quickly hit it off and became roommates, and Julie often came along with Lois when she was investigating a story. Then, a four-page backup story in *Superman's Girl Friend Lois Lane* #132 introduced the intrepid African American reporter Melba Manton. She was a newscaster for Metropolis's WGBS-TV, and in her short debut she saved an innocent man and solved a murder. Melba appeared several more times as a colleague of Lois, and in one story the two even teamed up to rescue Wonder Woman.

This assortment of smart, powerful women was indicative of another change in Lois's life: her newfound feminist leanings. There were sporadic mentions of Lois's support for women's lib during the Bridwell era; when Dave declared that he didn't want women fighting his battles, Lois responded, "Don't get uptight about women refusing to sit on the sidelines! . . . **You** don't want to be down-graded because you're **black! Don't** down-grade **us** because we're **women!**" But by the time Julie Spence first appeared, another editorial shake-up had led to new management for *Superman's Girl Friend Lois Lane*, and a feminist revolution for Lois Lane would soon follow.

Hear Her Roar

The seeds of this revolt had been germinating as far back as the final years of Mort Weisinger's tenure. After decades of putting up with

Superman's shenanigans, romantically and professionally, by the late 1960s Lois began questioning her relationship with the Man of Steel. When Superman forgot her birthday, it was the straw that broke the camel's back; in a two-part story from early 1968, Lois broke up with him and moved to Coral City, where she fell in love with an astronaut. She ended up back with Superman in Metropolis by the story's end, but two issues apart was quite a development for a series in which romantic strife rarely lasted more than a couple of pages.

Lois also developed new interests and abilities that didn't involve Superman. She became a volunteer nurse, and her medical training was soon a regular component of the series. She learned how to fight as well, mastering Klurkor, the Kryptonian form of karate. These self-defense skills helped her protect herself in dangerous situations, and made her a more capable investigative reporter. Lois took on risky assignments, like joining a motorcycle gang to get the inside story on their hazardous lifestyle. While leaping into danger was nothing new for Lois, now she was better able to handle herself and didn't need to rely on Superman so often. The series was still full of romantic silliness; in one issue, Lois romanced Comet the Super-Horse after she was turned into a horse by a sorcerer, and in another she tried to fight Wonder Woman when she was overcome with jealous rage after seeing the Amazon princess with Superman. But Lois was slowly starting to break out of her Silver Age mold.

At the same time, women across America were breaking out of their limiting societal roles as well. Tired of being treated as second-class citizens, they banded together to stand up against patriarchy, and the women's liberation movement swept the nation. *Sisterhood* and *equality* were the watchwords as they fought to improve women's roles in society. In politics, groups like the National Organization for Women worked to pass legislation, such as the Equal Rights Amendment, while local women's groups met for consciousness raising, protests, and, in more radical circles, discussions about perhaps just getting rid of men altogether.

By the early 1970s, superhero comics boasted a slew of strong, liberated woman. In Marvel's Spider-Man comics, Mary Jane Watson was a feisty, independent redhead who had no interest in being tied down in a relationship with Peter Parker. In the Bat-books, Batgirl had a PhD by day and fought criminals by night without any help from her namesake, and soon she was running for Congress. In Jack Kirby's *Mister Miracle*, Big Barda was a powerful, statuesque warrior who defended her escape artist husband from the evil hordes of Apokolips.

In *Wonder Woman*, DC's attempts at relevancy were disastrous, but Gloria Steinem and *Ms.* magazine soon swooped in to rebrand the superhero as a feminist icon. E. Nelson Bridwell's replacement on *Superman's Girl Friend Lois Lane*, Dorothy Woolfolk, was looking to do the same with Lois Lane.

As Dorothy Roubicek, she'd worked at DC in the 1940s as an assistant editor on *Wonder Woman*; she was the first female editor at DC, and the only one for many years. She later worked at Atlas and EC Comics, and married *Superman* writer Bill Woolfolk and had two children. After many years away from comics, Dorothy Woolfolk returned to DC in early 1971 and took over their entire romance line. *Falling in Love*, *Girls' Love Stories*, *Girls' Romances*, *Heart Throbs*, *Secret Hearts*, *Young Love*, and *Young Romance* were all under her control, and the stories began to develop a pro–women's lib angle, featuring protagonists with more agency who refused to settle for boys who didn't treat them properly.

Woolfolk added *Superman's Girl Friend Lois Lane* to her repertoire a year later, and she brought her feminist sensibilities with her. Jeff Rovin, an assistant editor on some of Woolfolk's books, recalls, "She was very much a feminist, and wanted Lois Lane and the love comics to reflect that." Soon after Woolfolk took over the book, she printed a letter from a fan that addressed her as "Miss Woolfolk." Her response to the letter ended with "And please, call me 'Ms.'"*

In the issue before Woolfolk's tenure began, Lois's sister, Lucy, met an untimely demise. Lucy was a regular character in *Superman's Pal Jimmy Olsen* throughout the Silver Age, working as a

---

* Lois responded similarly in that very issue when a cabdriver called her "Lady." She replied, "Don't call me 'Lady'! Call me **Ms.**!"

flight attendant and frustrating Jimmy with her fickle approach to dating, but in the early 1970s her frivolous adventuring took a dark turn. She became a spy for the 100, a powerful crime syndicate, and was killed while trying to break free of their evil clutches. The issue was written by Cary Bates; the young man replaced the aging Robert Kanigher, becoming the series' primary writer under Dorothy Woolfolk.

According to Bates, Woolfolk "wanted to push any boundaries with Lois she could (at least as far as DC was willing to allow at the time)," and her first issue completely changed the status quo of the book. The story began with a dazed Lois arriving back in Metropolis after she'd been missing for four weeks; her sister's death had affected her deeply, and she'd been out of touch for nearly a month while dealing with her grief. It was then that Lois first met her African American friend Julie Spence. After Julie saved her from some muggers, the two had a cup of tea, and hearing about Julie's life and problems snapped Lois out of her fog. She thought, "No amount of **self-pity** will ever bring my sister Lucy back . . . It's time I started taking a **good look** at this muddled world around me . . . and tried to help people in trouble . . . like Julie!"

The next morning, Lois strode into the *Daily Planet* offices in an all-red outfit, complete with short shorts and thigh-high boots. When Perry White told her that there were assignments waiting for her, Lois replied, "Here's an assignment for **you**, Perry—find yourself **another girl!** As of now, I'm no longer on the *Planet* staff!" Lois was sick of being told what to do, so she quit the *Daily Planet* to go freelance and only write the stories she cared about. She declared, "There's far **too much** injustice all around us to be ignored any longer!" Perry and Jimmy were stunned, but Lois just turned around and walked out.

Later that day, Superman caught up with Lois, and she explained her new approach to life. She said, "I've made a **vow** to myself—now that my **sister's gone**, I'm going to live my life for her and me . . . to make up for her death by doing **twice** as much in my lifetime." Dedicating her life to helping others meant a big change in her relationship with Superman as well. She told him, "I'm no longer the girl you come back to between missions! I can't live in your **shadow**—I've got things to do!" and broke up with him. Superman was understanding, telling her that he would respect her wishes.

This respect only lasted until the next issue. Superman kept interfering with Lois's investigation of the 100, telling her that it was too dangerous, but she refused to listen to him. When she reiterated her desire to do twice as much with her life, Superman snapped, "You're only being twice as **stupid!**" Lois told Superman to leave and "take your **super-male ego** with you!" As the Man of Steel flew off in a huff, he turned back to retort, "It'll be my **super-pleasure!**"

While their sniping back and forth was childish, Lois's internal monologues demonstrated both the maturity of her actions and the feminist motivations behind them. This wasn't a Silver Age tiff in which Lois was upset about an asinine perceived slight, and no super-kiss would fix the problem. After Lois ended things with Superman, she began to cry as she walked away, thinking, "That was **torture** for me! I . . . I'll miss him so much!" This was a difficult decision for her because she still loved Superman, but she realized that he was holding her back. She didn't want to be a damsel in distress whom he protected anymore; she wanted to be her own, independent woman.

But Superman just didn't get it. After their fight, Lois was again conflicted about her decision, and thought, "Oh, **Superman!** I care about you so much. Why can't you see life as it **is** today?" While warning Lois about investigating the 100, he kept repeating that fighting them was a man's job. At one point, Lois snapped back, "What would you like me to do, **Superman?** Spend my life cooking in the kitchen? Living only for my master . . . **man?**"

Free of Superman's chauvinism, Lois surrounded herself with sisterhood. She moved in with Julie Spence and two other women, Kristin Cutler and Marsha Mallow. Lois's roommates were also her companions when she went out investigating stories; they trekked up a dangerous mountain together when Lois was looking into a mysterious guru, and they all traveled to France to enjoy the Parisian nightlife when Lois covered the Trans-Europa Olympics. The roommates supported one another and referred to each other as sisters. In one issue, Kristin was having a difficult time and Lois was quick to remind her, "We women have to stick together."

By this point there was also another feminist heroine in *Superman's Girl Friend Lois Lane*. Since 1970, Lois's stories had run fourteen pages, followed by eight pages of "Rose and the Thorn." Created by Robert Kanigher and Ross Andru, Rose Forrest was the daughter of a Metropolis police officer who was killed by the 100. The shock of her father's death gave her a split personality: she spent her days as the calm, peaceful Rose, and took to the streets at night to hunt the 100 as the violent, vengeful Thorn. Thorn was a powerful, independent superhero from her first appearance in *Superman's Girl Friend Lois Lane* #105, and Woolfolk amped up the feminist content when she took over the book. One story featured a women's lib protest, with signs that proclaimed WOMEN'S RIGHTS and EQUAL SALARIES FOR EQUAL WORK!! In another issue, Rose worked for the campaign of Sylvia Charlton, an African American congresswoman who was running for the Senate.

There were more women behind the scenes as well. While the story that killed off Lucy Lane was written by Cary Bates, it was plotted by Irene Vartanoff, who went on to be a colorist on several Marvel books, and Deborah Anderson joined the series as Woolfolk's assistant editor.*

During this era, Lois stepped into the hero role. In *Superman's Girl Friend Lois Lane* #123, she snuck onto a rocket to investigate some suspicious activity, which was nothing new for Lois, but when things inevitably went bad, she was able to take care of it herself. While in space, Lois found a ship that belonged to the 100 and was attacked by two of their goons while out on a space walk. In a zero-gravity fight scene she flipped one and kicked the other, causing one of her attackers to think, "**Uhh!** She fights like a wildcat!" The 100's agents played dirty and put knockout gas in her air supply, but even when captured aboard the enemy's ship, Lois was still a formidable foe. She got the 100 captain to reveal his plan to hold the world ransom, slyly shut off the artificial gravity, and then flung herself at

---

* The story in *Superman's Girl Friend Lois Lane* #129 was credited to Maxene Fabe, a writer who worked on several DC books in the early 1970s, but in a recent interview she stated that she didn't write it, nor was she familiar with the story at all.

her captor and swung him by his feet into the wall, knocking him unconscious. Having taken control of the ship, Lois signaled Superman to come clean up the rest of the 100's agents while she piloted the vessel.

Lois didn't need rescuing anymore; when Superman showed up, they worked together to defeat the bad guys. Despite their relationship issues and Superman's sexist warnings, they teamed up to dismantle the 100. While covering the Trans-Europa Olympics, Lois suspected that a valuable diamond was hidden in the Olympic torch, so she strapped on a jet pack and interrupted the rocket race to ensure that the 100 agent posing as a participant wouldn't escape with the torch. She swooped in, grabbed the torch, and led the 100 agent on a high-speed airborne chase through Paris, where Superman ultimately nabbed the agent near the top of the Eiffel Tower. Lois was in the business of saving lives as well; when a local children's TV show hypnotized the citizens of Metropolis, Lois tackled a mesmerized man who was about to be hit by a car, prompting Superman to comment, "Nice bit of life-saving, Lois!"

Before long, though, old romantic tropes began to creep back into the series. In one issue, Lois fell in love with a new man when she learned that he had superpowers, only to have it end badly, and in another Superman taught her a lesson about the dangers inherent in marrying him. Not only was Lois back pining for Superman again, she also returned to the *Daily Planet*, and her roommates disappeared from the series. This return to the status quo was due to the departure of Dorothy Woolfolk, who abruptly left *Superman's Girl Friend Lois Lane* after only seven issues.

By the autumn of 1972, Woolfolk was gone not only from that book but from the entire romance line as well. Stepping in to take over *Superman's Girl Friend Lois Lane* was Robert Kanigher. He'd been a regular writer on the series and had editorial experience on a variety of DC books. Woolfolk had also been set to helm the upcoming relaunch of *Wonder Woman*, which would restore the heroine's superpowers and Amazon heritage. In the spring of 1972, *Ms.* magazine's celebration of Wonder Woman in their debut issue mentioned Woolfolk by name, cheering her appointment as the book's "first woman editor" and praising her "plans to decrease violence in the plots and return our heroine to the feminism of her birth." But when the Amazon Wonder Woman returned in January 1973, Kanigher was editing that series too.

According to DC Comics' editor in chief, Carmine Infantino, he fired Woolfolk. He said of her time editing the romance line, "That was a bomb. She was awful. She was always late. She did a lot of talking but no work. After a point, I had to get rid of her." He specifically recalled, "I tried her, and every couple of months, no books, no books, no books." However, the facts don't support his claims. All of Woolfolk's romance books came out each month, on schedule, and she also successfully transitioned several titles from six or eight issues a year to monthly series when she took over the line.

In a letter to Gloria Steinem written soon after her dismissal from DC, Woolfolk jokingly described herself as "a woman in her fifties victimized by male chauvinism and making it on her own." Many of her peers had little respect for her; according to Alan Kupperberg, who worked with Woolfolk, the other editors "always snickered at her behind her back" and called her names like "Ding-a-ling," "Wolf-gang," "Dotty Dorothy," and much worse. Kupperberg specifically singled out Infantino as one of the men who thought poorly of her.

They also looked down on Woolfolk because she edited the romance line, the bottom of the barrel in the company's publishing hierarchy. Moreover, her approach to editing was unconventional. Instead of hiring the same old creators, Woolfolk actively sought out new, young writers and artists for her books who didn't mesh well with many of the older men writing, drawing, and editing most of DC's titles. Infantino and his crew were certainly more modern than former editor Mort Weisinger, but they were in no way young and hip. Woolfolk's supposed lateness was clearly a pretense for her firing, and the real reason she was let go probably had more to do with her take-charge, staunchly feminist attitude not sitting well with the old boys' club that ran DC.

Woolfolk's departure was entirely unceremonious. When a letter in *Superman's Girl Friend Lois Lane* complained about a recent story, new editor Robert Kanigher brusquely replied, "Both the writer of, and the editor who bought 'Serpent in Paradise' are no longer in Eden." Kanigher gave Woolfolk an even crueler sendoff in *Wonder Woman*: the first issue of the rebranded series began with a sniper killing "Dottie Cottonman, woman's magazine editor." This may have been meant as a joke, albeit a tasteless one, but it suggests some personal animosity.

DC swiftly excised all of Woolfolk's feminist additions. The book's writers and artists remained the same after her departure, but their stories reverted to the series' previous status quo, and any mention of women's lib disappeared. Assistant editor Deborah Anderson was gone from the book's masthead just a few months after Woolfolk left, and she departed the romance titles she worked on as well. It was almost as if Woolfolk had never been there.

Woolfolk remained committed to bringing feminism to young audiences. Just weeks after she was fired, she spoke to a university class on mass communication about the role of women's lib in comic books. By the late 1970s, Woolfolk had moved from editor to creator, launching a successful series of mystery novels with Scholastic that starred Donna Rockford, a young detective.

Superman's Girl Friend Lois Lane was canceled two years after Woolfolk left, along with several other Super-books, and the characters were rolled into a new series, *The Superman Family*. Lois's adventures continued there, but at a lower page count and, for the first few years, with more reprints of old material than new stories.

But despite DC's thorough efforts to excise all of Woolfolk's feminist influence on Lois Lane, feminism was not a passing fad, and Lois's affinity for women's lib occasionally popped up in *Superman* and *Action Comics*. After Billie Jean King defeated Bobby Riggs in their famed Battle of the Sexes tennis match, the staff of the *Daily Planet* had their own gender showdown at a bowling alley, with the men of the office composing the "male chauvinist" team against the ladies' "women's lib" opposition, led by Lois. The men won, thanks to Clark picking up a 7-10 split, but at least Lois's feminist leanings were still alive.

5a

The Antifeminist Rebuttal

The reactions to Lois Lane's brief foray into women's lib were passionate, to say the least. Inside DC Comics, this new direction clearly went over poorly with the people in charge, given how quickly everything was undone once Woolfolk was removed from *Superman's Girl Friend Lois Lane*. The response from readers was equally intense, but not quite so one-sided.

The book's letter column highlighted differing reviews of Woolfolk's tenure. Albert Tanner wrote, "I must agree with those readers who feel Lois has become too much oriented toward 'social causes,' 'minority groups' and so on. [. . .] This applies to *Lois*' Women's Lib convictions also. [. . .] I'm sure the great majority of both men and women readers would not like her as a militant Women's Lib extremist." Gerard Triano echoed these sentiments when he asked, "Why must every ish [*sic*] allude to Women's Lib? I can't tell you how boring the subject has become." On the other hand, Jackie Cates praised the book's new direction: "After a long absence, I recently picked up the Lois Lane issue #121. I was very pleasantly surprised at the new Lois Lane . . . it is nice to see them catching up with the times." Eileen Stewart enjoyed the book as well; she was pleased that it "made Lois into a human being" and that "her stories have depth."

In response to the massive outpouring of both praise and condemnation, DC Comics added a second letter column to *Superman's Girl Friend Lois Lane*, bringing in a new columnist to "deal specifically with the new image of Lois." The introduction to the first column stated, "If the subject is so important to you and so controversial, it warrants its own special page in this mag." DC encouraged both sides to share their opinions, but while the column was described as an open forum to discuss women's lib, the new columnist had a clear agenda.

Alexander the Great

The man behind the new letter column was described as a "mystery columnist," and he went by the pseudonym Alexander the Great. An illustrated headshot that accompanied each column showed a man with black hair parted on the side, sideburns, a somewhat long face, and a slightly open mouth. The man was wearing a black bandit's mask, as if to further conceal his identity.

Alexander the Great made his position clear with his very first response in *Superman's Girl Friend Lois Lane* #124 from July 1972. Alan Wilson wrote in to complain about the series' new direction; he was a longtime reader of the book but now felt that "it's too much—I can't take it anymore!" Alan went on to say, "I don't see how you expect your readers to dig Lois. All she does is continually make more and more a fool out of Superman. And *that* certainly doesn't earn *my* respect!" Alexander certainly didn't dig Lois either, replying:

> Let's face it! She's always been such an obnoxious dame—is it possible for anyone—superhuman or not—to deal with such a personality? I don't think so. Women should know their place. Lois never has known hers. Superman should take a stand and put Lois in the place she deserves to be put in.

Alexander doubled down on his low opinion of Lois in response to Kathy Koralik, a self-described "old-fashioned girl" who wrote, "That Lois Lane is one rotten lady! [. . .] She must have a screw loose. Or maybe you editors do. How can you expect us to like the new Lois when she acts the way she does to Superman?" Alexander concurred enthusiastically:

I agree with you that any gal who gives up what Lois gave up must have a screw loose. Women keep marching and protesting for more rights, but the ones who **have** the rights take them for granted. Lois apparently never appreciated what she had—a good job and a great guy. So he bosses her around. So what? Maybe she's gone into a second-childhood—trying to be hip and not care about the solid things in life. Maybe she's just a loser and doesn't want to face it.

The insults kept coming over the column's next two outings. Alexander continued to batter the feminist movement, declaring, "Forget Women's Lib, if we gave them the world, they'd ruin it!" and "If we start to change the power structure, you females will be the losers." He also believed that men should respond directly to the feminist movement, suggesting, "If I were you, I'd get together with Superman and form Men's Liberation . . . to free us from those nutty Women's Libbers." He didn't forget about Lois either; when B. J. Reed requested "some more tender moments between Superman and Lois," Alexander declared:

As far as I'm concerned, Lois *has* a tender spot . . . but it's between her ears! Any chick who would snub Superman has to be *nuts*! I guess Lois feels if she can't have Supe, she'll cut him down! Stupid, huh?

Alexander also antagonized the young people who wrote anything remotely positive about women's lib. To a young man who suggested, "About the subject of Women's Lib, Lois is carrying it too far and Superman not far enough," Alexander replied, "What's the matter, kid, have you fallen for Lois or something? There is only *one* way to do things, and that's the *man's* way!" To a young woman who enjoyed the book's new direction, Alexander replied, "You must be going bananas!"

Not that positive comments about feminism were common in Alexander's column. The boys whose letters he printed were nearly all on his side, and even most of the girls were against Lois and her new direction. One wrote, "I think Lois is making trouble for us gals," while another argued, "Should Lois scream about her rights as a woman while in the same breath criticizing Superman for wanting to behave like a man? A woman's normal instincts are to be feminine and coy. A man's are to flex his muscles."

The Super-books' brain trust ended the column after three issues, replacing it with "The Boneyard," a column dedicated to readers pointing out mistakes in the comics. Alexander the Great's departure was as unceremonious as Dorothy Woolfolk's: there was no announcement that it was over; they just stopped publishing it and it was never mentioned again.

The column was a bizarre contrast to the stories in *Superman's Girl Friend Lois Lane* at the time, and its brief tenure leaves far more questions than answers. Alexander's treatment of Woolfolk was particularly odd. When he turned the column over to Woolfolk so she could answer a question, Alexander griped, "And now I am forced to give some space to a mere woman." His final column put down Woolfolk in back-to-back responses: Alexander replied to an anti–women's lib letter with "Who knows what evil lurks in the heart of Editor Woolfolk? Women's freedom is one of them, of course, and, crusader that Ms. W. is, she'll use any medium to fight for her sense of justice." Then in response to a complaint about a story, he wrote, "As for the issue being a 'mess,' it was edited by a . . . woman! (BLECCH!)"

These shots at Woolfolk could mean that the column was a satirical, hyperbolic take on anti–women's libbers and Woolfolk was in on the joke, but they could also mean that someone higher up at DC was behind the column and was putting her down. Woolfolk's firing and the subsequent scrubbing of all of her changes suggests the latter, but the column's ludicrously over-the-top sexism suggests that it might not have been meant to be taken seriously.

Marc—on the Man's Side!

Over on DC's romance titles, Woolfolk's tenure on *Young Love* offers a very similar situation. A few months after Woolfolk took over the book and began to steer it in a more feminist direction, a new male columnist appeared. "Marc—on the Man's Side!" purported to offer the male view on the romantic troubles of the girls who regularly wrote in to the series. In the first column, a girl asked if she should intentionally let her boyfriend, Fred, win games because he was miffed when she beat him at mini-golf. Marc replied, "Let me first say that you are a fool! No girl should try to beat a boy at a game. What are you trying to do, banana-head? Lose Fred?" Another girl was upset that her boyfriend dumped her after she gained some weight, and Marc responded, "Control isn't your problem, TOTAL GROSSNESS IS!" He suggested going on a doctor-prescribed diet, and wished her, "Good luck, fatso!"

The column continued in this vein. Marc was soon down on women's lib as well; in *Young Love* #94, he called women's lib "a movement or group of ladies who try to get permission from men to do things which, once they got permission, they wouldn't want to do anyhow." He was even more over-the-top than Alexander, ending one column by declaring, "Some of you beasts don't deserve getting the benefit of my colossal brilliance." The reaction to Marc was so fervent that it led to a two-page response in *Young Love* #95 called "The Girls Strike Back!" in which readers expressed their outrage at Marc, as well as offering a few supportive letters. This was followed a few months later with another two-page special column that printed a variety of letters for and against women's lib. Comics scholar Jacque Nodell suggests, "They were using the character of Marc to work in the concepts of the Women's Movement and gauge reader interest." Marc's abrasive responses may have been a way to fire up readers of *Young Love* to try to get them talking about women's lib.

Nodell also calls Marc a character, which is certainly the case. There was no real Marc—or Alexander, for that matter. The columns were assigned to assistant editors or perhaps even farmed out to freelancers, and they may not have had the same writer on a month-to-month basis. The art of Alexander probably looked nothing like the person(s) who wrote the column, and the photograph that accompanied each installment of "Marc—on the Man's Side!" was purportedly a picture of a letterer who worked in DC's offices.

Alexander didn't last long enough to inspire a pro–women's lib response in his column. Thus his rants stand as an odd relic that showcases anti–women's lib rhetoric from both Alexander and his readers. "Marc—on the Man's Side!" ran for much longer, but if Woolfolk was trying to spark a positive discussion of women's lib, the net result was poor. While Marc inspired a lot of anger in readers, it often took the form of name-calling rather than substantive discourse. In the special column with letters for and against women's lib, the against letters made a much stronger case for their viewpoint. The anti–women's libbers presented a firm advocacy of traditional gender roles and the importance of wives and mothers. Meanwhile, one of the pro–women's lib letters read, "I like the way women stand up for their rights. I think, however, that it is stupid the way they burn their underwear." The one consistent voice throughout the column was Marc decrying women and feminism.

There are indications that Woolfolk may have realized that the Marc experiment had taken a wrong turn. The last issue of *Young Love* before she was fired included a mail-in ballot for readers to vote on whether Marc should be allowed to continue his column given his harsh views on women's lib. When the results were announced eight months later, Woolfolk was long gone, and Marc remained a fixture of the series for another three years.

6

As the Daily Planet Turns

*W*hile Lois Lane experimented with women's lib in the early 1970s, big changes were afoot at the *Daily Planet*. The Galaxy Broadcasting System, a multimedia conglomerate run by the ruthless mogul Morgan Edge, bought the newspaper. Lois stayed at the *Daily Planet*, apart from her brief resignation during Dorothy Woolfolk's run, but Clark Kent moved to the television division and became an anchor for WGBS-TV's nightly news program. The new job came with a new attitude; the bumbling oaf of decades past was replaced with a more confident, hipper Clark. He traded his fusty blue suit and fedora for modern, stylish fashions, and was even profiled in *Gentlemen's Quarterly*.

These changes were part of DC Comics' larger attempts to become a more relevant publisher. *Action Comics* and *Superman* had sold well throughout the 1960s, but overall DC was steadily losing ground to Marvel Comics. The Super-books were split up across a variety of editors after Mort Weisinger left, but the main man at the helm was Julius Schwartz. Schwartz had been an editor at DC since the 1940s, but had always been forward thinking. He engineered the revival of DC's superheroes at the dawn of the Silver Age, and he ran the Bat-books during their wildly successful run in the 1960s, transitioning the property from campy hijinks to the tales of the Dark Knight.

One of Schwartz's most lasting contributions to the Bronze Age was *serialization*, a process of storytelling by which each issue built on what occurred in the previous installment. Until the 1970s, issues of *Action Comics* and *Superman* were entirely self-contained. No matter how momentous the adventure, each story ended with a return to the status quo, and understanding the next issue was in no way dependent on having read the previous one. As a result, nothing significant ever changed, and relationships didn't really develop. With the move to serialization, each issue became a crucial chapter in a larger story, part of a richer world with a deeper history.

Marvel's superhero comics had been serialized from the beginning, which is probably why DC embraced this method of storytelling. It also made good financial sense, because now readers couldn't miss an issue. If they did, they'd be lost, so they had to buy all of them. This fundamental shift in story structure changed the tone of the Super-books dramatically, and had a significant impact on the depiction of Lois Lane.

A Superpowered Soap Opera

With the cancellation of *Superman's Girl Friend Lois Lane* in 1974, *Action Comics* and *Superman* became Lois's primary vehicles. Lois appeared every other month in a short feature in *The Superman Family*, but *Action* and *Superman* were full-length, monthly series. However, with the new focus on serialization, Lois rarely took center stage. The primary story line always featured Superman, engaged in battles of wits and/or fists with dastardly villains over multi-issue arcs. With the main plot focused on superhero adventuring, it was up to the subplots to carry the emotional side of the book. Thus, Lois, Clark, and the rest of the Galaxy Broadcasting System populated story arcs that focused primarily on interpersonal conflict. Basically, the goings-on in the *Daily Planet* building became a soap opera.

In the old days, things were simple at the *Daily Planet*. Lois and Clark showed up for work, got an assignment, and filed the story by the end of the issue. There were occasional arguments and drama, but everything was resolved by the last page and reset to zero when the next issue began. With serialization, every interaction was now far more complex. Resentment from past disagreements lingered. Previous flirtations colored conversations and could spark jealousy or scorn.

Lois was quickly slotted into a romantic role. There wasn't a lot of space for newspaper journalism; Superman took care of the series' action, while Clark's television job handled the majority of news-related story points. All that was left for Lois was an increasingly complicated string of romantic entanglements.

While such a role was nothing new for Lois, this time it came with a twist. In *Superman* #297 from March 1976, Lois and Clark were out at a business lunch when a boorish coworker, sports reporter Steve Lombard, slapped Clark on the back, causing him to spill his drink down his suit. Clark was already frustrated in his Superman persona due to an ongoing plot thread that had him intermittently losing his powers, so when Steve continued to poke fun at him, he lost his cool. Clark flipped the table on top of Steve, unloading the table's contents on his surprised colleague.

Lois was intrigued. She showed up at Clark's door that evening with a bag full of groceries, and the two shared homemade beef bourguignon by candlelight. After dinner, the pair retired to the couch, where they ended up kissing. The following morning, Lois was ebullient; she waltzed into the *Daily Planet* offices singing "I Feel Pretty" from *West Side Story*.*

In the past, Lois's interest in Clark had always been transitory, but this time it stuck. The next issue began with Lois and Clark walking down the street hand in hand, with a bracelet made of hearts on Lois's wrist. Soon they were officially a couple, openly kissing at the *Daily Planet* while Lois threw around words like "relationship." Even when Clark's Superman frustrations got sorted and he returned to his mild-mannered self, they stayed together.

---

* Or rather, a non-copyright-violating version thereof. Lois's exact lyrics were "I feel pretty, I feel lovely" followed later by a "la la la la la la la la."

Drama of course followed, though initially the couple weathered the storms. Lois was furious when she saw Clark talking to a self-professed celebrity groupie, but in the next issue she surprised Clark in his apartment with another beef bourguignon to apologize for her jealousy. She explained, "I thought you were **two-timing** me, you old **devil!**" Then she decided, "I'm a mature woman, a **liberated** lady! If I **want** a man, I should go **get** him! So here I **am!**" *

Clark's Superman duties also complicated the relationship. Early in their courtship, Lois and Clark were heading to dinner when Clark heard news of a strange creature attacking a lab. To get out of the date without raising Lois's suspicions, he slyly used his heat vision to blow out the wheel of a taxi, which caused it to skid into a fire hydrant and spray Lois with water. With her dress and makeup ruined, the date was off and Clark was free to fly off as Superman.

Lois was calm about this first cancellation, making up the date with Clark later that night with yet another homemade beef bourguignon, but her placability waned as Clark's desertions mounted. His escapes quickly lost any cunning; when Supergirl was hurt deep in outer space a few issues later, Clark just panicked. He babbled as he shoved Lois out the door, "I've got a **splitting headache**, a **bad stomach, trick knee** . . . pick any of the above! In a word, I can't have **dinner** with you—so please, **go home!**" Lois didn't take this kindly at all. She kicked Clark's door, called him a bozo, and shouted, "If I never see you again, it'll be **too soon!**"

Clark's hasty exits prompted a frank discussion of their relationship in the following issue. Lois was so frustrated by Clark's hot-and-cold attitude that she'd asked Perry White to assign her to another city. After baring her soul to Clark, she stepped into the washroom for a moment to wipe her tears, while Clark received news that someone was in trouble. He shot the doorknob off the washroom door with his heat vision, locking Lois in, and flew off as Superman to save the day. He then promptly forgot that he'd left Lois locked

---

* To this latest version of Lois, a liberated lady got her man by strapping on a frilly apron and cooking him a meal.

in his apartment. When he finally remembered and let her out six hours later, Lois was furious.

During their discussion, Lois had revealed that she saw Clark as a consolation prize, because she was still in love with Superman. Some readers, however, had other ideas about what was really going on. Having keenly observed the past year of comics, Brian Uhlenbrock wrote in to the *Action Comics* letter page to present his theory: Lois knew that Clark was Superman. "When Clark first kissed Lois in that historic scene in *Superman #297*, he forgot himself and kissed her as he would **normally** . . . as he has many times in his **super-identity!**" He argued that Lois realized this immediately, and that's why she pursued Clark and gave up her habit of trying to prove that he was Superman. Perhaps tellingly, the editor didn't respond to that part of Brian's letter, and instead briefly replied to another point he made.

Brian may have been on to something. After the washroom incident, Lois was struck with an alien disease that put her out of commission for several issues. By the time she woke up, Clark had realized the error of his ways and immediately proposed to her, but her response was conditional. She replied, "I'll say '**Yes**' . . . without a moment's hesitation . . . **if you tell me right now—that Clark Kent is Superman!**" Clark was briefly torn between protecting his secret and getting to be with the love of his life, but ultimately he murmured, "I . . . I'm **sorry**, Lois . . . I . . . **can't** tell you that . . ."* He quickly left the hospital room as a tearful Lois turned away in sorrow.

Reactions to the botched proposal were mixed, but they showed an evolution in the way readers saw Lois. In the Silver Age, the vast majority of readers sided with Superman/Clark and blamed Lois for whatever ills befell her. A decade later, some still put the blame on Lois, but belief had spread that Lois was doing more than chasing unfounded suspicions and that, after all these years, she had actually figured out Clark was Superman. Even some of her critics

---

* In response to this turn of events, the book's omniscient narrator completely flipped out. To Lois, the narrator admonished, "**Superman is proposing to you!**—But **must** you make him **say** it? This is **it**—the moment you've **dreamed** of for **years**! Don't **spoil** it!" To Clark, the narrator pleaded, "**Forget** that you **shouldn't** reveal your secret to Lois—not here . . . not like this! **Forget** all that—just **do** it!"

acknowledged the possibility; they just thought that she should have accepted the proposal and let Clark tell her the truth in his own time. Other readers sided with Lois, like Mike Flynn, who wrote, "She feels so much for **Superman** that she honestly felt he would have the guts—and love—to simply affirm a fact to her." In fact, only two of the eight letters addressing the proposal referred to Lois negatively, and those who were frustrated were upset with the writers and editors more than Lois. This suggests that the series' audience had grown more mature and that readers now better understood the mechanics of making comic books and were less likely to be angry at a fictional character. But the letters also showed a fondness for Lois and an appreciation of her intellect that had been absent from the letter columns for some time.

The first act of this soap opera saga came to a calm close soon after the proposal. When Lois next appeared, she was at work and unperturbed, chatting with Clark amiably and even suggesting that they should try to be friends. The fallout from the rebuffed proposal was minimal, but a new twist was just around the corner in the form of a returned rival, Lana Lang.

Lana had disappeared from the Super-books in *Superman's Girl Friend Lois Lane* #109 in April 1971. She was tired of waiting around for Superman and took a job as a European correspondent for the Galaxy Broadcasting System. Lana was barely mentioned, much less seen, for the next few years, except in the letter columns in which diehard fans occasionally demanded her return only to be told there were no plans to bring her back. This all changed with a surprising announcement at the end of *Superman* #317 in November 1977: Lana Lang wasn't just back in Metropolis, she was Clark's new coanchor on the nightly news.

When Lana first returned, she and Lois appeared to be close friends. They shared a cab to work, and Lana offered Lois some advice on her awkward relationship with Clark. But this camaraderie was fleeting. After the duo were attacked by the monstrous Solomon Grundy, they returned to work, where their boss Morgan Edge was looking for some pictures from Superman's fight with the creature. Lana immediately responded, "I suppose **Lois** was too **panic-stricken** to phone in **her** story to the *Planet*—but **I** called a film crew . . . and got footage that'll scoop **every reporter** in town!"

Immediately after Lana embarrassed Lois in front of her boss, she finagled a lunch date with Clark right in front of Lois, even though she knew that they'd just broken up. Even worse, Clark told Lana that he was taking her to "this cute little French restaurant that makes the **best boeuf bourguignon** I've **ever had**," sharing his and Lois's favorite dish with Lana while insulting Lois's cooking in the process. Lois was incensed: "Well, if he thinks I've treated him shabbily **before**—he hasn't seen the **half** of it yet!"

Lana's return sent Lois into a downward spiral. In the issue following Lana's Solomon Grundy scoop, Perry White found Lois asleep at her desk in the middle of the night. Perry observed, "Lois has been going after every story with a **vengeance**," and noted that she was trying to outscoop Galaxy Broadcasting System's television news division as if "she had some kind of personal **vendetta** against it!" He wanted Lois to slow down, fearing she'd have a nervous collapse, but she refused to go home and soon shot off in the *Daily Planet*'s helicopter on the trail of another big story.

Before long, Lana and Lois's old competitive games were in full swing again. In *Superman* #324, Lana gave Lois a false scoop that sent her across town so that Lana could cover the real story. A confrontation soon followed, in which Lois proclaimed, "I ought to pull out your flaming red hair by its **mousy brown roots!**" Lana nonchalantly replied, "Sorry about the **scam**—but like they say . . . 'All's fair in love and **journalism**'!"

Their renewed rivalry was further exacerbated when Lois began dating Superman again. They'd lost contact while Lois was dating Clark, but Superman's powers went haywire soon after the breakup, and Lois was there to help him concentrate and get them under control. Seeing Lois put herself in harm's way to help him made Superman realize how much she loved him, and he declared, "**Lois, forgive** me . . . for what a fool I've been all these years! For all the wonderful things I refused to see in you . . . all the love I felt . . . and refused to **admit**." Superman's contrite remarks served as a sort of apology for the past few decades of lessons and rudeness. From then on, Superman treated Lois not as an impetuous child but as a grown woman who deserved his respect.

Romance soon bloomed. Superman visited Lois's apartment to bring her a gift, a Kryptonian wish-ring, and the two had dinner together.* The news of this relationship didn't sit well with Lana; her time in Europe hadn't cured her infatuation with the Man of Steel at all. Lana was stunned when Lois showed her the ring Superman gave her, and Lois only made matters worse. When Lana suggested going to dinner so that she could apologize for how she'd been treating Lois, Lois accepted the apology but passed on the dinner invite, intentionally needling Lana by telling her that she already had plans to go out with Superman. A furious Lana thought, "She's so blasted **casual** about her affair with the big lug I could **strangle** her! The way she takes him for granted—it's **disgusting**! She doesn't **deserve** him!"

The battle for Superman came to an abrupt close in *Superman* #332 when Superman took matters into his own hands. Lana tried to put the moves on Superman after he saved her from yet another evil menace, but he wasn't having any of it. He responded, "Do you think I'm **blind?**—or **stupid?** Do you think I **don't know** how you've been **chasing after** me since you returned to **Metropolis**—pulling those stunts on poor **Lois** to ace out 'the competition'?" When Lana objected and tried to declare her love, Superman cut to the core of things as he said, "You're not in love—you're **star-struck**! You want **reflected glory** . . . what you **imagine** to be the **glamor** of being '**Mrs. Superman**'!" As Superman flew off, Lana banged on her patio door and yelled after him, before eventually hanging her head in sorrow.

Superman returned to his old tricks with Lana, teaming up with Lois to pull an elaborate ruse and teach Lana a lesson about trust to emphasize that he neither trusted nor loved her. In short, he treated Lana like he used to treat Lois. Superman, and his writers, hadn't actually moved on from his patronizing ways, they'd just stopped unleashing them on Lois.

---

* Lois again strapped on her frilly apron to cook the meal, replicating a Kryptonian dish that Superman suggested. Superman was certainly treating Lois better than he had previously, but old dynamics continued.

After a few years of romantic stability, by 1983 Lois's relationship with Superman had achieved an equilibrium that neither party was happy with. Superman remained concerned about protecting Lois from his enemies and preserving his secret identity, and thus was unwilling to commit and occasionally struggled with how far he'd let the relationship progress. Lois wanted more from Superman, in both a solid commitment and in his actual presence because he was off saving the world so often.

This impasse was further complicated by Clark and Lana. After Superman shut her down for good, Lana set her sights a little lower and found herself attracted to her coanchor. Just as Lois and Superman's relationship neared a breaking point, Lana began to pursue Clark, and soon the two were dating. The super-two-timer had even less room for Lois in his life, and so she decided to move on.

Lois requested an international assignment, and Perry White proposed a set of interviews with Middle Eastern leaders that would set her up for a Pulitzer Prize and keep her out of Metropolis while she reevaluated her life. When she ran into Clark as she left Perry's office, Lois declared, "I'm not waiting for **Superman** to make all my dreams come true. I don't think I'm waiting for **Superman** any more **at all**." But a few days later, when the interviews had fallen through, Superman showed up in Egypt and she agreed to fly off with him to talk about life and their relationship. Lois then returned to her family home to think things over, not telling anyone where she'd gone.

In the meantime, the Middle Eastern leaders again changed their minds about the interviews and Lois was nowhere to be found, so Perry sent Lana instead. At her family home, Lois decided that she was through with Superman, and her feelings were only confirmed when she flipped on the television and saw Lana conducting her interviews. She yelled, "**The sneaky, sniveling, conniving witch!**" and blamed Superman, believing that he had taken her away from Egypt so that Lana could get the story.

Lois immediately returned to Metropolis, where she attacked Lana at a party celebrating her Middle East success. She threw her drink in Lana's face, which prompted Lana to dunk Lois's head into the punch bowl. Lois then tackled Lana to the ground and was straddling her when she noticed a poster of the Man of Steel. Lois burst into tears and clawed at the poster, crying, "It wasn't **you** I was lashing out at . . . it was **him!** For not loving me **back** the way I loved him!" The unseemly catfight ended with Lois bawling on Lana's shoulder as they commiserated over their frustrations with the Man of Steel.

Fan response to this brawl broke down along gender lines. Male readers seemed to love it, with Jim Toste writing, "As a younger reader, I'd never see [sic] the two L.L.s at each other's throats before, so pages 15 and 16 were a special treat." Andrew Maclaney commented, "I also enjoyed the scene (and I do mean *scene*) between Lois and Lana." Four other male letter writers responded with similar enthusiasm to the issue. The only voice of dissent was the sole female letter writer, Jeanne Williams, who wrote:

> Halfway through *Superman* #388, I began to wonder if I'd picked up one of my old issues of *Lois Lane* by mistake. Just when I was secure in the thought that, whatever else might happen, Lois and Lana's cat-fighting days were over, they start up again. This could set the women's movement back at least a decade.

Jeanne brought up a valid point. This comic from the 1980s recycled plotlines that were worn out in the 1950s, reducing its female characters to hysterical satellites of the primary male character. Nabbing a man, be it Clark or Superman, was all Lois and Lana were after. Their roles in the books consisted of little else.

Moreover, their professional lives were being marginalized in an era in which journalism was reaching new heights in America. While Lois romanced Clark, the shock waves from the Pentagon Papers and the Watergate scandal were still reverberating across the country. Her rival returned to the scene soon after Barbara Walters joined the *ABC Evening News*, but Lana was too busy sabotaging Lois and chasing Superman to do much actual reporting. Over the fifteen years that Julius Schwartz edited the Super-books, more than twenty women won Pulitzer Prizes, but in *Action Comics* and *Superman*, the female reporters were wrapped up in their love lives.

Solo Adventures

When *Superman's Girl Friend Lois Lane* was rolled into a shorter feature in *The Superman Family* in 1974, Lois only got a new story once every three issues, while the issues in between reprinted some of her more cringe-worthy Silver Age adventures.* The series' retro fixation wasn't helped by the addition of "Mr. and Mrs. Superman." This new feature was set in a version of the Golden Age in which Lois married Superman and spent most of her time trying not to accidentally reveal Superman's secret identity to the world.

Then, in 1977, a new creative team brought Lois's solo series into the modern day. Tom DeFalco was a young writer who had been working at Archie Comics, and *The Superman Family* was one of his first superhero jobs, while artist Win Mortimer had been drawing comics since the 1940s but still brought a modern style to the book. Together, they showcased the heroic side of Lois and made her the star of a new cast of characters.

In their first story, in *The Superman Family* #185, Lois investigated an elderly vigilante who was attacking known muggers across Metropolis. After getting some clues from Inspector Henderson, a recently introduced comic book version of the police officer from the 1950s *Adventures of Superman* television show, Lois met an informant at a dive bar, where she was attacked by a lecherous goon.† She dispatched him easily with a martial arts maneuver and continued her research, only to be attacked again by a pair of muggers. Lois made quick work of them as well, throwing one into the other and leaving them both stunned. Superman showed up after the fact, and the only useful thing he did was fly Lois across town to nab her target after she discovered the vigilante's true identity.

DeFalco and Mortimer's Lois was capable of saving herself, and Superman's role in the feature soon diminished. He was replaced by the Human Cannonball, a brash and inexperienced superhero

---

* Her sporadic new stories were an odd departure from her usual newspaper reporting; the first arc involved Lois aiding a spy agency with the help of the ghost of a dead agent.
† In a nod to Tom DeFalco's history with Archie comics, the oversized goon was named "Moose" Mason.

whom Lois took under her wing. As his alter ego Ryan Chase, he invented a jet pack and decided to dress up in a green costume with a spherical black helmet to fight crime. However, he needed someone to teach him the ropes, and no one knew more about superheroes than Lois Lane.

The Human Cannonball was comically bad at superheroics and could do little more than barrel into villains with the power of his jet pack. Lois was responsible for all of the brain work, and she ended up doing a lot of the actual crime-fighting as well. When the duo went undercover to expose a group that stole and sold babies, the Human Cannonball blew their cover and Lois swiftly took out a gunman and the mastermind while the Human Cannonball exclaimed, "Nice move, Lois! But **I'm** the **super-hero** here!"

Lois and the Human Cannonball were joined by Lois's old friends from Little Africa, Dave Stevens and Tina Ames, who had appeared infrequently in the Super-books since *Superman's Girl Friend Lois Lane* ended. While Dave had been the focus of their stories in the past, Tina took center stage in *The Superman Family* for an arc in which she saved Dave and gained energy-based superpowers. Lois's team-up with Tina also brought back the feminist dialogue that had been missing from Lois's adventures since Dorothy Woolfolk departed; when a masked villain declared, "Gentlemen do not battle ladies," Lois retorted, "**Women's lib** changed that! We now get **equal rights**." Then after the villain taunted, "Don't you know females aren't supposed to engage in combat?" Lois hit him twice as she replied, "Try telling **that** to **Wonder Woman!**"

DeFalco and Mortimer also poked fun at old comic book tropes, and in one clever scene they flipped the script on a classic romance-comics moment. A common setting for romance comics was a hospital, where a shy young nurse would fall in love with a dashing doctor and eventually get him alone and kiss him passionately. This was exactly what happened when Tina was in the hospital in *The Superman Family* #193; a doctor and nurse locked lips while thinking, "My world explodes whenever Nancy kisses me!" and "What a man! I can feel the ground shaking!" This dialogue would have fit perfectly in a Silver Age romance comic—or a Silver Age Lois

Lane story, for that matter—but the couple with their eyes closed were missing the real action. In the previous panels, Lois fought a squad of villains while proclaiming, "Ever since **women's lib**, we girls have been entitled to equal fight scenes—I just want **my share** of the action!" As the doctor and nurse kissed, Lois intruded on their romantic interlude by bursting into the room atop a villain she'd just tackled off of a hover board. She pummeled the goon, asking, "Are you holding **back** because of my sweet, retiring disposition—or have you already **lost** consciousness?"*

DeFalco and Mortimer's tenure was short-lived. They moved on to other projects after a year and a half and were replaced by writer Gerry Conway and artists Bob Oksner and Vince Colletta. The new team's run was a mixed bag of sexiness and scoops; in one issue, Lois investigated a weight-loss camp and spent most of the story in lacy underwear and short shorts. In another, she joined a corrupt roller derby team and took down the whole group single-handedly.

Conway's most interesting issue was a special full-length story in *The Superman Family* #200 in 1980 that was set in the future. Lois and Clark were married, and after raising their daughter for sixteen years, Lois was set to return to work full time, only to find out that she was pregnant again. Lois met this news with unabashed fury, slamming her helmet against her motorcycle, stomping through her home, and yelling at Clark, "All those **hopes** I had for restarting my career **full time**, now that our daughter is almost grown—**shot!**" After a conversation in which Lois told Clark, "I don't regret having been a **wife** and **mother**—but that isn't all I want," Clark agreed to quit his day job and stay home with the baby so Lois could keep working. The story was an unconventional approach to pregnancy for the early '80s that directly dealt with the tension between work and home life and ultimately showcased Lois's devotion to her career.

Conway was soon replaced by Marv Wolfman, whose main arc involved an amnesiac Lois falling in love in a seaside New England town. Wolfman didn't last long either, and was followed by Paul

---

* This satisfying moment of the new supplanting the old is made even better by the knowledge that in the 1960s Win Mortimer worked on many of the DC romance comics.

Levitz. The mixed bag continued with Levitz, whose first issue was again heavy on Lois in her underwear but also had her pitching a grenade out of her window and jumping from a moving car after disarming a would-be kidnapper.

Throughout *The Superman Family*'s run, Lois's feature continued to be called "Superman's Girl Friend Lois Lane."* The title was always accompanied by an introduction, though it changed with the creative teams and reflected their approach to the character. During DeFalco and Mortimer's run, the header read:

> She's smart—she's successful—she's beautiful—she's Metropolis' best reporter—and sometimes—she's . . . Superman's Girl Friend Lois Lane.

This introduction led with Lois's intelligence and accomplishments, putting her appearance third and deemphasizing her romantic leanings while highlighting her own achievements over her relationship with Superman.

This was completely reversed during Conway's and Wolfman's time on the book:

> Before **Clark Kent** came to work at the *Daily Planet*, **she** was there . . . a beautiful, resourceful, determined reporter—never known to give up until she gets her **story!** No wonder she was a **natural** to become . . . Superman's Girl Friend Lois Lane.

Clark led off the introduction, continuing a trend common in this era. Rather than being introduced on their own merits, many female character introductions began with their connection to a male character. Supergirl was "trained by her **cousin, Superman,**" Batgirl was "the daughter of Gotham City's police commissioner," and the Huntress, a hero in an alternate universe, only began fighting crime

---

* For one issue during Paul Levitz's run, *The Superman Family* #213, the feature was simply titled "Lois Lane." It reverted back to "Superman's Girl Friend Lois Lane" with *The Superman Family* #214.

after "the **darknight detective** of the world we call **Earth Two** hung up his cowl." Meanwhile, male characters' introductions rarely mentioned female characters at all, even those key to their backstory. The only exception was Hawkman, whose introduction mentioned his wife, Hawkgirl.

After Lois's connection to Clark was established, the introduction then moved on to her physical appearance. This too was common for female characters. Batgirl was called "the dominoed daredoll," Black Canary was a "blond bombshell," and Wonder Woman possessed "the beauty of Aphrodite." The attractiveness of male characters never came up.

The introduction then moved to Lois's job, but ultimately her relationship with Superman was portrayed as the logical culmination of her life's work. It's not surprising that Conway's and Wolfman's stories focused more on romance and putting Lois in appealing outfits than those of their predecessors.

When Levitz took over the feature, the new introduction hit a midway mark between the first two:

> Award-winning reporter . . . incomparable electronic journalist
> . . . adventurer . . . explorer . . . even trouble-maker . . . she's a
> little bit of them all. But though her by-line is world-famous,
> she's best known as . . . Superman's Girl Friend Lois Lane.

Levitz didn't reference her appearance at all, instead focusing on her career before calling her a "trouble-maker" and declaring that her professional achievements paled in comparison to her relationship with Superman. In the end, Levitz leaned into "Superman's Girl Friend" where DeFalco had found a way to downplay it.

Despite the constant reminder that Lois's primary role was as the love interest of the Man of Steel, readers of *The Superman Family* enjoyed the stories that focused on her independence and abilities. Kent Phenis was pleased that "the emphasis is now on showing what a fine reporter Lois is." After a Superman-less story in which Lois foiled jewel thieves and got a big scoop in the process, Daniel Fogel remarked, "Lois handled herself well and proved she's as capable as any super-hero." However, at the end of the day DC Comics wanted Lois to be known for her romance with Superman, and they stuck with this defining trait even as the entire universe collapsed around them.

Whatever Happened to the Man of Tomorrow?

The Superman Family was canceled in 1982, and after the Middle East interview snafu and subsequent catfight with Lana, Lois's role in *Action Comics* and *Superman* petered out as those series entered an odd limbo. After nearly fifty years of publishing comic books, DC was about to reboot its entire line with the crossover miniseries *Crisis on Infinite Earths*, an event that would combine DC's disparate fictional universes and streamline continuity. In anticipation of this new universe, the Super-books lost their soap opera vibe; everything was going to be rebooted anyway, so they put out barely connected filler stories, bringing back some fan favorite creators for short arcs and basically waiting out their inevitable demise.

In September 1986, to cap off *Action Comics* and *Superman* before the reboot began, DC published special final issues of both series that composed the two-part story "Whatever Happened to the Man of Tomorrow?" Alan Moore, already a comic book icon for his work on *Marvelman* and *Swamp Thing*, wrote the story; Moore's now-legendary *Watchmen* launched the week before his Superman finale began in *Superman* #423.* For art, DC brought in Curt Swan, the most beloved and definitive Superman artist of the past half century.

Their story was set in a future in which Superman had been dead for a decade, and Lois recounted his final days to a *Daily Planet* reporter who was writing a story for a commemorative issue. Lois

---

* When discussing Alan Moore's role in the history of a famed female character, it's relevant to point out that while he is a legendary writer who's arguably shaped the modern comic book industry more than any other creator, his work has been justifiably critiqued for its treatment of women. He'd later have the Joker sexually assault and permanently paralyze Barbara Gordon, a.k.a. Batgirl, in *Batman: The Killing Joke*, and many of his books involve the assault and rape of female characters, often as a significant character moment.

Lane had become Lois Elliott; after Superman's death, she married a man named Jordan and together they had a young son named Jonathan. Lois's interview served as a framing device for Superman's final battle. All of Superman's chief villains rallied against the Man of Steel, manipulated by an evil, punk-rock version of Mister Mxyzptlk. After his secret identity was exposed and the *Daily Planet* was attacked, Superman took all of his friends to his Fortress of Solitude, which was soon besieged by his enemies.

Lois had very little to do in the issues apart from cry about her circumstances. Lana Lang took a stand, teaming with Jimmy Olsen to dip into Superman's reserve of super-serums so that they could fight toe-to-toe against Superman's foes. Lana died in the ensuing battle but was able to kill Lex Luthor, the parasitic host of the alien supervillain Brainiac, before she was electrocuted. Lois's sole contribution to the proceedings was pointing out that Superman could use his Phantom Zone projector on Mister Mxyzptlk, though when he did the fiendish imp attempted to transport himself back into his own dimension and the dual forces killed him. Ashamed at having committed murder, Superman subjected himself to gold Kryptonite to permanently remove his powers and walked out into the harsh Arctic tundra, where he presumably died of exposure. A body was never found.

The story's twist ending in *Action Comics* #583 revealed that Jordan Elliott was actually Superman, and that their toddler son was already strong enough to crush coal into diamonds. After fifty years of trying, Lois had finally ended up with Superman, giving up her career at the *Daily Planet* to become a housewife in suburbia. "Whatever Happened to the Man of Tomorrow?" is widely regarded as one of the best Superman stories of all time, but it was hardly a strong showcase for Lois. Luckily, a new universe and a new Lois Lane were just around the corner, and she would soon be back at the *Daily Planet* with a vengeance.

Jerry Siegel and Joe Shuster, DC Comics publicity photo, 1942
Siegel (sitting) and Shuster (standing) cocreated Lois Lane. She was added to their ever-evolving Superman pitch in 1935.

Joe Shuster's first Lois Lane sketch, 1935
The sketch was based on model Jolan Kovacs, who later dated Shuster but ultimately married Siegel. COPYRIGHT © 2015 JOE SHUSTER ESTATE, J. MICHAEL CATRON, AGENT

Action Comics #1, cover by Joe Shuster, DC Comics, 1938
The first appearance of Lois Lane. She reluctantly went on a date with Clark Kent, slapped a bully, and then pitched a story about Superman to her editor after the Man of Steel told her not to.

TOP LEFT: *Action Comics #29*, cover by Wayne Boring, DC Comics, 1940

Superman rescues Lois Lane, who was a perpetual damsel in distress throughout the 1940s. Trying to get front page scoops often just resulted in her capture.

TOP RIGHT: *Superman #16*, cover by Fred Ray, DC Comics, 1942

Lois was madly in love with Superman and not at all interested in Clark Kent. This love triangle lasted for decades.

BOTTOM LEFT: *Superman #57*, cover by Wayne Boring and Stan Kaye, DC Comics, 1949

Every so often in the Golden Age, the tables turned, and Lois gained superpowers and got to be the hero for an issue.

Joe Shuster artwork from "The Bride Wore Leather," *Nights of Horror* **#7, Malcla Publishing Company, 1954**
Shuster fell on hard times in the 1950s and ended up drawing fetish art for seedy pornographic magazines. Doppelgängers of Clark Kent and Lois Lane made regular appearances in his art.

Kurt Schaffenberger's audition art for *Superman's Girl Friend Lois Lane***, 1957**
This test page helped Schaffenberger become the regular artist on Lois's new solo series, where he became known for his expressive artwork. IMAGE COURTESY OF HERITAGE AUCTIONS (WWW.HA.COM)

Lois Lane in Superman short *The Arctic Giant*, Fleischer Studios, 1942
Voiced by Joan Alexander, this first big-screen incarnation of Lois ended most of the early shorts with a front page story.

Joan Alexander in a publicity photo for the Mutual Broadcasting System, 1942
Alexander also voiced Lois Lane on the *Adventures of Superman* radio show throughout the 1940s.

Publicity photo of Noel Neill as Lois Lane in *Superman* serial, Columbia Pictures, 1948
Neill reprised the role in 1950's *Atom Man vs. Superman* serial, as well as the later seasons of the *Adventures of Superman* television show.

Phyllis Coates as Lois Lane in *Adventures of Superman*, Warner Bros., 1952
Coates played Lois in the first season of the television show as a tough and fearless reporter. IMAGE COURTESY OF PHOTOFEST (PHOTOFESTNYC.COM)

George Reeves and Leonore Lemmon, 1959
Reeves played Clark Kent / Superman in *Adventures of Superman*, and his relationship with this L.L. may have led to his untimely demise in 1959. IMAGE COURTESY OF PHILIP S. DOCKTER

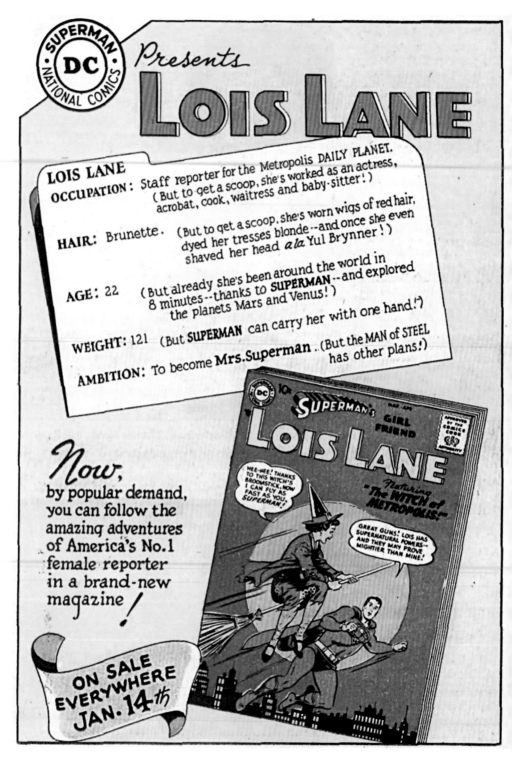

DC Comics advertisement for *Superman's Girl Friend Lois Lane* #1, 1958

Lois launched her own series in 1958, a remarkable feat for a female character, but this ad makes clear that her ambition was "to become **Mrs. Superman**."

DC Comics advertisement for *Superman's Girl Friend Lois Lane* #5, 1958
Lois was ashamed of her appearance after a growth ray caused her to gain weight, so she hid her face from Superman.

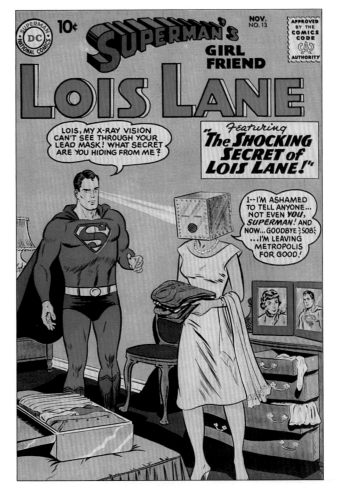

Superman's Girl Friend Lois Lane #13, cover by Curt Swan and Stan Kaye, DC Comics, 1959
When Lois was tricked into thinking her face had turned horribly ugly, she encased her head in a lead box so Superman couldn't see it with his X-ray vision and prepared to move away from Metropolis.

TOP LEFT: *Superman's Girl Friend Lois Lane* #16, cover by Curt Swan and Stan Kaye, DC Comics, 1960 Superman pretended that Lois had "Kryptonite vision" to teach her a lesson about touching his stuff, one of her many lessons from the Man of Steel in the Silver Age.

BOTTOM LEFT: *Superman's Girl Friend Lois Lane* #21, cover by Curt Swan, Stan Kaye, and Kurt Schaffenberger, DC Comics, 1960 When Lois Lane and Lana Lang got superpowers, the two grown women fought over who would marry Superman.

BOTTOM RIGHT: *Archie's Girls Betty and Veronica* #59, cover by Bob White, Archie Comics, 1960 Meanwhile, Betty and Veronica, two teenagers, treated their beau like a puppet.

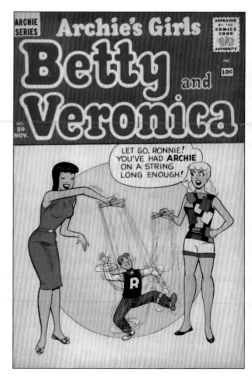

TOP: DC Comics Advertisement for *80 Page Giant Magazine* **#14, 1965**
A compilation of several stories in which Lois battled her many rivals for Superman's affection.

RIGHT: *Superman's Girl Friend Lois Lane* **#19, cover by Curt Swan and Stan Kaye, DC Comics, 1960**
In this "imaginary story," Lois finally achieved her dream and married Superman but found little wedded bliss. Most of the imaginary stories ended with Lois in tears.

TOP LEFT: DC Comics advertisement for *Superman's Girl Friend Lois Lane* #80, 1968.

In the late 1960s, Lois became increasingly frustrated with Superman's shenanigans.

TOP RIGHT: *Superman's Girl Friend Lois Lane* #106, cover by Curt Swan and Murphy Anderson, DC Comics, 1970

Lois turned herself into an African American woman to write a story about Metropolis's Little Africa district in this bizarre attempt at addressing race issues.

BOTTOM LEFT: *Superman's Girl Friend Lois Lane* #110, cover by Dick Giordano, DC Comics, 1971

Lois again aimed for racial understanding but instead fell into clichés as she took the side of Native Americans in a clash with land developers.

TOP RIGHT: *The Superman Family* #182, cover by Curt Swan and Neal Adams, DC Comics, 1977
After her own series was canceled, Lois starred in a regular feature in *The Superman Family*, still titled "Superman's Girl Friend Lois Lane."

BOTTOM LEFT: *Lois Lane: When It Rains, God Is Crying* #1, cover by Gray Morrow, DC Comics, 1986
Lois investigated missing children cases in *When It Rains, God Is Crying*, a dark, gritty miniseries written by Mindy Newell.

BOTTOM RIGHT: *Lois Lane: When It Rains, God Is Crying* #2, cover by Gray Morrow, DC Comics, 1986
Despite being emotionally shaken by her grisly investigation, Lois ultimately got her story in the miniseries' conclusion.

Margot Kidder in *Superman: The Movie*, Warner Bros., 1978
Kidder played Lois Lane in four Superman films, portraying a smart and relentless Lois for a new generation of fans. IMAGE COURTESY OF PHOTOFEST (PHOTOFESTNYC.COM)

Kate Bosworth, publicity photo for *Superman Returns*, Warner Bros., 2006
Bosworth portrayed Lois in Bryan Singer's underwhelming 2006 film. After Superman disappeared, Lois married someone else and had a child.

Amy Adams, publicity photo for *Man of Steel*, Warner Bros., 2013
The multiple Oscar nominee played Lois in Zack Snyder's 2013 film and its 2016 sequel, *Batman v Superman: Dawn of Justice*.

TOP RIGHT: *Action Comics* #662, cover by Kerry Gammill and Brett Breeding, DC Comics, 1991

DC relaunched the Super-books in 1986, and five years later Clark Kent finally told Lois that he was Superman, months after they got engaged.

BOTTOM LEFT: *The Death of Superman* collection, cover by Jon Bogdanove and Dennis Janke, DC Comics, 1993

Lois was front and center during the most famous and bestselling Superman story of all time: his death.

BOTTOM RIGHT: *World Without a Superman* collection, cover by Tom Grummett and Doug Hazlewood, DC Comics, 1993

Lois remained front and center after Superman's death, becoming the glue that held the disparate Superman books together in the months that followed.

Teri Hatcher, publicity photo for *Lois & Clark: The New Adventures of Superman*, Warner Bros., 1993

Hatcher played Lois Lane for four seasons on the ABC series. She took center stage in the first season, but superhero antics dominated the later years of the program's run.

Erica Durance, publicity photo for *Smallville*, episode "Crossfire," Warner Bros., 2009

Durance joined *Smallville* as Lois Lane in the show's fourth season and remained on the program until its tenth and final season.

Lois and Superman, publicity image for *Superman: The Animated Series*, Warner Bros., 1996

Dana Delany voiced a snarky and beloved Lois in this program, as well as its spinoffs *Justice League* and *Justice League Unlimited*.

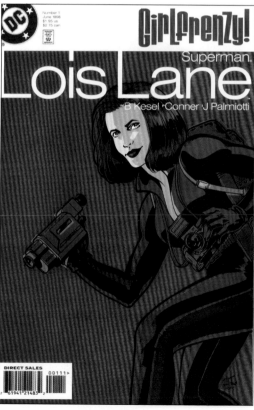

TOP LEFT: *Superman: The Wedding Album*, cover by John Byrne, DC Comics, 1996

Lois Lane and Clark Kent tied the knot in this special "Event of the Century!" issue. Lois's role as Superman's wife soon took over most of her comic book appearances.

TOP RIGHT: *Superman* #168, cover by Ed McGuinness and Cam Smith, DC Comics, 2001

In one of her rare story lines set outside of her home life with Clark, Lois teamed up with Batman to fight Lex Luthor.

BOTTOM RIGHT: *GirlFrenzy! Superman: Lois Lane* #1, cover by Leonard Kirk and Karl Story, DC Comics, 1998

After Lois's Silver Age series ran for over one hundred issues, DC's short-lived "Girlfrenzy!" line was one of her few, brief opportunities to headline a book in the Modern Age.

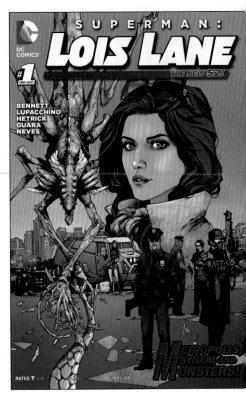

TOP LEFT: *Action Comics* #796, cover by Dan Jurgens and Bill Sienkiewicz, DC Comics, 2002

In the early 2000s, Lois "died" repeatedly to provide emotional story fodder for Superman.

TOP RIGHT: *Superman: Lois Lane* #1, cover by Kenneth Rocafort, DC Comics, 2014

Lois has had little to do in the New 52, DC Comics' relaunched comic line, apart from this one-shot issue.

BOTTOM LEFT: *Lois Lane: Fallout* by Gwenda Bond, Switch Press, 2015

Lois might not have much to do in the comics, but a teenage Lois is the star of this well-received young adult novel.

Women Writers

By the early 1980s, Lois Lane had appeared in nearly a thousand comic books over the course of more than forty years, and not a single one was written by a woman. Irene Vartanoff helped plot an issue of *Superman's Girl Friend Lois Lane*, Maxene Fabe was credited on an issue of the series that she didn't actually write, and Lois's only female editor had lasted just seven issues before being replaced. Apart from that it was all men.

This stark lack of female input is not at all unusual for the super-hero comics industry. Superman didn't have a woman writer on a regular series until Louise Simonson came aboard *Superman: The Man of Steel* in the early 1990s. No Batman book was helmed by a woman until Devin Grayson took over *Batman: Gotham Knights* in 2000, and no female artists drew an issue of *Batman* until Becky Cloonan in 2012, a whopping seventy-two years after the series began. Even Wonder Woman wasn't immune; while Joye Murchison wrote several issues of *Sensation Comics* and *Wonder Woman* in the 1940s, she went uncredited. There wasn't a woman in the amazing Amazon's byline until Danette Thomas cowrote *Wonder Woman* #300 in 1983.

Thus, it turns out that Lois was ahead of the curve when it came to female writers, albeit by a slim margin. In 1982, a year before *The Superman Family* was canceled, the writing of the "Superman's Girl Friend Lois Lane" feature passed from Paul Levitz to Tamsyn

O'Flynn. For the first time in her long history, the words coming out of Lois's mouth were written by a woman.

Tamsyn O'Flynn

Tamsyn O'Flynn grew up reading comic books in Queens, New York, but left the funny books behind when she entered Adelphi University. After graduating with a degree in psychology, O'Flynn picked up comics again after she saw *Superman: The Movie*, and she soon began writing in to DC's letter columns. Her neat and well-written letters impressed the editors so much that they invited her to visit DC's offices; they later hired her as a proofreader and put her in charge of the letter columns of several series. O'Flynn stepped in as the regular writer of the Lois Lane feature beginning with *The Superman Family* #214, with Bob Oksner staying on board as the feature's artist.

Her first story had Lois stumble onto a missing and presumed-dead billionaire who wanted to give up his past riches for the simpler life he now enjoyed. Lois agreed to protect his secret, but the billionaire's greedy nephew suspected he was still alive, went through Lois's notes, and set out to kill his uncle to ensure his inheritance. After piecing together what was afoot, Lois arrived just in time to stop the homicidal nephew's plan and save the billionaire's life.

O'Flynn's Lois also expressed a disinterest in romance; when she dropped off Clark Kent at his apartment after work, he leaned in and Lois thought, "Oh no! Don't tell me he's going to kiss me goodnight!" She was happily spared from a smooch when Clark had to take off because Superman was needed. Later on, Lois caught the bouquet at the billionaire's wedding, and while she momentarily daydreamed about marriage, Superman never came up. In fact, Superman was absent from the entire story. Lois figured out the nephew's plan on her own, got herself to the scene of the crime, and disarmed the big, strong villain with her martial arts skills.

Even in small moments, O'Flynn highlighted key aspects of the character that other writers had neglected. Lois's feminist leanings were mentioned on the first page, as the narration revealed that she was returning from a weeklong convention of the National Organization for Women. Later, Lois got to pick the restaurant for the *Daily Planet* staff's monthly dinner outing, so she went out on a limb and chose a sushi restaurant, telling a disgusted Jimmy Olsen, "Blame my insatiable curiosity—I'll try anything **once!**" It was just a short scene, but it showed Lois's adventurousness and added some humor to the book.

O'Flynn's first story served as a template for the rest of her *Superman Family* run. Lois would meet someone, help them with a problem or a mystery, defeat the bad guys by herself, and usually get a good story out of it. She did all of this without Superman; while Clark popped up occasionally, Superman appeared rarely, and then only in flashbacks to past issues as Lois worked on a book about her best stories, a running plotline through O'Flynn's tenure.

The tortured romance plots that dominated Lois's time in *Action Comics* and *Superman* stories of the era were nowhere to be found. At most, there were occasional flirtations with men whom Lois met in the course of her investigations, which quickly fell by the wayside as Lois neared the targets of her front page scoops. With O'Flynn at the helm, Lois took down gangsters, thieves, and murderers with aplomb. Her Lois was confident and carefree, constantly smiling and always calm and collected, even in the most precarious circumstances.

O'Flynn's stories went over well with readers, including Alan Moore, who praised her work in a 1983 article about women in comics. DC must have liked her work as well, because when *The Superman Family* was canceled only nine issues after O'Flynn came aboard, she and Lois were back together just three months later as the backup feature in the second issue of a new series, *The Daring New Adventures of Supergirl.** It was the same creative team, but a lot had changed.

First, Lois was no longer "Superman's Girl Friend." The feature was simply titled "Lois Lane," and with a new title came a new

* The Lois Lane feature didn't appear until the second issue, because the back end of the first issue was taken up by a fifteen-page preview of a new *Masters of the Universe* miniseries. Surprisingly, this He-Man preview had more panels featuring Superman than the whole of O'Flynn's "Lois Lane" run in *The Superman Family*.

introduction. O'Flynn's run in *The Superman Family* had kept the Levitz-era introduction, which praised Lois's intellect and achievements but considered them trumped by her relationship with Superman. For *The Daring New Adventures of Supergirl*, O'Flynn took a different tack:

> Reporting is her job . . . her career . . . but even more, it's her life. Where trouble goes, she follows . . . in relentless pursuit of truth and the ultimate story. She's an ambitious, tough-minded lady with independence on her mind and in her actions . . . but she's also a heartbreakingly caring lady, lavish with her time and energy when it comes to people. Relentless . . . ambitious . . . tough . . . caring. She's . . . Lois Lane.

This lengthy and somewhat hagiographic description led with Lois's work and talked about her as a person while leaving her appearance, her romantic aspirations, and Superman entirely out of it. It set up Lois as the star of the feature, on her own merits rather than because of her affiliation with anyone else.

The feature also had a new supporting cast. Mark Spencer, a gofer at the *Daily Planet* with dreams of becoming a reporter, was a constant presence, along with Jamie Gillis, a female photographer who had been introduced during Gerry Conway's tenure. Inspector Henderson and Perry White were regular side characters, while Clark Kent and Superman were notably absent; neither the Man of Steel nor his alter ego appeared in any of the new "Lois Lane" stories.

The structure of the feature shifted as well. While O'Flynn's stories in *The Superman Family* were self-contained, complete adventures, her "Lois Lane" stories in *The Daring New Adventures of Supergirl* were serialized, each issue ending on a cliff-hanger that led into the next installment.

These ongoing adventures were more melodramatic than the quick, action-packed tales of *The Superman Family*, but Lois herself was the grounded center of the feature. Arcs dealt with a teenage supermodel's familial problems, psychic newspaper stories written the day before the events described happened, and the burgeoning romance between Jamie and Mark. While there was a lot of angst and tears from the side characters, Lois stayed above the emotional fray. She was busy stopping kidnappings, freeing her captured friends, and solving mysterious murders.* Lois worked closely with the police and earned the deep respect of Inspector Henderson, who called her "the **best** darned investigative reporter I know!" Her only involvement with romance was sporadically giving advice to Jamie or Mark as their relationship progressed. Apart from that, Lois was all business.

After seven issues, O'Flynn was replaced by Joey Cavalieri, who wrote the feature for another four issues before "Lois Lane" was dropped from *The Daring New Adventures of Supergirl*. The series wasn't long for the world anyway; Supergirl was killed in 1985 during *Crisis on Infinite Earths*.

The story entitled "There's No Fool . . ." in *The Daring New Adventures of Supergirl* #8 was not only O'Flynn's last Lois story but also her last credited comic book story. O'Flynn dropped out of the comic book world, but Lois soon returned in a new miniseries from another female writer.

Mindy Newell

In the early 1980s, Mindy Newell was working as a nurse when she read about DC Comics' New Talent Program in an issue of *Action Comics*. She sent in a pitch and soon became a regular freelancer for the publisher, writing for series like *Amethyst, Legion of Super-Heroes*, and *Wonder Woman*. In 1986, Newell approached editor Dick Giordano about writing a Lois Lane miniseries in which Lois investigated missing and abused children, a high-profile topic in the 1980s after several child abductions captured the national media's attention.† A key component of her pitch was that Superman wouldn't appear in the story; the comic would be all about Lois.

---

* The feature's main murder mystery victim was Kristin Cutler, one of Lois's roommates from her women's lib days, who had inadvertently gotten involved with a mobster and was killed because she planned to go to the FBI.
† The miniseries dealt with several gruesome topics, including kidnapping, child abuse, and sexual assault, so please consider this a trigger warning for the rest of this chapter.

Giordano liked the pitch and teamed Newell with artist Gray Morrow, and the first issue of *Lois Lane: When It Rains, God Is Crying* hit comic book shops in August 1986.

The story picked up soon after Lois's Middle East interview debacle. While there were no real repercussions for Lois missing the interviews in *Action Comics* or *Superman*, Newell's Lois was on the outs at the *Daily Planet*, sidelined with smaller stories. When she learned that the body of a young girl had been found in the river, it was her first big scoop in some time, and she had to work hard to convince her editors to let her cover it. Lois's initial story became a longer feature piece about missing children, and she was quickly consumed with an expansive, grisly investigation.

Newell grounded the series in realism, eschewing the usual beats of superhero comics in favor of a straight newspaper drama that spanned two oversized issues. She spoke to the FBI, state children's services, the police, and doctors and nurses to learn about the topic from every angle, and poured all of her research into the story to present an accurate account of America's child abduction problem. There were no silly romantic games, Lois didn't make amusing quips while disarming bad guys with Kryptonian martial arts, and Superman never swooped in to save the day. Instead, the comic centered on Lois methodically, almost obsessively, digging into a gruesome and troubling story.

Gray Morrow's gritty and lifelike art added to the book's realism, as did colorist Joe Orlando's muted color palette; there was no bright, cartoonish imagery. Along with the main story, Newell wrote a multipage prose section in each issue that discussed real-world child abductions. She offered safety tips and information, along with a lengthy list of resources for every possible aspect of the topic, from support groups to hotlines to do-it-yourself fingerprint kits so you could have all of your child's information on record.

Newell's Lois was a woman on a mission who, as the investigation unfolded, became increasingly lost in the dark story. She was brusque with her friends, sharp with her bosses, and she put her story above everything else. Lois's friends and coworkers worried that she might be headed toward a breakdown, and frequently referenced the Middle East fiasco and her recent breakup with Superman as evidence that she was trying to bury her problems with her work. They were concerned that the dark subject matter would be too much for the supposedly fragile Lois, and that she'd collapse under the weight of it all.

The subject matter certainly was dark; Newell didn't shy away from the gruesome realities of child abduction. Lois interviewed a woman whose two-year-old daughter was missing for nine months, during which time she was regularly beaten and raped by her captors. The child was found, but the previously happy little girl was now a subdued, skittish ghost of her former self despite extensive therapy. Later in the issue, Lois covered dual missing babies on the same day: one was stolen from a hospital while another was found stuffed in a garbage pail. This was not a book for the faint of heart.

Even Lana Lang became part of Lois's heavy investigation. She revealed to Lois that during her mysterious time away in Europe, she not only gotten married and had a son, but her son had been kidnapped and killed by a gang of Italian terrorists. In one of the book's most unsettling scenes, Lana told Lois that the terrorists sent her the baby's ear as proof that they had him, and that she still had the ear, now black and dried up, in a safe deposit box because she couldn't bear to part with it.

Over the course of the investigation, this bleak subject matter clearly wore on Lois, but despite her friends' concerns she made it through. She finished her article, and the miniseries ended with Lois attending the funeral of the young girl whose death had started the whole story. Lois's friends were there with her, fences presumably mended after a month of her angrily brushing them off and dismissing their worries as she focused solely on her work.

With a relaunch of the entire Super-line just around the corner, *Lois Lane: When It Rains, God Is Crying* immediately became obsolete. In response to a favorable letter about the book in the letter column of the newly launched *Adventures of Superman* series, editor Andy Helfer promised that another Mindy Newell–penned Lois Lane miniseries was on the way, but the book never materialized. Newell wrote a few other series in the years that followed, including cowriting a run on *Wonder Woman* with George Pérez, but facing an increasingly unstable comic book market she returned to nursing in the mid-1990s. As for Lois, it would be more than a decade before her name adorned the cover of another comic book.

7

Lois Lane on Screen, Part 2: Movies

The airing of *Adventures of Superman*'s final episode in early 1958 marked the beginning of a lengthy drought for live action versions of the Superman comics. There were a couple of cartoon shows through the years, but for over two decades the only place to see live action Lois and Superman was in a brief run on Broadway. *It's a Bird . . . It's a Plane . . . It's Superman* was a musical scripted by David Newman and Robert Benton, with songs by Charles Strouse and Lee Adams. Adams was a Tony Award–winning lyricist for *Bye Bye Birdie*, while Strouse would go on to write the music for the megahit musical *Annie*, and Newman and Benton would earn Oscar nominations for the film *Bonnie and Clyde*, so the creative power behind the show was considerable.

The plot of *It's a Bird . . . It's a Plane . . . It's Superman* centered on Superman defeating an evil scientist while romancing Lois Lane. Lois was played by Patricia Marand, who was nominated for a Tony for Best Performance by a Featured Actress in a Musical for the role, one of the show's three nominations. Marand had several solo songs, including the show's main number, "It's Superman"; a ballad called "What I've Always Wanted"; and a song she sang while being captured, "I'm Not Finished Yet." The last number included lyrics like "Superman won't let me die / He will plummet from the sky / Why he's on his way I'll bet," and the very dramatically vocalized, "You've tied my hands but you can't tie my spirit!" The constant references to Superman may be why none of Lois's songs have had much life outside of the show.*

The production debuted at the Alvin Theatre in March 1966 to generally positive reviews, but the audience failed to materialize and the show closed in July after 129 performances. It was resurrected in 1975 as a television special on ABC starring Lesley Ann War-ren as Lois, but that version bombed with both critics and viewers. However, a new Lois was on the horizon. Superman was on his way back to the silver screen, and Lois Lane was about to be redefined for a new generation.

Superman: The Movie

In the early 1970s, father-and-son film production team Alexan-der and Ilya Salkind were riding high on a successful run of mov-ies, including a hit adaptation of *The Three Musketeers*. Ilya, the younger Salkind, suggested that they continue in the action vein and adapt Superman, arguing that the character's iconic status would give them an automatic blockbuster. It took a while to convince his father, but eventually the Salkinds purchased the rights from DC Comics and Warner Bros. and began development on *Superman: The Movie* in 1975.

Although Alexander Salkind had been slow to get on board with Superman, once the rights were purchased he went all out. He hired *Godfather* author Mario Puzo to write the script, and Puzo's five-hundred-page screenplay was so massive that the Salkinds decided to split the saga into two films that would be shot simultaneously. The script was rewritten several times, including a draft by David

---

* While Lois's songs are long forgotten, "You've Got Possibilities," sung by Linda Lavin as new character Sydney Carlton, has been recorded by several artists and has become a standard among nightclub singers.

Newman, cowriter of the Superman musical, and his wife, Leslie. Leslie focused on Lois Lane in particular, rewriting her dialogue almost entirely to ensure that she came off as a tough, modern woman.

The Salkinds considered a wide array of directors, including a young Steven Spielberg. They worried about Spielberg's inexperience, plus he was reportedly over budget on the shark movie he was in the middle of shooting, so the Salkinds decided to pass. Ultimately they hired Richard Donner; he'd worked mostly in television but the success of his latest film, *The Omen*, won him the job.

Even before they hired Donner, the Salkinds had locked down Marlon Brando as Superman's father, Jor-El, and Gene Hackman as underworld schemer Lex Luthor, banking on the actors' star power to help the movie's chances. For the lead role, the Salkinds had such a hard time that they even screen-tested Alexander's wife's dentist because he resembled Superman. After an exhaustive search, the relatively unknown Christopher Reeve was cast as the Man of Steel.

The search for Lois Lane was less bizarre but certainly thorough. Big names like Barbra Streisand, Natalie Wood, and Raquel Welch were considered for the part but didn't pan out, while Anne Archer, Liza Minnelli, and Stockard Channing were some of the many actresses who auditioned for the role. At the end of the screen-testing process, the producers were torn between two choices: Channing and Margot Kidder.

Kidder was born in the remote town of Yellowknife, Northwest Territories, in Northern Canada, and later moved into more populated regions of the country, where she had steady work in Canadian film and television in the late 1960s. She moved to America in the early 1970s and received acclaim for a variety of film roles, but as the *Superman* casting process got under way, Kidder was essentially off the grid, on a ranch with her young baby and husband. The marriage was falling apart and she hated ranch life, so Kidder reached out to her business contacts in search of a new role and was sent the *Superman* script. The producers flew her to London to audition, and Donner was sold on her the second that she tripped into the door as she entered the room. Her enthusiastic albeit clumsy energy was exactly what he was looking for, and Kidder won the part.

Simultaneous shooting on *Superman: The Movie* and *Superman II* began in London in 1977 and lasted for more than a year and a half. It was already budgeted to be the most expensive production of all time, and as filming went on the costs continually exceeded the original estimates. Halfway through, the filmmakers had to put the shooting of the second film on hold to complete the first one. The Salkinds grew concerned that they wouldn't recoup their investment, but when the film debuted in December 1978 it shattered the American weekend box office record and went on to earn almost six times its massive budget globally.

The film was an origin story for Superman, beginning with the destruction of Krypton and Clark's childhood in Smallville, Kansas, before he moved to Metropolis to get a job at the *Daily Planet*. Kidder didn't appear as Lois Lane until more than forty-five minutes into the movie, but when she finally showed up she was a force of nature.* When first introduced to Reeve's bumbling Clark, she completely ignored him and instead swept through Perry White's office to pitch a series of articles about a string of senseless killings in the city. Later that day, Lois and Clark were mugged as they left the office, but instead of handing over her purse she dropped it on the ground and kicked the mugger in the face as he bent down to pick it up. Lois had a tough exterior, be it toward potential rivals or toward muggers, though she did eventually warm toward Clark.

This Lois was wholly committed to her job. After she turned down a dinner date with Clark because she was going to the airport after work to grill the president as soon as he stepped off Air Force One, Clark asked, "Goodness, don't you ever let up?" Lois replied, "What for? Hmm? I mean, I've seen how the other half lives. My sister, for example. Three kids, two cats, and one mortgage. Yech! I would go bananas in a week!"

Lois continued to display her commitment to the job when she became the first person whom Superman saved. The helicopter that was going to take her to the airport got caught on a loose cable and

---

* There was a short glimpse of Lois as a child earlier in the movie. She was a passenger on a train who was surprised to see a young Clark Kent outrunning the locomotive. Fittingly, her mother was played by Noel Neill.

careened off the top of the *Daily Planet* building, throwing Lois out of the cockpit. As she plummeted toward the ground, Superman swooped in and caught her, telling her, "Easy, miss. I've got you." Lois responded with one of the film's most iconic lines: "Y-You've got me? Who's got you?" Once Superman set her safely back on the roof and turned to depart, Lois had the journalistic wherewithal to call out to him, "Wait . . . who are you?" Only when Superman was gone did she finally succumb to the shock of the moment and fall to the ground in a faint.

As the film progressed, it managed the rare feat of introducing a romantic element to Lois's story without compromising her reporting prowess. Superman chose Lois for his first interview, and their conversation on her balcony was both thorough and flirtatious. Lois was clearly smitten with the Man of Steel. Her first two questions were "Are you married?" and "Do you have a girlfriend?" Things only heated up from there, with Lois posing innuendo-laden questions like "How big are you—how tall are you?" and asking Superman to use his X-ray vision to guess what color underwear she was wearing. Kidder and Reeve's chemistry permeated the scene, yet Lois remained on task, asking all of the relevant questions in the midst of their flirtations to compile a solid profile of the new hero. The scene ended with a romantic flight through Metropolis and was followed by Lois giving Superman his name and getting a front page exclusive interview: "I Spent the Night with Superman."

From then on, Lois was less of a factor in *Superman: The Movie*, as Lex Luthor commandeered a pair of nuclear missiles and took over the plot. The extent of Lois's involvement in the film's conclusion was as a damsel in distress. When she was killed as a result of one of Luthor's missile attacks, a distraught Superman flew around the world so fast that he went back in time and was able to stop both missiles, thus saving her life. Lois did end the movie with a line that well captured the character's confident nature: when Jimmy remarked that Superman seemed interested in Lois, she nonchalantly replied, "Who knows, someday, you know, if he's lucky . . ."

After the film's blockbuster debut, Margot Kidder became a breakout star. In 1979 she shared top billing with James Brolin and Rod Steiger in another hit film, the frightening classic *The Amityville*

Horror, and the following year she was back in the newsroom again in *Superman II*, this time with a bigger role.

There was no forty-five-minute wait for Lois Lane this time around. Ten minutes into *Superman II*, Perry White sent his "best reporter" to Paris to cover a hostage situation involving terrorists with a nuclear bomb at the top of the Eiffel Tower. He said to Clark, "If I know Lois Lane, she'll not only come back with a Pulitzer Prize story, but a one-on-one interview with a hydrogen bomb titled 'What Makes Me Tick.'" The movie then cut to Paris, where Lois snuck past the police and into the Eiffel Tower, hid underneath the elevator cab, and ascended to the terrorists' base point to cover the story. She got another front page article out of the trip, titled "Merci Superman: French Terror Scheme 'Bomb.'"

Lois's biggest scoop came later in the film, when she and Clark investigated a story at Niagara Falls. Noticing that Clark disappeared every time Superman showed up, she made the obvious connection. She was so sure that she'd figured out Superman's secret identity that she bet her life on it, throwing herself into the raging rapids of the river below them believing that Clark would turn into Superman and save her. He did no such thing, instead surreptitiously using his heat vision to break off a large tree branch for Lois to grab onto. Clark even fell into the river trying to help Lois as she neared the shore, and Lois had to drag them both to dry land.

As they warmed up in their hotel room next to a roaring fire, Lois was embarrassed about being so wrong about Clark, but she was suddenly proved right. Clark tripped and fell hands first into the fireplace but emerged entirely unscathed.* Now that the jig was up, Lois and Clark/Superman revealed their romantic feelings for each other and flew off to the Fortress of Solitude for their first date.

A holographic representation of Superman's mother that was encoded in the Fortress's crystalline computer informed him that to date a human, Superman would have to become mortal himself.

---

* In Richard Donner's original plan for the film, instead of Lois learning Clark's secret because of an accident, she pulled out a revolver and shot him. He then admitted he was Superman, and chastised Lois that she could have killed Clark if she was wrong. Lois replied, "With a blank? Got ya."

Superman chose Lois over his superpowers and subjected himself to a "molecule chamber" that rendered him powerless. Lois was touched by the gesture, but it was ill-timed; a trio of Kryptonian prisoners, led by the fiendish General Zod, had escaped from the Phantom Zone and were taking over the Earth.

With Superman depowered, the tough-guy role fell to Lois. When a local goon in a small-town diner beat up Clark, Lois jumped on top of his attacker and had to be restrained by the restaurant's owner. Later, when Zod and his cohorts stormed the *Daily Planet* offices, Lois punched his right-hand woman, Ursa, square in the jaw, though it had little effect on the powerful warrior. Superman without super-powers was generally useless, but Lois was as fierce as ever. After Superman's powers were restored and he tricked the invading Kryptonians into losing theirs, Lois continued to fight, knocking out Ursa with a strong punch in the film's final battle.

Superman getting his powers back meant that he and Lois couldn't be together. Lois assured Superman, "You don't have to worry. I'll never tell them who you really are." But she was grief-stricken over the end of their relationship. Wanting to spare her that heartache, Clark gave Lois a hypnotic kiss that removed her memory of the last few days, after which she returned to her normal self and Clark again became just another guy at the office to her. The memory wipe was designed to reset the status quo for the next movie, and it was presented as an act of compassion rather than a sign of mistrust. Still, Superman doing so without her permission was an odd callback to the Silver Age days of Superman thinking he knew what was best for Lois.

Altogether, *Superman II* was a strong showcase for Lois's bravery, intellect, and strength. The film also added to her growing list of endearing eccentricities. In *Superman: The Movie*, Lois had been the reporter who didn't know how to spell, while in *Superman II* she extolled the health benefits of drinking fresh squeezed orange juice every day while she smoked a cigarette. Kidder's Lois Lane had her quirks, but she always got her story.

While the two films were initially supposed to be shot simultaneously, for portions of *Superman II* Lois looked noticeably thinner and had a different haircut. This was because after the second film was put on hold so that Richard Donner could finish the first, the Salkinds fired him over creative and financial differences. *Superman II* was a patchwork of Donner's original footage combined with footage shot months later by new director Richard Lester, who also had several scenes rewritten. The change in director didn't go over well with many in the cast; Gene Hackman refused to return for 1983's *Superman III*, which would again be directed by Lester, and while Margot Kidder agreed to reprise her role, she was very public about her support for Donner and her displeasure over his departure.

Perhaps not coincidentally, Kidder found herself with a much smaller part in *Superman III*. Lois showed up near the beginning of the film to explain that she was going to Bermuda on a lengthy vacation, and she wasn't seen again until the end of film, when she returned to work with a tan and "a front page story that's going to blow the lid off of corruption in the Caribbean." Lana Lang, played by Annette O'Toole, replaced Lois in the role of Superman's love interest, but Lois didn't miss out on much. Left to his own devices without Donner's work to build on, Lester produced an uninspired, slapstick-heavy film that went over poorly with both critics and audiences.

As a result of *Superman III*'s poor performance, the Salkinds sold the rights to Superman to Cannon Films, a production company best known for making B-movies. The cast agreed to return for a fourth Superman film; Reeve was swayed when the producers allowed him to have input on the story, and even Gene Hackman came back as Lex Luthor. Sidney J. Furie was hired to direct,* and in 1986 filming began on *Superman IV: The Quest for Peace*, which pitted Superman against Nuclear Man, a villain controlled by Luthor and fueled by nuclear energy.

Shooting went badly on every level. Cannon continually slashed the film's budget, and the end result looked shoddy, with subpar special effects and reused stock footage throughout. Tensions ran

---

* Furie holds the rare distinction of having been nominated over the course of his career for both a Palme d'Or (for *The IPCRESS File*) and a Razzie Award (for the 1980 remake of *The Jazz Singer*).

high on set as well. While the cast had been like a family back in the Donner days, Kidder recalls that Reeve was "really full of himself because he'd written part of it," and the two of them bickered constantly. Ultimately, Kidder thought that *Superman IV* turned out to be "a dreadful piece of shit," and audiences agreed.

The film again had Superman manipulating Lois's memory. Superman was conflicted over what to do about the world's nuclear weapons after a child asked him to just get rid of them all, so he decided to talk to his closest friend about it. Clark revealed to Lois that he was Superman, and the two relived their flying scene from *Superman: The Movie*. After they talked, Superman felt much better and casually erased Lois's memory with another super-kiss. *Superman IV* combined the worst parts of its predecessors when it came to Lois Lane. On top of the hypnotic smooch, Lois was a key player in a supposedly comedic double date scene with Clark and Superman that was reminiscent of Lester's slapstick shtick.

But Lois wasn't without her strong moments. When a new publisher bought the *Daily Planet* and turned it into a trashy tabloid, Lois ferociously fought against the changes. Later, when the world thought that Superman was dead after Nuclear Man defeated him, Lois had faith that he was still alive and took his cape to Clark. Despite the various memory wipes, Lois knew that Clark was Superman and, without saying so explicitly, gave him a pep talk and told him that she still believed in him. Lois was too smart for even Superman's memory wipes to overcome.

The film series' significant drops in quality weren't enough to tarnish its legacy, and today Margot Kidder's Lois Lane is generally regarded as the most iconic version of the character. A brash, unstoppable exterior hiding a kind interior became the standard for Lois moving forward across all media, though her portrayals in subsequent Superman films have yet to reach the bar set by Kidder.

Superman Returns

Warner Bros. began to develop a new Superman film in the early 1990s. The project remained in limbo for over a decade, costing the studio millions of dollars as they pursued new scripts and directors only to have each attempt fall through. Tim Burton, McG, Wolfgang Petersen, and Brett Ratner were all attached to direct before Bryan Singer took the reins in 2004. Fresh off launching the wildly successful X-Men film franchise, Singer brought new life to the project, and *Superman Returns* hit theaters in 2006.

The film was a quasi-sequel to *Superman II*. Ignoring *Superman III* and *Superman IV*, it began with Superman returning to Earth after a five-year absence. Singer retained the aesthetics of Donner's original films and referenced them constantly, even copying the casting strategy. He used old footage of Marlon Brando as Jor-El, cast a known star, Kevin Spacey, as Lex Luthor, and hired an unknown actor, Brandon Routh, to play Superman.*

Singer looked at several actresses for Lois Lane, including Claire Danes and Keri Russell, while Kevin Spacey lobbied for his costar from the film *Beyond the Sea*, Kate Bosworth. Bosworth was born in Los Angeles and moved throughout the country several times with her family before she started acting in New York as a teenager. Her big break came in the surfing film *Blue Crush*, and she followed that up with several starring roles. Singer liked her work and gave her the part.

On paper, Lois Lane had a lot of strong moments in *Superman Returns*, but some odd story choices and an uninspired performance from Bosworth muddied the end product. Singer's tale put Lois in a new position; during Superman's absence, she'd gotten engaged to Perry White's nephew Richard and had a child. She'd also written an article titled "Why the World Doesn't Need Superman" that earned her a Pulitzer Prize. When Superman came back to Earth, he found an antagonist instead of an ally.

Lois was introduced on board an airliner with a space shuttle strapped to its hull, where she was covering the first midair shuttle launch. A mechanical failure caused the shuttle's rockets to fire while it was still attached to the plane, rocking the vessel and injuring the

---

* Noel Neill also cameoed as a rich woman seduced by Lex Luthor into bequeathing him her fortune.

event's hostess, so Lois got out of her seat to help get the hostess strapped in. As the plane spun out of control, the now-unbelted Lois careened around the cabin until Superman saved both the airliner and the shuttle. Back on the ground, Lois didn't care at all about Superman's return, instead pursuing the story behind the electromagnetic pulse that had disrupted the launch and blacked out most of Metropolis. This was the right course of action, seeing as Lex Luthor was behind it all. When Superman tried to talk to her later in the film, she declared, "The world doesn't need a savior and neither do I."

However, Lois's dismissiveness seemed like the anger of a jilted lover rather than the result of any real journalistic conviction. Her son was revealed to be Superman's child, presumably the product of their Fortress of Solitude tryst in *Superman II*, and she began to warm to the Man of Steel again after he took her flying. She ended up saving him near the end of the film, bravely diving into frigid water to rescue him after Luthor stabbed him with a Kryptonite shard and he fell into the sea. After Superman ultimately foiled his nemesis's plan, Lois visited him in the hospital, kissed him, and wrote a new article titled "Why the World Needs Superman."

In his review of the film, Roger Ebert wrote, "Lois Lane has lost her dash and pizzazz," a sentiment echoed by many reviewers and fans; Bosworth's Lois lacked the brashness and snark that Kidder had brought to the role. Her flat performance undercut Lois's occasional strong moments, and her lack of chemistry with Routh made the awkward romantic plotline even less effective.

This incarnation of Lois was also the only one of the five modern live action versions who didn't figure out that Clark Kent was Superman.* To be fair, most of the other Loises had more time to put it all together; Bosworth only had one film. *Superman Returns* was moderately successful, bringing in just under $400 million worldwide, but its box office total was less than that of Singer's latest X-Men film, and audiences didn't react well to a deadbeat dad Superman or a story that leaned heavily on a film franchise that had ended two

---

* Including Lois's two live action television incarnations, discussed in chapter 9.

decades before. A planned sequel was canceled, and Warner Bros. brought out a brand new film, with a new Lois, seven years later.

Man of Steel

The superhero film market of the twenty-first century has been a tale of two approaches. Marvel developed a reputation for movies that were bright and funny, while DC's biggest success was the gloomy and serious *Dark Knight* franchise. When Warner Bros. decided to relaunch Superman, they hired the *Dark Knight* creative team to develop the project along the same lines. A new addition to the team was director Zack Snyder, who was known for his adaptations of the weighty comic book classics *300* and *Watchmen*.

The new film, titled simply *Man of Steel*, was a somber affair. The bright colors traditionally associated with Superman were muted. The climactic fight scene resulted in mass destruction and death, including Superman murdering his foe. There were few smiles, let alone laughs, over the course of the film. It was meant to be a real-world take on superheroes that dealt seriously with the genre. Snyder later said of the movie, "I really wanted to show the violence is real, people get killed or get hurt, and it's not fun or funny."

Henry Cavill starred as Superman and Michael Shannon played the malevolent General Zod. Well-known actors like Kevin Costner, Russell Crowe, Laurence Fishburne, and Diane Lane costarred in supporting roles, and for Lois Lane, Snyder turned to a multiple Academy Award nominee.

Snyder had met with several actresses about the role, including Jessica Biel, Mila Kunis, and Olivia Wilde, but Amy Adams soon rose to the top of the pack. Adams was born in Italy to American parents; her father was in the military, and she moved often during her childhood. After high school, Adams had a regular musical theater gig in Minneapolis for several years before she relocated to Los Angeles to pursue a film career. She found steady work, including a guest spot on *Smallville*, and struck it big with the Disney film *Enchanted* in 2007. Her film career exploded from there; when Adams was cast as Lois Lane four years later, she'd already received three Academy Award nominations, and she's been nominated again since then.

Adams had been a fan of Lois since she watched *Superman II* at a sleepover with her gymnastics team as a young girl. She loved the film so much that she made tinfoil bedsheets for her Barbie dolls, mimicking the metallic bedding in the Fortress of Solitude. Adams auditioned for the role on three different projects: Brett Ratner's failed Superman film, Bryan Singer's *Superman Returns,* and finally *Man of Steel.* Her audition and meeting with Snyder sold him immediately.

Initially, Adams's Lois was a bright spot in the perpetually dour *Man of Steel.* In her first scene, she muscled her way into covering an American military investigation of what appeared to be a Soviet submarine found frozen in the Arctic ice. After getting a cold shoulder from the commanding officer, Lois snuck onto the ship, which was actually an ancient Kryptonian scouting vessel. She was injured by the ship's defense system and saved by a mysterious superpowered man, who then disappeared.

Perry White refused to print her story, considering it too outlandish, so she leaked it online and set about finding her mystery man. Unlike every previous incarnation of the character, Lois discovered that Clark Kent had superpowers right away, before he even arrived in Metropolis or unveiled himself to the world as Superman. She didn't know his name and he'd used an alias to get into the Arctic site, but she tracked him back through reports of spectacular feats until she landed in Smallville and then at the front door of the Kent farmhouse.

Having quickly established Lois as a brilliant and unstoppable reporter, *Man of Steel* then demonstrated that she was in it for the truth, not the front page story. After she met Clark and heard his story, she dropped her article despite the anger of the now-interested Perry White. Clark was afraid that the world wasn't ready for him, and she agreed and kept his secret. She protected it even when Zod threatened to attack the Earth if its citizens didn't hand over Kal-El. Lois took off running when the FBI came to interrogate her about her mysterious stranger, and after they captured her she refused to talk, instead leaving the decision of whether or not to reveal himself up to Clark.

He did reveal himself, but as Superman and not Clark, and from then on Lois became a nonfactor in the film. She traveled with

Superman to Zod's ship as a hostage but served as little more than a puppet as the computerized ghost of Jor-El walked her through escaping. Also, she and Superman fell immediately in love despite having spent barely five minutes of screen time together. They drifted down to Earth in a romantic slow spin after escaping Zod's ship, and Lois spent the rest of the movie breathlessly following Superman from scene to scene, her face set in an expression of concern and her eyes slightly welled up with tears.

While Adams's Lois could be tough, she didn't have the brashness usually associated with the character, and her dialogue lacked snap. However, *Man of Steel* established a unique status quo for Lois and Clark moving forward. The film ended with Clark getting a job at the *Daily Planet*, presumably thanks to Lois. With Lois having figured out his secret at the very beginning, the franchise seems poised to skip the secret identity shenanigans that have traditionally undermined her intellect and instead portray Lois as a smart, capable partner to both Clark and Superman as the characters are incorporated into Warner Bros.' plans for a DC Comics cinematic universe.

7a

Parodies and Homages

Three months after *Superman: The Movie* broke box office records on the big screen, Margot Kidder took to the small screen to host *Saturday Night Live*. She reprised the role of Lois Lane in a sketch in which Lois and her new husband, Bill Murray as Superman, hosted a party for their superhero friends.* Dan Aykroyd played the Flash, John Belushi was the Hulk, Garrett Morris appeared as Ant-Man, and Jane Curtin played Lana Lang.

After Superman stepped out to get some ice and Clark Kent arrived at the party, Lois confided in Clark that she wasn't happy being married to Superman. She declared, "I can't tell you how incredibly dull he is! I mean, he's so kindhearted and all that, but he's so boring sometimes I think I'm gonna lose my mind." She also mentioned Superman's sexual inadequacies; Superman was a virgin on their wedding night, while Lois was used to dating more experienced and enthusiastic men like the Hulk. Clark was so upset by these revelations that he revealed his secret identity to everyone at the party and shooed them out, ending the scene.

The sketch was scattered and a bit flat, playing to sporadic laughs. Nevertheless, it said a lot about how people saw Lois in this

---

* Another Lois, Teri Hatcher from TV's *Lois & Clark*, would host *Saturday Night Live* in 1996. While she didn't play Lois, her monologue centered on her inability to recognize cast members when they were wearing glasses.

era: Superman was presented as old fashioned and square, while Lois was a frank modern woman.

This was just one of many spoofs on the Man of Steel across a variety of media in the decades following his 1938 debut. While Superman was often the focus of these parodies, the depiction of their various Lois Lanes illustrates how the public perception of the character has evolved over time.

Looney Loises

One of the earliest parodies of Superman was a superheroic rodent who appeared in a series of cartoon shorts created by Paul Terry of Terrytoons beginning in 1942. While today the character is most commonly known as Mighty Mouse and wears a yellow and red costume, originally he was called Super Mouse and his costume was blue and red to more directly ape Superman. Looney Tunes tackled similar ground in 1943 with *Super-Rabbit*. In this cartoon short, altered carrots turned Bugs Bunny into Super-Rabbit, and the opening was an impressively accurate homage to the Fleischer Studios' animated Superman shorts. However, neither Terrytoons nor Looney Tunes saw fit to include a Lois Lane analogue. It seems that while Superman was wildly popular in the early 1940s, Lois hadn't yet been cemented as a key component of his mythos.

By the late '40s, with Mighty Mouse renamed and his shorts revamped into their familiar "Here I come to save the day!" operatic style, an alliteratively named damsel in distress had become a regular part of his cartoons. Pearl Pureheart was constantly captured and ultimately rescued by Mighty Mouse at the end of each short, but in the meantime she fiercely fought back against her captor. When she was eventually subdued, she remained upbeat. In one short, Pearl nonchalantly powdered her nose while tied to a speeding vehicle; in another she worked on needlepoint while she was tied to the tracks of a roller coaster, singing, "I'm not worried, ha ha, hee hee hee! My hero's on the way and he will rescue me." Pearl's depiction perhaps owed more to westerns than to the superhero genre, but her pluck and calm are reminiscent of several of Lois's early adventures in comics, radio, and cartoons.

Direct Lois clones began to appear in other DC comic books around this time as well. In 1948, a photojournalist named Vicki Vale debuted as a romantic interest for Batman. Two years later, Lana Lang appeared as Superboy's childhood sweetheart. Both alliteratively named women were inquisitive and tenacious and spent most of their time trying to decipher the secret identity of their beau. It's clear that the decision-makers at DC Comics at the time believed that Lois's key characteristic was her quest to link Clark Kent with Superman, so the writers copied that trait onto their new female characters.*

In the midst of all this secret identity hysteria, *MAD Magazine* #4 took a different tack with its parody "Superduperman" in April 1953. Written by Harvey Kurtzman with art by Wally Wood—both heralded as comic book legends today—the story was a huge hit for *MAD*, and it helped to establish the satirical tone of the magazine in its early days, when it was still finding its voice. Clark Bent was a lowly assistant copyboy who turned into Superduperman, an arrogant and powerful hero, while Lois Pain was a star reporter who had no time for the sniveling Clark. When Clark saved all his money to buy Lois some expensive jewelry, she replied, "Yawn! Another pearl necklace! Waddit set you back, creep?" and quickly dismissed him: "Thanks, creep! Now go away, boy! You bother me!" Clark begged to be allowed to smell her perfume for a minute, but she refused him.

At the story's end, Superduperman revealed his secret identity and boorishly taunted Lois: "Now you'd give your bottom dollar for me to sniff your perfume I supposen't!" Lois was not interested and shouted, "**Hands off!** So you're Superduperman instead of Clark Bent! . . . Big deal! Yer **still** a creep!" This version of Lois was self-assured and not interested in romance with Superduperman at all. Instead, she served as the voice of her creators' critique of the Man of Steel. With "Superduperman," Kurtzman and Wood exaggerated the creepiness and arrogance they saw in Superman, deglamorizing

---

* In 1956, a female reporter named Iris West debuted as a love interest for the Flash, and in the years that followed she was surprisingly unconcerned about secret identities. This may be due to Lois moving away from that obsession, or DC's writers learning to differentiate their female characters.

the muscle-bound hero; Lois Pain's disdain for both Clark Bent and Superduperman echoed their sentiments. Their Lois was confident and independent, and too smart to fall for a jerk like Superduperman.

"Superclod," a 1956 sketch on *The Ernie Kovacs Show*, was clearly influenced by Superduperman, but the satire was much softer. Kovacs played Clark as a bit of a buffoon, knitting away at his desk while Lois, played by Edie Adams, typed out a big story. When Clark asked Lois out on a date, she responded, "I simply won't go out with a poor excuse for a man. Why, you're . . . you're . . . pusillanimous!" She later said, "If only you could be more like Superclod! Now there's a man!" Kovacs's Superclod was as broad as his Clark. He wore a silly metal hat, couldn't see without his glasses, and had to get help to open the window so he could fly out of the office. At the end of the sketch, an exhausted Superclod flew off, asleep, while Lois just shook her head at the camera.

Both Clark and Superclod were clownishly incompetent, while Lois was the one who had it together. Compared with the *MAD* parody, the sketch incorporated rather than inverted Lois's typical traits: she noticed that Clark looked a lot like Superclod, and she was interested in Superclod and not Clark. But ultimately, Lois was depicted as an ace reporter and even realized what a dolt Superclod was. Her reputation as an intelligent journalist was becoming a defining trait.

This continued on television screens in 1964 with the children's cartoon *Underdog*. The hero of the show was a canine spoof of Superman with a red costume and a blue cape. His secret identity was the "humble and lovable" Shoeshine Boy, but when danger arose he'd leap into a phone booth and emerge as a superhero. Onlookers would call out, "It's a plane!" "It's a bird!" "It's a frog!" to which he always replied, "Not plane, not bird, nor even frog, it's just little old me, Underdog."

A female reporter completed the Superman parody. Sweet Polly Purebred, voiced by Norma MacMillan, was a television news anchor, often referred to as "TV's top reporter." * Her primary role

---

* In the 2007 live action *Underdog* film, Sweet Polly was voiced by Amy Adams, who would go on to play Lois Lane in *Man of Steel*.

on the show was as a damsel in distress. Villains regularly captured her specifically to lure Underdog into a trap, and she frequently sang, "Oh where, oh where has my Underdog gone? Oh where, oh where can he be?" to summon the hero. *Underdog* stories extended across four episodes, and Sweet Polly was guaranteed to be in harm's way in at least one, and often more, of the installments.

At the same time, Sweet Polly was a respected reporter who never shied away from a big story. When her network's ratings were down and an executive wanted to send her to an island with a giant ape, Sweet Polly replied, "How wonderful!" When she interviewed a scientist about to investigate dangerous ocean phenomena, she said, "Oh, how thrilling! I wish I could come along and televise the whole thing for our viewers!" and ended up accompanying him. Sweet Polly went undercover, flew airplanes, and even traveled into space on multiple occasions to get news stories. She always got captured at some point, but she was adventurous nonetheless. Furthermore, Underdog was regularly captured as well; he was clumsy and comically inept at times, and often ended up trapped with Sweet Polly. Occasionally, Sweet Polly even got to be the one who freed them both.

By the late 1960s, Lois analogues were receding into the background of Superman parodies. Gilbert Shelton's *Wonder Wart-Hog* was a spoof of the Man of Steel that was popular in the underground comics scene, starring a "timid, mild-mannered reporter" named Philbert Desanex who transformed into the titular hero. The first few stories in 1962 featured Melody Lane, a fellow reporter who suspected a connection between Philbert and Wonder Wart-Hog. Her primary purpose was to relay news to Philbert that spurred him into action, but she disappeared after the first few stories. Marvel's Superman parody "The Origin of Stuporman" in 1968 had its Lois, Locust Pain, appear in only two of the story's panels, exclaiming, "Oh, **Stupey**, it's just **divine** of you to keep **rescuin'** little ol' me!" With the *Adventures of Superman* television series long past and Marvel comics outselling the old-fashioned Superman comics, Lois Lane appeared to be fading from public view.

She returned to the fore in two parodies from 1969, but Lois fans had little reason to celebrate, as both pieces subjected the character to graphic sexual violence. In a new Wonder Wart-Hog tale in

R. Crumb's *Zap! Comix* #4, Gilbert Shelton introduced a reporter named Lois Lamebrain. Wonder Wart-Hog stripped her and groped her when she passed out, raped her with his snout after she woke up and laughed at his small penis, and then killed her when he sneezed while raping her. Perhaps influenced by this tale, Larry Niven's essay "Man of Steel, Woman of Kleenex" appeared in *Knight: The Magazine for the Adult Male*. Niven argued that because "one loses control over one's muscles" during an orgasm, if Superman had sex with Lois then he "would literally crush LL's body in his arms." Ultimately, "Kal-El's semen would emerge with the muzzle velocity of a machine gun bullet" and "he'd blow off the top of her head."

These pieces are less a commentary on Lois Lane than a reflection of the countercultural boundary-pushing common during the sexual revolution of the late 1960s. People were dealing with sex openly and frankly for the first time, but in some circles this came with ingrained misogyny and childish, grotesque attempts at humor. Primarily male spaces like men's magazines and underground comics, in particular, became avenues for male writers and artists to engage in their bizarre fantasies; *Zap! Comix* publisher R. Crumb called his comics a means for "getting rid of all this pent-up sex rage." As a result, they were often awash with crude, sexually violent images.* Such pieces said far more about their creators than their subjects.

A decade later, *Superman: The Movie* reignited the Superman craze and *MAD Magazine* brought back Superduperman in 1979 to do a parody of the film. It was a goofier, cornier strip than the original; Krypton was called Krapton, the farmers who found baby Superduperman named him Cluck after their favorite chicken, and Superduperman fixed the splitting San Andreas Fault with a giant zipper. The art was different as well, with Mort Drucker's iconic caricature style replacing Wally Wood's classic cartooning.

Instead of bringing back Lois Pain, the new strip introduced Lotus Lain, and the sharp satire of the original strip was traded for

---

* The rampant sexism and lack of support for female cartoonists in the underground comics scene led to women starting their own publications, like *Wimmen's Comix* and *Tits & Clits Comix*.

silly cynicism. *MAD* poked fun at Lotus's inability to see that Cluck Kennt was Superduperman; during their rooftop meeting, she said, "Y'know, if you were wearing **glasses**, you'd look **exactly** like someone I **know**, but I **can't** quite think **who** . . . !" and later exclaimed, "I got it!! **Henry Kissinger!**" When Lotus named the new hero Superduperman, he sarcastically replied, "**Great!** And I'm going to call you **'Old Eagle Eye'!**"

MAD's *Superman II* parody a few years later continued in the same vein. When Lotus noticed that she'd never seen Cluck and Superduperman together, she jubilantly declared, "**You're deliberately avoiding him!! Right?!**" After Lotus finally realized the truth, Superduperman asked her, "Was it because we have the **same build** and the **same features?** . . . Because we have **identical speaking voices?** . . . Because back at the hotel, I slept in **red and blue jammies** with a **big 'S'** on them?" This clueless take on Lois Lane wasn't a critique of the character so much as emblematic of a weariness with the tropes of the genre and of movies in general. The first strip ended with Superduperman telling Lotus that he brought her back to life because the Warner Bros. executives "**reminded** me that **without** Lotus Lain, there's no **'Superduperman II'!**"

However, *MAD*'s angle that it was ridiculous for Lois not to realize that Clark was Superman came at the same time that comic book readers began to believe that Lois actually knew Clark's secret. Both views were indicative of a public perception of Lois as a smart investigative reporter, clever enough to put the pieces together. *MAD* took it to comical extremes, but there was some respect for Lois underneath the many jokes they made at her expense.

8

A Whole New World

*L*ois didn't have much to do as *Crisis on Infinite Earths* ripped
across DC Comics' parallel universes. The crisis in question
was an intergalactic, multiversal war against a creature from an
antimatter universe bent on destroying all of space and time. Entire
universes were wiped from existence, and the plan to defeat the evil
Anti-Monitor involved traveling back to the dawn of time for a massive battle. Lois was an ace reporter, but this was definitely a job for
Superman, along with scores of other superheroes.

The heroes ultimately won, of course, and the result was a single
streamlined universe in which all of DC's characters coexisted. The
other Earths that had appeared throughout the Silver and Bronze
Ages were gone as DC Comics entered what both fans and historians refer to as the Modern Age.* This new universe came with a
partial reboot. Some of DC's characters, like Batman and the Flash,
retained significant portions of their pre-*Crisis* continuity; most of
the Silver Age frivolity was forgotten, but their Bronze Age history

---

* The "Mr. and Mrs. Superman" feature in *Superman Family* had been set on Earth-Two, a
world where stories of Golden Age heroes continued, and Earth-Two's Superman played a
key role in defeating the Anti-Monitor. Ultimately he, Earth-Two's Lois, Earth-Three's hero
Alexander Luthor, and Earth-Prime's Superboy survived the crisis in a pocket universe,
but they weren't seen again until two decades later in *Infinite Crisis*.

was left largely intact. Other characters, like Wonder Woman, were rebooted entirely, their past adventures wiped away and replaced with brand new stories.

Superman was a logical target for a complete reboot. After nearly fifty years of comics, the history of the Super-books had become too cumbersome. There were multiple iterations of each villain, Superman's powers had reached almost godlike levels, and relationships were severely strained after decades of romantic ups and downs. DC chose to start over from the very beginning with Superman, retaining key components of his mythos but otherwise wiping the slate clean. The man given the task of creating the new Man of Steel was John Byrne, a writer and artist who brought new life to all of Metropolis's citizens, especially Lois Lane.

John Byrne's New Lois Lane

Today, most comic book fans know John Byrne as a bit of an eccentric crank who spends a lot of time on his personal message board grousing about the comic book industry and the world in general. While he still writes and draws comics, he works primarily for smaller publishers; he hasn't done a comic at DC or Marvel in several years. But in the 1980s, there were few creators as popular as John Byrne.

Byrne had made a name for himself at Marvel, drawing and later co-plotting Chris Claremont's historic run on *X-Men* starting in 1977. He drew famous story lines like "The Dark Phoenix Saga" and "Days of Future Past," both of which were later adapted in the X-Men film franchise. Byrne also drew *Avengers* and *Captain America*, and wrote and drew a very well-regarded five-year run of *Fantastic Four*.

When Byrne moved to DC Comics to relaunch the Super-books, he received a significant amount of creative control. He was the writer and artist of both *Action Comics* and *Superman*, the two flagship Superman titles. The new series *Adventures of Superman* launched at the same time with Marv Wolfman writing and Jerry Ordway on art, but before long Wolfman was out and Byrne was cowriting that book as well. Byrne so dominated the Super-books that editor Andrew Helfer felt unneeded and left the books, and new editor Mike Carlin mostly just stayed out of Byrne's way.

Byrne's run began with *The Man of Steel*, a six-issue miniseries that laid out Superman's revised backstory before Byrne relaunched the monthly series. The first issue, which debuted in October 1986, also introduced readers to the new Lois Lane. Byrne later said of his take on Lois, "I wanted Lois to be a three-dimensional character who had more to her than just wanting to nail Superman as the ultimate catch." When Lois first appeared, she was on board an experimental space plane, covering its maiden flight for the *Daily Planet*. After a jet collided with the plane, Clark Kent used his powers in public for the first time, grabbing the vessel and landing it safely.* As Clark ran off to avoid detection, Lois bounded out of the space plane and yelled, **"HOLD IT RIGHT THERE, BUSTER!!!"** But the mysterious hero disappeared, and subsequently adopted the iconic cape and tights to protect his civilian identity during future rescue missions.

Throughout the book's second issue, Lois was hot on his trail. Perry White told her to go get the story and Lois promised, "As good as got, Chief! Tell the rewrite boys to stay close to their phones— **Lois Lane** is on the job!!" She scoured Metropolis trying to find the newly costumed hero, whom she'd dubbed "Superman" in her article about the space plane, but she kept missing him; he always took off just before she arrived on the scene of his latest feat. Lois remained determined because, as she explained to her pilot as she prepared to jump from a helicopter to a roof below in pursuit of Superman, "I didn't win my Pulitzer Prize by sitting in front of a word processor all day!"

In the end, Lois took matters into her own hands by intentionally driving her car off a bridge and into a river. After Superman rescued her and dropped her off at home, he turned to leave but she shouted, **"COME BACK HERE!!!"** Impressed by Lois's tenacity, Superman

---

* Byrne simplified Superman's early life, doing away with classic elements like Krypto the Superdog, his Fortress of Solitude, and his teenage adventures as Superboy. Instead, Clark used his powers in public for the first time as a grown man in Metropolis. He didn't even learn about his Kryptonian heritage until after he became Superman.

stayed and granted her a short interview before returning to his duties. In the old days, Lois would have been all aflutter at meeting Superman, but this time it was Superman who came away infatuated. As he flew off, he thought, "She's quite a woman, Lois Lane. **Quite** a woman! And quite a **reporter**, too!"

Byrne's Lois was a tireless, award-winning reporter, and the 1988 miniseries *World of Metropolis* showed how Lois's journalistic inclinations dated all the way back to her childhood. As a young girl, Lois's class visited the *Daily Planet* offices on a field trip, and Lois knew more about the newspaper's history than the reporter assigned to lead the tour. She was awed to come across then-reporter Perry White; when he got into an expletive-laden argument about journalistic integrity with his editor, Lois cheered, "Attaway t'go, Mr. White! You **tell** him!"

Young Lois was back at the *Daily Planet* a few years later, declaring that she'd be "the best darn reporter this paper has ever had!" and lying about her age to try to get a job until her sister ratted her out, telling Perry that Lois was only fifteen. They got kicked out of the *Daily Planet* offices, but Lois heard something about Perry investigating Lex Luthor on the elevator ride down. Later that night, Lois broke into Luthor's building and, although she was caught and tossed out, absconded with a piece of paper that she'd hidden in her mouth. She went back to the *Daily Planet* the next day and the paper proved useful for Perry. Lois worked for him from then on.

But as great a reporter as Lois was, back in the present day she missed out on the scoop of the century. By the time she'd typed up her first interview with Superman, a new reporter named Clark Kent showed up at the *Daily Planet* with his own interview with the Man of Steel. He was hired straightaway, and his story ran on the front page before Lois made it back to the office with her now-redundant article.

Lois was apoplectic, and remained so for some time. When the fourth issue of *Man of Steel* jumped ahead eighteen months, she was still furious. Lois was forced to work with Clark on a story, and she referred to him as "swine" and a "big dope," belittling him the entire time they were together. She even remembered the exact number of days since Clark had outscooped her.* When *Superman* relaunched with a new first issue in January 1987, Lois's anger hadn't let up. After weeks of trying, Clark had convinced Lois to go jogging with him, but she still referred to him as "the **weasel** who beat me to the first **exclusive** on Superman."

A year later, Lois learned why he was able to get the scoop, and her fury reignited. While visiting Clark's home town of Smallville to cover a story, she ran into Clark's high school sweetheart, Lana Lang, and she was hugging Superman.† After putting things together and asking Superman point blank if he was Clark Kent, Ma and Pa Kent bailed out their son by telling Lois that Superman was Clark's adopted brother.‡ Lois flipped out, shaking her finger at Superman and yelling, "You big **jerk!** You and Kent have been having just the **best** time, haven't you? Tossing me a story, every now and then, just to keep me **going. Playing** with me." She stormed out, and was still mad at the end of the issue even after Clark, Lana, and Superman had all tried to calm her down.

Clark was especially keen to pacify Lois because he'd fallen in love with her. The jogging date in *Superman* #1 had been one of several attempts on Clark's part to get Lois to like him. In a reversal of the pre-*Crisis* dynamic, Clark was now the center of the romantic hijinks; he constantly wooed Lois, but she wasn't particularly interested in romance. She hated Clark, and while she liked Superman well enough, she was too busy chasing down stories to spend much of her time mooning over him.

Clark wasn't Lois's only suitor. Lex Luthor, reimagined as a corrupt business tycoon, also carried a torch for Lois and was similarly rebuffed. When Lois and Clark went to cover a soiree on the

---

* "Seventeen months, two weeks, four days, and an odd number of hours."
† Lana Lang was no longer Lois's vivacious big-city rival. She remained a small-town girl, and she never really got over the fact that Clark had moved to Metropolis, leaving Smallville, and her, behind. Lana was also unwittingly involved in an attack by the Manhunters, a group of interstellar robots, which caused her even more emotional trauma. She flitted in and out of the Super-books during the Modern Age but was never the strong presence she used to be in the pre-*Crisis* comics.
‡ The adopted brother ruse came up occasionally after this issue, but it was such a flimsy cover story that it soon fell into disuse and was forgotten.

businessman's yacht, Luthor sent Lois a designer dress that she assumed was a loaner and so she wore it.* While on the boat, Luthor told her that it was a gift and declared, "You know full well how much I **desire** you. Give me the chance, and I could make you the **happiest** woman in the world." The gift was both an affront to Lois as a journalist and a romantic advance that disgusted her, so she immediately took off the dress and wore Clark's suit jacket instead. She later disarmed a hijacker and blasted machine gun fire at the other men who were attempting to take over the yacht, all in heels and a suit jacket.

The new Lois handled herself well in dangerous situations, which came up often seeing as she actively sought them out. She went under-cover to find a wanted extortionist, beating up his goons when her wig fell off and exposed her identity. She broke into a paramilitary camp to rescue Jimmy Olsen, taking out several well-armed soldiers in the process, including one wielding a bazooka. Even when she came up against powerful supervillains, Lois was unfazed; when the Kryptonite-powered Metallo nabbed her, she just taunted, "Where the heck did you pick up a **cornball** name like that?" Lois was a tough gal who had no time for romance, but that soon changed.

Romance Blooms

After a couple of years unattached, romance developed for Lois and Superman, just not together. Superman had a brief dalliance with Wonder Woman until they decided to instead be friends. Lois dated Jose Delgado, a former boxer who fought crime in Metropo-lis's Suicide Slum as the superhero Gangbuster, but the relationship soured when Delgado became involved with a company owned by Lex Luthor. Single again, Lois slowly turned her gaze toward Clark.

Their relationship developed in fits and starts. Lois's anger at Clark began to thaw during John Byrne's tenure; she wasn't yet inter-ested in him, but she wasn't pleased when someone else was. After

---

* She also got a trendy haircut to match the dress. The new Lois's hair was chestnut brown, and she cut it short in a style that she kept for several years after.

she skipped out on a lunch date with Clark in *Superman* #11, Lois stopped by his apartment that evening for dinner and found their new coworker, gossip columnist Cat Grant, already there. From then on, Lois had nothing but animosity for Cat. Even when Cat tried to be friendly with Lois, asking about her mother's health when she heard that she was ill, Lois immediately shut her down and insulted Cat for not covering real news.

By 1988, Byrne was displeased by his perceived lack of support from DC Comics. He felt that editorial was more interested in catering to the whims of fandom than backing his vision for the Super-books, and he resented that DC continued to use the pre-*Crisis* Superman in all of its licensed properties. Frustrated and no longer having fun, Byrne quit. *Action Comics* briefly became a weekly book in which Lois was barely featured, while Jerry Ordway took over *Superman* and Dan Jurgens wrote and drew *Adventures of Superman*. Writer Louise Simonson and artist Jon Bogdanove joined the team in 1991, launching a fourth series, *Superman: The Man of Steel*.

With new creators at the helm and editor Mike Carlin working to keep all of the books in sync, Lois's hatred of Clark disappeared for good. When one story arc had Superman trapped deep in space, Clark was "missing" on Earth and Lois went to his apartment to look for clues. Instead of feeling glad to be rid of a hated rival, Lois cried for her lost friend. She missed Clark again months later when he left the *Daily Planet* to become managing editor for the magazine *Newstime*, so much so that she even asked him on a date so that they could catch up. Unfortunately for Lois, she was the victim of bad timing; Clark was under the influence of the Eradicator, a sort of Kryptonian warrior AI, and with his new martial inclinations he had no interest in social interactions and rudely rebuffed Lois's invitation.

In May 1990, after Superman defeated the Eradicator, Clark returned to the *Daily Planet*. He apologized to Lois for his rude behavior, and she gave him a big hug and agreed to a dinner date. The date was interrupted by a mysterious attack at LexCorp, though this time Lois was the first to abandon the dinner to go cover the story, leaving Clark free to take off as Superman. When they picked up again later that night, Clark boldly declared his intentions: "Maybe you want this relationship to proceed at its own pace, Lois, but I think life is too short to sit and wait." He kissed her, and Lois kissed him back.

From then on, Lois and Clark were a couple, and romance quickly took over Lois's plotlines yet again. Since all of the current Super-books focused on Superman as the dominant character, Lois was already relegated to a handful of pages in most issues. Now, with the romance in full bloom, the content of her sparse appearances shifted. Instead of chasing stories and fighting villains, Lois went on dates with Clark. The entirety of her role in *Superman* #45, the issue after their first date, was going to the hairdresser to get a new look and talk about her burgeoning relationship.

The whirlwind romance led to a proposal just six months later. While the cover of *Superman* #50 proclaimed it the "Historic Engagement Issue!" Lois wasn't included on the cover. Instead, the art was simply Superman breaking through a brick wall. Inside, Lois appeared on only seven of the book's forty-eight pages.

Clark's proposal was rather subdued. After a visit to the Kent farm, his mother snuck an heirloom engagement ring into his shaving kit. Lois and Clark went to lunch at a diner and Clark awkwardly pulled out the ring, told Lois his mom had given it to him, and asked, "I've thought this over for a **long** time, Lois . . . would you—I mean, **will** you be my—" and Lois interrupted with a surprised, "**Wife?**" There was no bended knee, no declaration of love, just a casual proposal while they waited for Clark's tuna melt to arrive. Lois asked for some time to think it over, but the reader got very little insight into her thought process. Superman fought bad guys for the rest of the issue, and the story finally returned to Lois in its last pages, as she visited her sick mother in the hospital. Not knowing about the proposal, Lois's parents both expressed their high opinion of Clark, and when Lois found Clark waiting for her outside the visitor's area, she agreed to marry him.

The anticlimactic proposal was followed a few issues later by a more surprising and emotional event: Clark revealed to Lois that he was Superman. Lois actually got to be on the cover of *Action*

Comics #662 for this one. A shocked Lois needed a couple of issues to process the news. She wasn't angry or upset, admitting, "In my heart I think I've known for a long time, but my brain would always dismiss the notion." Her concerns were more practical, ranging from the added stress of being married to a superhero to his alien physiology and whether they'd age at the same rate.

As she pondered Clark's revelation, the Super-books launched an arc in which Superman was trapped in time and flitted through various eras, from the Jurassic period to Camelot to the thirty-first century. The story unfolded over several issues, during which Lois was limited to a panel or two set in the present in which she worried about Superman's disappearance. When Superman finally returned, his secret identity reveal was three months past in publishing time and had become the new status quo. Lois and Clark carried on as a happily engaged couple without the comics showing a definitive moment of acceptance from Lois.

In these two pivotal, life-changing moments for Lois, Superman's narrative overshadowed hers entirely. Such is the lot of a secondary character, but the writers had chosen to present obvious qualms on Lois's part that were then never addressed. Instead, she was swept along with the flow of the story. Either her trepidation was simply a plot device to add tension to these big events and the writers had no intention of following up on it, or the threads the authors intended to weave into their stories fell by the wayside as Superman's primary narrative took over again. Whatever the case, Lois was underserved by her creative teams in these key moments.

They continued to put her misgivings on the back burner as the engagement went on. After Clark had to ditch Lois on a series of dates to fly off as Superman, Lois considered whether this was the sort of life she truly wanted. Being constantly worried and left alone wasn't what she'd imagined when she agreed to marry Clark, but her trepidation again disappeared in a sudden about-face. Instead of being concerned about her own happiness, Lois focused on Superman's greatness and turned her dissatisfaction on herself. She wrote an editorial for the *Daily Planet* called "Time for Thanks . . ." in which she chastised the citizens of Metropolis, and herself by proxy, for being ungrateful for Superman and exhorted her readers to appreciate all the good he did.

In another issue, Clark got angry at a guy who was flirting with Lois. He acted so aggressive that Lois responded, "What's your problem, anyway? **Testosterone** poisoning?" Clark then got mad at Lois, and his attitude bothered her so much that the couple ended up in a heated argument by the end of the issue. Then, when Clark revealed that he had just been jealous, Lois melted, kissed him, and declared, "As if there could ever be **anyone** for me but you," once again dismissing her own legitimate concerns.

Clark wasn't the only jealous one in the relationship. When Superman got amnesia and found himself engaged to the princess of a lost island tribe, Lois came after him with a vengeance. In a rare cover appearance, Lois battled the nearly nude princess, who was clothed only in a small thong and a flower garland that barely covered her breasts. Lois pulled her hair while the princess did the same to her with one hand and clawed at Lois with the other. Their fight continued inside the issue until Superman broke it up. It wasn't Lois's finest moment.

Lois and Clark's relationship didn't often bring out the best in either party, but Lois's compassionate, heroic side came through in one particular story in which she stubbornly refused to listen to Clark. In the apartment next to her fiancé's, a husband regularly abused his wife, but the woman refused to press charges after Superman intervened. Clark decided to stay out of things, feeling that he shouldn't get involved until the wife wanted him to. After hearing the violence through the walls while visiting Clark, Lois immediately decided that Clark was wrong and ran to help. Ultimately, the woman left her abusive husband and sought help from a women's shelter thanks to Lois's involvement.

Lois also remained a tough, story-minded journalist in her infrequent solo adventures. Blockhouse, a gargantuan supervillain, kidnapped Lois in *Superman: The Man of Steel* #8, and her first reaction was nonchalant annoyance that he'd destroyed the mailbox where she'd just deposited the Christmas cards she'd spent hours writing. But she then thought, "Still, if I'm lucky, this might turn into a **story!**"

She also fought back against her superpowered captors despite being ridiculously outclassed, battling them until she was subdued. Lois was her most confident, assertive self when she got out from under Superman's shadow, and a lengthy break from the Man of Steel was just around the corner.

Doomsday

For better or for worse, Lois and Clark were headed toward marriage, but outside forces soon derailed the Super-books' master plan. Warner Bros. was developing *Lois & Clark: The New Adventures of Superman* for television, and the producers wanted to start at the beginning of their relationship, stretch out the romantic tension, and then marry them after a few seasons. Not wanting the comics to get too far ahead of the show and steal its thunder, DC Comics' brass decided to postpone the wedding, leaving the Superman creative team scrambling for an overarching story line for the upcoming year.

The writers of the Super-books met annually with editorial staff to decide the major plot points for the next twelve issues of each series, and Jerry Ordway had a running joke each year in which he suggested that they just kill Superman. While brainstorming a replacement story line after the marriage was nixed, editor Mike Carlin remembered Ordway's joke, and the more he thought about it, the more it grew on him. Perhaps motivated by frustration at their original plans being postponed, the writers were on board with the idea and a plot was hatched: in the autumn of 1992, the Man of Steel would die.

This murderous scheme reflected the comic book landscape of the time. In the late 1980s, miniseries like Alan Moore and Dave Gibbons's *Watchmen* and Frank Miller's *The Dark Knight Returns* presented violent, often gruesome stories set in a world of super-heroes. The violence was part of a critique of the genre, portrayed as a symptom of the insanity necessary to don a cape and fight crime in a world of superpowered beings. The books were very popular, and the rest of the industry tried to follow their dark lead, but in doing so they kept only the violence and forgot the critique. Massively muscular, gun-toting, homicidal antiheroes were soon all the rage, and this broader thirst for violence bled into previously wholesome mainstream titles.

Superman's killer was Doomsday, a giant grey creature covered with bony spikes. He escaped from a subterranean capsule out in the country and cut a swath of destruction toward Metropolis. The Justice League tried to stop him but they barely slowed him down. Soon, Superman and Doomsday were fighting toe-to-toe in the heart of Metropolis, landing punches so powerful that the shock waves shattered windows across the city. After several issues, bloodied and beaten, with his costume torn to shreds, Superman finally landed the decisive blow against Doomsday, but then he too went down and died in Lois's arms.

The Man of Steel's death in *Superman* #75 garnered media attention around the world, selling nearly three million copies, and fans were clamoring to find out what happened next. Lois had been given very little to do over the course of the battle apart from worrying for Superman. While she showed her bravery when she and Jimmy were cornered by Doomsday, distracting the monstrous creature so that Jimmy could escape, Superman dominated the books. But with the death of Superman, Lois was suddenly the best-known character in the fictional world of Metropolis. She became the main star of all four Super-series at a time when the Super-books had never been more popular, and she acquitted herself like a true hero.

Lois was shell-shocked in the immediate wake of Superman's death, but she got right back to work. She returned to the *Daily Planet* offices and wrote the tragic cover story, typing it up as tears streamed down her face. Lois maintained her composure despite the horrific events of the day, and she continued to protect Superman's secret identity by pretending that Clark was one of the many people missing in the rubble of downtown Metropolis.

As the grand funeral of her fiancé neared, Lois fought through overwhelming grief to be there for the people she loved. She wasn't sure she'd be able to attend the service, fearing the sadness would be too much to bear, but she went and stood together with her friends from the *Daily Planet*. She'd been scared to reach out to the Kents, feeling tremendous guilt at having been there while their son was killed and not being able to help, but after the funeral she picked up the phone. The Kents came to Metropolis right away so that they could all grieve together. The Super-books portrayed Lois's sorrow, and in doing so they also portrayed her strength.

After Superman was buried, a mysterious flood in Metropolis had Lois out chasing stories again. She tracked the source of the flood to an explosion near Superman's tomb, and was appalled to find out that the tomb had been broken into and the body was missing. Through her underground sources, Lois learned that Project Cadmus, a scientific research center, had stolen the body, and so she donned a wet suit and scuba gear and snuck into their facility from the river. She incapacitated the doctors who got in her way and found Superman's body, but she had to leave it there when the guards were called. Lois escaped and wrote up the story for the *Daily Planet*, then set about getting the body back.

Needing more firepower, Lois teamed up with Supergirl.* They planned a more direct breach of Project Cadmus's headquarters, but Supergirl left Lois in the woods near the lab for fear she'd get hurt during the dangerous mission. Lois was undeterred and quickly teamed up with the Outsiders, a motorcycle gang who patrolled the area, and drove into Cadmus on a high-tech bike to help with the mission. She and Supergirl then returned Superman's body to the burial site, giving Lois a bit of closure, though the body wouldn't remain there for long.

With Superman dead and reburied, the Super-books took a three-month break. The massive popularity of the story line had caught everyone by surprise, so the editors and creative teams came up with a big, bold plan for the follow up. All four Super-books would carry on, and each would feature a new replacement Superman. When the new Supermen premiered in June 1993, Lois was the glue who held the line together. With Superman's body once again missing, she investigated each new hero and acted as the reader's guide to each

---

* This Supergirl wasn't Superman's cousin Kara, who had yet to be reintroduced following Superman's post-*Crisis* reboot. Instead she was a "protoplasmic matrix," a shape-shifting artificial life-form from a pocket universe, who patterned herself after Superman. When her universe was destroyed, she came to the primary universe's Earth and became a superhero based in Metropolis.

character, judging whether or not he was the real Superman and, if not, whether he was worthy to carry his mantle.

The "Reign of the Supermen" arc launched in *Action Comics* #687 with a hero called the Last Son of Krypton. He looked like Superman but had a slightly different uniform, yellow sunglasses, and a casual disregard for the well-being of criminals. When he rescued a prop plane that nearly crashed in Metropolis, Lois was immediately on the scene and, in a callback to *The Man of Steel* #1, shouted, "**HOLD IT RIGHT THERE, BUSTER!!!**" She spoke to the new hero, and while he knew about Clark's double life and that he was engaged to Lois, he told her, "Kent is gone. There is only Superman now." Despite his inside knowledge, Lois wasn't sold on the Last Son of Krypton, especially as he continued to mercilessly assault criminals and clash with other superheroes. Lois's doubt proved well founded: the Last Son of Krypton was actually the Eradicator, who had drawn power from Superman's body to create his new form and thus absorbed some of his memories.

Lois met the Metropolis Kid, also known as Superboy, in *Adventures of Superman* #501 when he showed up at her desk at the *Daily Planet*. The teenage hero rocked a leather jacket, sunglasses, and an earring, and claimed to be Superman, but Lois wasn't buying it. Superboy was eager for attention and press coverage, and Lois's brusque responses led him to reveal that he was actually a clone of Superman, quickly solving that mystery.

The identity of the third Superman wasn't a mystery for readers; he was John Henry Irons, an inventor who built a metal suit so that he could fight crime in Suicide Slum as the Man of Steel. As he selflessly saved lives, eschewing news coverage and trying to keep the other Supermen in line, Lois was impressed. She gave him the ultimate endorsement to readers in *Superman: The Man of Steel* #23 when she thought, "The **others** seem to have Superman's face, his body, his costume . . . the Man of Steel seems to have his **soul**."

The new hero with the best claim to being the real Superman was the Man of Tomorrow, also known as Cyborg Superman because of the many cybernetic replacement parts across his body. When he met Lois in *Superman* #78, he said that the cyborg technology repaired the extensive damage from his fight with Doomsday. She asked him to prove he was Superman, and he claimed that his memory was foggy but he could recall a farm in Kansas and the name Kent. She took him to a scientist familiar with Superman, who confirmed that Cyborg Superman's cybernetic parts were Kryptonian in nature and that his DNA matched Superman's exactly.

Lois followed all of the Supermen closely, tracking their movements and their interactions with one another, suspicious of all of them but the Man of Steel. When Cyborg Superman complimented Superboy, telling him, "I wish I had that much confidence in my powers when I was your age," Lois knew he was a fake. Clark had told her that his powers developed slowly, and that he wasn't very powerful as a teen. Lois had caught Cyborg Superman in a lie.

A few issues before, the intergalactic warlord Mongul had launched an attack on Earth and completely obliterated Coast City. As the four Supermen flew off to fight the invasion, Lois had serious concerns about Cyborg Superman. Initially, she was too dejected to do anything about it; the new Supermen had given her hope that she would get her fiancé back, and now her hopes were thoroughly dashed. But she was Lois Lane. She pulled herself together and marched into Perry White's office to announce, "I don't trust the **cyborg**, Perry. I'm going to **Coast City!**" When Perry said it was too dangerous, she went anyway.

Lois warned the Man of Steel and the other heroes about Cyborg Superman, and again her suspicions proved accurate: he was working with Mongul. As the heroes prepared to attack Mongul's ship, yet another Superman emerged from the ocean in a Kryptonian battlesuit, sporting a black uniform and long hair. Lois was both incredulous and annoyed, having been through this four times before, and still didn't believe he was Superman even when he knew Clark's favorite movie was *To Kill a Mockingbird*. It was only after they had a moment alone and he reeled off fact after fact that only Clark could know that she allowed herself to believe that Superman had returned.*

---

* As it turned out, the Eradicator had stolen Superman's body and was keeping it in suspended animation in a Kryptonian regeneration chamber, using it like a battery to power his new form. This eventually woke Superman up, though there was also a running story line in which Pa Kent had a heart attack, met up with his son in something resembling limbo, and saved him from succumbing to the pull of the Kryptonian afterlife.

All told, Superman was only dead for nine months, and his return meant the end of Lois's role as the thread that held the Super-books together. Her previous solo ventures had centered on Lois fighting bad guys and getting great stories, and there was certainly some of that over this six-month stint, but alongside the heroics there was also a story of a different kind of strength, as Lois dealt with her grief and persevered.

8a

Lucy Lane, Riot Grrrl

As an upper-middle-class woman with a steady job, Lois Lane was a bit of a square. She wasn't frumpy or out of touch, but there was nothing alternative about her. By 1990, she was not only financially secure but also in a stable relationship, so her day-to-day life was relatively settled apart from the occasional threat of supervillains. Lois may have been an everywoman in comparison to the exotic and exciting lives of the many superpowered women who populated the DC Comics universe, but relative to the average American woman, Lois led a life of privilege.

Throughout the 1990s, Lois's sister, Lucy Lane, was a means to explore the life of a normal American woman in ways stories about Lois couldn't. Lucy had been a staple of the Silver Age Super-books as a foil for other characters; she was Jimmy Olsen's fickle girlfriend, and her untimely death led to Lois's brief feminist revolution. In the post-*Crisis* universe, Lucy had her own side adventures that delved into feminist subcultures and issues like poverty, race, and unplanned pregnancy. While Lois flew through the sky with Superman, Lucy was the Super-books' woman on the street.

Investigating Lucy Lane

Over the first few years of the new universe, Lucy appeared only sporadically. Superman's misbegotten clone Bizarro cured her temporary

181

blindness in a *Frankenstein*-esque issue of the *Man of Steel* mini-series, and she had occasional dialogue in hospital scenes during the running story line in which Lois's mother was ill. Lucy became a more regular presence when she started to date Jimmy Olsen in 1991, though not all of her stories were exactly relevant to modern readers; in one three-issue arc, she was shot by Deathstroke the Terminator and then turned into a vampire.

Outside of her vampiric interlude, Lucy's dalliance with Jimmy gave her a key role in a much more relatable story arc. When Jimmy was laid off from the *Daily Planet*, he wasn't able to land a new job and soon found himself kicked out of his apartment. He slept in his car for a while, but then his car was impounded and he had nowhere to go. Jimmy was too embarrassed to ask his friends for help, instead relying on homeless shelters for food and a place to sleep. Ashamed of his predicament, Jimmy avoided Lucy, but she saw him at a shelter where she was volunteering. When he ran away, Lucy told Lois and Clark what happened and together they reached out to their friend and helped him get back on his feet. Lucy continued to date Jimmy despite his hard times, and the two remained a couple for several years.

Dating Jimmy had its ups and downs and he wasn't always a good boyfriend, but Lucy found camaraderie with a group of women after a major disaster hit Metropolis. Lex Luthor leveled most of the city with sonic missiles, and while Superman fought the many villains who took advantage of Metropolis's weakened state, Lucy wandered around and met some women who were digging through the rubble of a music shop to find instruments. They weren't musicians, but they wanted to form a band and decided that getting some instruments would be a good first step. A perplexed Lucy asked, "But what about **Superman**? He's fighting for his **life**—for **our** lives!" Margo shrugged her off: "We'd only play the demeaning roles of cheerleader, girlfriends, or victim, Lucy!" These ladies weren't at all interested in engaging in superhero adventures, with their limited roles for women; they were going to do their own thing. They called themselves the Riot Grrrls.

The group's name was a direct reference to the riot grrrl movement, which developed in the early 1990s. Young women in the alternative punk scene were frustrated by their lack of a voice not only in the subculture but in society as a whole. They began to make their own zines and start punk bands to voice their opinions and express their anger at the constant misogyny of the world around them.* Riot grrrls were politically motivated with a do-it-yourself mindset, and their music, art, writings, and protests addressed women's issues and demanded that women's voices be heard.

Lucy Lane's Riot Grrrls resembled the early days of Bratmobile, a famed real-life riot grrrl band. Bratmobile put out zines and talked up their "band" for months before they learned any instruments and actually played together. It would be a long while before the Riot Grrrls made music,† but in a smattering of appearances in 1994 and 1995, they exposed Lucy to a feminist subculture that was barely covered by the mainstream media, much less corporate-owned comic book publishers. Given the Super-books' audience, the politically radical messages on topics like rape and sexuality that were common in the riot grrrl movement weren't presented. Nonetheless, the Riot Grrrls were radical relative to the rest of the DC Comics universe. They talked about the importance of women "taking the **lead,** taking **responsibility**—defining **themselves**" and critiqued the lack of strong roles for women in the world of superheroes. They even thought about becoming superheroes themselves when they caught a bad guy while Superman was busy elsewhere. The Riot Grrrls were also a stark change of pace from the sea of thin white women who dominated the superhero genre. The band was ethnically diverse, with women of varying sizes, all with strong personalities and differing perspectives.

While the Riot Grrrls weren't around for long, Lucy's time with them led her to become a more mature, self-assured character.

---

* Many riot grrrl zines repurposed images of female superheroes, adopting the women as icons of female strength and power. Wonder Woman was a particular favorite, but Lois Lane made it to the cover of the sixth issue of *Riot Grrrl*, a zine from Washington, DC, alongside Wonder Woman and Supergirl.

† In cameo appearances years after their initial arc with Lucy, the Riot Grrrls had a top-ten hit with their song "Kryptonite Love" in 1996 but were playing a homecoming dance in 1997.

She broke up with the often-absent Jimmy, and when he protested that he'd been calling her, she replied, "Yes . . . asking me out at a **moment's** notice! At **all** hours! At **your** convenience!" Lucy realized that she wanted to date a man who respected her, and soon began a relationship with Ron Troupe, a reporter at the *Daily Planet*.

Ron was kind and attentive, the complete opposite of the flighty Jimmy. Lucy met him while visiting the *Daily Planet* offices and they became friends, attending a Pearl Jam concert together when she couldn't get ahold of Jimmy. Their relationship grew slowly in the background of the Super-books, but eventually they fell in love.

The relationship pushed some boundaries, because Ron was African American. In 1995, when Lucy and Ron started dating, a Gallup poll found that only 48 percent of Americans approved of interracial marriage, and the comics explored this attitude. Ron's sister made it very clear that she didn't want Lucy at their parents' anniversary party solely because of the interracial issue, and Lucy's old-school, military-general father had reservations about the relationship as it became more serious. Such opinions were the minority, however; the main cast of the Super-books were behind Lucy and Ron unequivocally.

They remained supportive when Lucy got pregnant while dating Ron. While the story took a chaste, responsible stance by having Lucy clearly state that they'd only had sex once and used protection, the comics didn't shy away from tackling the difficulties of an unplanned pregnancy head-on. Lucy's first response was "This is a **nightmare! It can't** be **true!** How can this have **happened?**" Tears welled in her eyes as she worried about how her parents would respond, and she feared her mother's anger and her father's disappointment. She decided to visit a women's clinic, because "before I do **anything,** I need to know for sure." That "anything" was tellingly vague. Abortion was never discussed specifically by Lucy, but she thought a lot about her "options" and left the clinic with pamphlets about keeping the baby, adoption, and abortion.

Ultimately, she decided to keep the baby, and she and Ron were soon engaged, but it wasn't all smooth sailing. Ron had recently been let go from the *Daily Planet* and Lucy didn't have a job either, so they had to scramble to find work so that they could be prepared for their new arrival. Lucy got a desk job at the airline for which she used to be a flight attendant, while Ron gave up his journalistic dreams and took a job at a bank just so that they would be guaranteed a steady paycheck.

Lucy and Ron got married in late 2000, and Lucy had a baby boy a few months later. They named him Sam, after her father, and the birth turned out to be the end of Lucy's decade-long role as a regular side character. The Super-books got caught up in an inter-galactic crossover, and when it was done the books moved from interconnected stories to disparate arcs, and Lucy was forgotten in the shuffle. She and a toddler Sam appeared briefly in 2004 to take care of an injured Lois, but that was the end of this version of Lucy.

As the real-world, street-level counterpart to Lois Lane, Lucy had offered a unique perspective not often seen in superhero comics until she faded out of sight, but when she returned in 2009 she'd been eaten by the superhero machine. The 2000s had an odd tendency toward big event comics that turned familiar female characters into villains. For example, Scarlet Witch, a former member of the Aveng-ers, wiped out almost all of mutantkind in Marvel's *House of M*, and Jean Loring, the ex-wife of the Atom, became a murderer in DC's *Identity Crisis*. When the Super-books centered a massive crossover around the establishment of a new planet of Kryptonians in Earth's solar system, Lucy was one of the primary antagonists.

The story line introduced Superwoman, ostensibly a Kryptonian but later revealed to be a secret weapon of the American military under the command of General Sam Lane. They'd devised a spe-cial suit that gave Kryptonian powers to a human soldier, and they disguised her as Superwoman so that she could better spy on the Kryptonians. Superwoman was an enforcer and an executioner, a tool to help the paranoid military prepare for a possible Kryptonian invasion. Ultimately, in a shocking unmasking at the end of *Supergirl* #40, Superwoman was revealed to be Lucy Lane before she was acci-dentally killed when her suit ruptured during a fight with Supergirl.*

---

* This Supergirl was Superman's cousin Kara, who debuted in the post-*Crisis* universe in 2004. The "protoplasmic matrix" Supergirl had undergone a number of changes over the years, and even starred in her own series, but the character became increasingly convo-luted. Her book ended in 2003, after which DC introduced a new Supergirl that more closely followed her simpler classic origin.

Her backstory was revealed in *Supergirl Annual* #1, and the character had been changed entirely; Ron and their son were gone without explanation, and the vast majority of her history had been erased. In the past, Lucy and Lois had always been close, bonding over their father's stern military nature. They supported each other despite their different life paths, and they had each other's backs no matter what. The annual told a completely different story, casting Lois as their father's favorite daughter and Lucy as the child who could never quite measure up. Lucy became bitter and resented Lois's success, and when their father was presumed dead after an alien attack, she joined the military so that she could finally do something to make him proud. Her military career led her to the Superwoman program, where she learned her father was actually still alive. She became his faithful soldier, obeying him unquestioningly.*

The treatment of Lucy Lane was indicative of a broad, cavalier disregard for female characters. The tapestry of her history, written and illustrated by scores of comic book creators as they explored so many underrepresented facets of the lives of American women, was wiped out entirely just so DC could have a surprising reveal of Lucy as Superwoman and then kill her off. It was a fate that befell many female characters who were sacrificed for shock value during blockbuster comics events throughout the 2000s.

Through a twist of superhero pseudoscience, Lucy later came back to life, but her DNA had been altered to make her a human/Kryptonian hybrid. She was hidden away in S.T.A.R. Labs, where scientists worked to restore her human self. Lois visited the facility briefly to remind Lucy of the woman she used to be, but she remained a crazed zealot, fiercely loyal to her father's xenophobic plans.

Soon after, DC Comics rebooted their entire comic book line again and both the riot grrrl and Superwoman were wiped from continuity. Thus far in the new universe, Lucy Lane is a nonfactor.

---

* Scarlet Witch and Jean Loring also had men at the core of their turns to villainy. Scarlet Witch wiped out mutants to get back at her father, and Jean Loring became a killer to get her husband back. These stories in which male creators drove female characters into villainy are an interesting, albeit wholly inadvertent, cautionary tale about what can happen when men, real and fictional, are at the center of everything.

9

Lois Lane on Screen, Part 3: Television

The Man of Steel returned to the small screen in 1988 for the syndicated half-hour television series *Superboy*. Although Alexander and Ilya Salkind had sold their Superman movie rights to Cannon Films after *Superman III* underperformed, they retained the televison rights, and Alexander Salkind and syndication company Viacom were both very intrigued by a pitch for a show about Clark Kent's college years. *Superboy* ran for four seasons and included episodes penned by notable comic book writers like Cary Bates, Mike Carlin, and Denny O'Neil.

Lois Lane wasn't part of the show at all, though Noel Neill did make a guest appearance in the fourth season. Instead, Lana Lang was Superboy's love interest, and Stacy Haiduk's portrayal of the character was the show's only constant during its run. Superboy and Lex Luthor were both recast after the first season, supporting characters disappeared and were replaced with new ones, and the show's setting and tone changed several times. Haiduk's consistent presence anchored the show through its many attempts at retooling; Ilya Salkind later said that she "was out of this world. She was the one who made the show."

Superboy was canceled in 1992 due to legal pressure from Warner Bros. They'd regained the films rights to Superman from Cannon Films and wanted to launch their own television show. Not wanting audiences to be confused by two programs with two different continuities, Warner Bros. filed a lien against the Salkinds and forced them to end the program. Their new show, *Lois & Clark: The New Adventures of Superman*, debuted on ABC a year later, with Lois Lane as its star.

Lois & Clark: The New Adventures of Superman

While developing the program, Warner Bros.' top pick for showrunner was Deborah Joy LeVine, a former lawyer turned writer-producer who had made a few television movies and worked on shows like the legal drama *Equal Justice*. Not only had LeVine never run a show before, she'd also never even read a comic book. Growing up, her parents were strict about what she read and never allowed comics in their home, and she didn't read the few comic books that her brother was able to sneak into the house. Skeptical but curious about the job, LeVine read every Superman comic book that she could get her hands on. While the superhero action didn't much appeal to her, she loved the dynamic between Lois and Clark and pitched a romantic comedy set primarily in the *Daily Planet* newsroom. Warner Bros. liked the idea and casting soon began.

The search for Clark was a long one. Although LeVine saw Dean Cain early in the process, she wasn't sold on him until after she'd auditioned dozens of other men. For Lois, however, LeVine found her woman right away when Teri Hatcher came in. Hatcher was born in Palo Alto, California, and studied acting at San Francisco's American Conservatory Theater before getting a job as a San Francisco 49ers cheerleader in the mid-1980s. She soon moved into acting full time, working steadily for several years in small television and film roles, most notably a guest appearance on *Seinfeld* in which she spoke the famous line "They're real . . . and they're spectacular."

Hatcher's charm, humor, and beauty were exactly what LeVine wanted for her Lois Lane, though she did mention to Hatcher that her hair was currently too long for the part. Hatcher was so keen to get the role that when she returned for her callback audition, she'd had her hair trimmed to a short bob. Impressed by both her acting skills and her dedication, LeVine gave Hatcher the part.

LeVine saw Lois at the forefront of the show and had a very specific vision for the role. The producer later recalled, "I wanted her to be an astute businesswoman, I wanted her to be smart, I wanted to make her just a great, modern woman." Lois wouldn't simply work with Clark, she would be his boss. The show was almost called *Lois Lane's Daily Planet*, but the network ultimately settled on *Lois & Clark* instead.

The series' two-hour pilot, which aired in September 1993, began with a disheveled, bearded ruffian entering the *Daily Planet* building. The ruffian went to a desk and used a pair of scissors to cut off the bandages that were binding her breasts and then, with the help of Jimmy Olsen, pulled off her beard before exclaiming, "I nailed 'em cold!" The show then cut to the ruffian, now cleaned up and wearing a sharp skirt suit, standing next to the *Daily Planet* proofs for her latest front page story, "Million Dollar Car Theft Ring Exposed" by Lois Lane.

Lois was the unequivocal star reporter of the *Daily Planet*, and she knew it. When Jimmy told her that Lex Luthor never gave one-on-one interviews, she confidently replied, "Well, he's never met Lois Lane before either." Later paired with newbie reporter Clark Kent, Lois called him a "hack from Smallville" and informed him that "you are low man, I am top banana, and that's the way I like it."

Although her self-assurance bordered on arrogance, throughout the pilot she demonstrated that it was warranted. Lois investigated the explosion of a rocket after her sources informed her that someone was sabotaging the space program. She broke into a restricted warehouse to get pictures of the wreckage, then took out an attacking goon, disarming him of his switchblade and knocking him out cold. Fearing the worst about a new rocket's upcoming launch to ferry colonists to an international space station, she found a way to sneak on board, located a bomb, and stopped the launch countdown so that the threat could be dealt with. Lois had some help along the way from a caped hero, but she was the driving force behind saving the launch and its many passengers.

The pilot also showed a softer side of Lois. Her sister told her that she needed to get out more and meet a guy, and that to do so she had to stop being so smart and so intense. Lois replied, "I'm just being myself, and if they're not man enough to handle it then I guess I'll just wait for someone who is." Being so intimidating left Lois lonely; after her conversation with her sister, she watched a cheesy romantic movie and cried to herself.

Her job always trumped her love life. She went on a date with Lex Luthor, partly in hopes of getting an interview with him, and when the date ended with a kiss instead of an exclusive story, she was furious with herself for not getting a hard-hitting interview rather than happy about the date. She didn't make the same mistake at the end of the pilot, when the caped hero flew her back to the *Daily Planet* after they saved the rocket. Lois was clearly smitten with him, but she stayed focused on wrangling an exclusive interview before naming him "Superman."

Lois showcased her reporting skills throughout the first season, writing exposés on corrupt congressmen, faulty nuclear plants, and more. She constantly put herself in danger to get these stories, often going off on her own to do so. She went undercover as a nightclub singer to investigate the mob, refused to stop looking into a murder she'd witnessed even though numerous people were also trying to have her killed, and broke into buildings all across Metropolis.

Her penchant for trespassing was indicative of a larger disdain for laws and authority. When Lois felt that she was in the right, she acted like the rules no longer applied to her because she was on the side of truth and justice. Early in the season, when federal agents showed up at the *Daily Planet* with a warrant to interview Lois about Superman, she was entirely uncooperative, offering them nothing but contempt and sarcasm. In a later episode, Lois believed that a man convicted of murder was innocent, and when he escaped prison she let him stay at her apartment while she tracked down the real killer.

Above all else, Lois was dedicated to journalism. When Earth was in danger from an asteroid, she refused a spot in Luthor's protected bunker because she wanted to be in the middle of it all, covering the story. In another episode, the *Daily Planet* staff was taken hostage, and while everyone else was morose and frightened, Lois exclaimed, "This is going to make an incredible story. I mean, how many journalists get this type of opportunity to be in the belly of the beast, part of the event, not just a casual observer?" As a smile spread across her face, she laughed, "It's like being one of those guys in a Baghdad hotel." Lois put herself in danger because she loved it; that's where the good stories were.

Lois's pursuit of the truth at all costs wasn't entirely pure. There was a definite sense that she enjoyed the glory of the front page and the prestige of being a top reporter. It wasn't enough that the truth came out; Lois had to be the one to tell the story and get the credit for it. She stole Clark's leads, threw elbows to get to the pay phone first after a press conference, and didn't put much effort into stories that she thought were beneath her. When Lois and Clark met a crying mother who asked them, "You've both been writing about the kidnappings, haven't you?" Lois's first response wasn't to comfort the grieving woman but to point out that she'd actually done most of the work for the articles, not Clark.

Throughout *Lois & Clark*'s first season, Lois was by far the most nuanced character on the show. Clark was a perpetual Boy Scout, and the program's other two female characters made up a literal mother/whore dichotomy. K Callan played Clark's mom, who was there primarily to support him and do things like sew the Superman costume and cook meals. Cat Grant, played by Tracy Scoggins, was the *Daily Planet*'s gossip reporter and spent nearly all of her screen time spouting innuendo-laden dialogue and trying to hook up with various men, most often Clark.

Lois's season-long story arc was also a gendered cliché. While Lois tracked down a front page scoop in each individual episode, the plotline that ran through all of the episodes was a romantic one, with Lex Luthor courting Lois. This culminated in their engagement as the season drew to a close, and their wedding in the season finale. While Clark, Perry, and Jimmy spent the final episode tracking down evidence to prove that Luthor was a criminal mastermind, Lois was completely out of the action as she fretted about her wedding and her burgeoning feelings for Clark.* She ultimately decided not to marry Luthor on her own, before Clark and the gang showed up to stop the wedding and have Luthor arrested, a redemptive end to a plotline that never reflected well on her.

The first-season finale also marked the end of Deborah Joy LeVine's tenure as showrunner. While the show was a moderate success despite airing against some stiff competition, network executives wanted more of Superman fighting bad guys and less of Lois bossing around Clark; they were still irked that Lois's name came first in the title. LeVine wasn't interested in making a show like that, so she left the program and was replaced by a team of producers. They took Lois out of the spotlight and brought Superman to the fore, and the show's next three seasons were a mixed bag for Lois.

The character didn't change so much as the show changed around her. Lois was still a top reporter and her nuances remained, but the show itself was bigger, less interested in the goings-on at the *Daily Planet*. The second season brought in comic book villains like the Prankster and Metallo, and more fantastical plotlines involving time travel and clones.

It also ramped up the romantic tension between Lois and Clark when the two began dating midway through the season. Lois, suspicious by nature and gun-shy after her relationship with Luthor proved to be such a mistake, was hesitant at first, but once she and Clark began dating things progressed quickly. In the season finale, Clark decided to tell Lois that he was Superman, but they kept getting interrupted whenever they tried to talk. When he finally got Lois alone at the end of the show, Clark went another way; instead of confessing his dual identity, he asked her to marry him. The season ended on that cliff-hanger.

Season three began with another twist: in response to Clark's surprise proposal, Lois plucked off his glasses and replied, "Who's asking, Clark or Superman?" In the season-two finale, Lois had

---

* Lois's mother in the wedding episode was played by former Lois Lane Phyllis Coates, though in later episodes the generally reclusive Coates was replaced by Beverly Garland.

allowed Superman to stop her heart to fool a gang of villains who were blackmailing him. When Superman caressed her face before putting her in suspended animation with his freezing breath, Lois recognized that his touch was the same as Clark's. Initially, Lois was furious with Clark for not telling her sooner, but ultimately she decided to postpone her answer not out of anger but so that she could get adjusted to this new information before she decided. And then later in the episode she single-handedly defused a bomb, because she's Lois Lane.

For more than five decades across various media, Superman had kept Lois in the dark. She was perpetually duped, cast in an adversarial role in which she was constantly outsmarted. The recent reveal of Clark's secret indentity in the comics had downplayed the implications of this knowledge; the focus stayed on Superman and kept Lois, and her concerns, in the background. But on *Lois & Clark* the revelation added a new dynamic to their relationship, and to the Superman mythos in general. Lois and Clark became coconspirators, and both were better because of it. Lois could be a better reporter because she had constant access to Superman's powers via Clark, while Superman could be a better superhero because he could rely on Lois's insights and her covering for him. More significantly, the power dynamic shifted dramatically. While Lois had always bossed Clark around, viewers knew that the joke was on Lois, because Clark was actually Superman and was continually manipulating her. With the secret revealed, Lois and Clark became equal partners.

This new role suited Lois well. She even took the superhero reins when Superman's powers were transferred to her for an episode, donning a purple uniform and mask to take to the skies as Ultra Woman. But as the third season progressed, the story lines became increasingly bizarre, and hard-hitting journalism was sidelined.

Lois proposed to Clark early in the season and the wedding took place soon after, but the Lois who married Clark was revealed as a fake. Lex Luthor had kidnapped the real Lois to force her to be with him, replacing her with a frog-eating clone. The clone Lois subsequently fell in love with Clark and set out to murder the real Lois, who escaped from Luthor, lost her memory, and decided she was a lounge singer from a pulpy romance novel. The situation took several episodes to resolve and dominated most of the second half of the season.

The fourth season was somewhat less ridiculous, though not without its quirks. When Lois and Clark prepared to tie the knot for real, their plans were nearly thwarted by the maniacal Wedding Destroyer, played by guest star Delta Burke. The wedding only came together because of the intervention of what appeared to be a guardian angel, a character who had never been seen before and who didn't show up again. The silliness continued through the year with villains like Lex Luthor's fiendish son and that mischievous imp from the fifth dimension, Mister Mxyzptlk. However, there were more grounded moments as well. In one episode, Lois became interim editor of the *Daily Planet*, and in a two-parter she was able to beat a murder rap after she was framed for the crime.

The producers ended their fourth season in the spring of 1997 thinking that they'd be back for a fifth. They closed the finale with a cliff-hanger in which Lois and Clark found a mysterious baby in their apartment shortly after learning that they couldn't conceive their own child. However, the show's audience was steadily declining, perhaps a victim of the curse many programs face when they end the dramatic will-they-won't-they tension by having the two main characters get together. Over the course of the fourth season, ABC had moved *Lois & Clark* to a new time slot and then to a new night, but the ratings only fell further. Ultimately the network decided to cancel the show, and the cliff-hanger went unresolved.*

Smallville

Clark Kent returned to television screens just four years later, this time without Lois Lane. After plans for a show about a young Bruce Wayne were killed because Warner Bros.' feature film division was

---

* Producer Brad Buckner and writer Tim Minear later revealed that the baby was Kryptonian royalty from the future, a descendant of Lois and Clark sent back in time so that they could protect him from assassins.

developing *Batman Begins*, production company Tollins/Robbins hired writers Alfred Gough and Miles Millar to create a program starring a young Clark Kent instead. They pitched *Smallville*, a show about Clark's high school years in his rural hometown. The duo proposed a strict "no tights, no flights" rule for the show: it would be about Clark and his journey to become Superman, not about the actual superhero. Warner Bros. was on board and found a home for the show on its own broadcast network, the WB. The network was known for dramas about teen angst, and *Smallville* fit right in.

Tom Welling starred as Clark Kent, and the show chronicled the development of his burgeoning superpowers and his awkward social life. He befriended a young Lex Luthor, played by Michael Rosenbaum, pined for Kristin Kreuk's Lana Lang, and got advice from his wise parents, played by *The Dukes of Hazzard*'s John Schneider and *Superman III*'s Annette O'Toole. The show had a "freak of the week" structure that tied back into Clark's origin: when his spaceship crashed in Smallville, it brought with it a Kryptonite meteor shower, and the alien rocks endowed the local townspeople with bizarre abilities. Clark investigated this phenomenon with the editor of his high school newspaper, Chloe Sullivan, an original character played by Allison Mack who filled the classic Lois Lane role of a snarky, inquisitive reporter with a soft spot for the hero. Whenever the infected citizens got out of control, Clark used his new powers to save the town. *Smallville* was an instant hit, breaking the WB's ratings record with its premiere episode in October 2001.

After three seasons, Clark and Lana's romantic drama was beginning to get stale and Millar and Gough wanted to change the show's dynamic by bringing in Lois Lane, but Warner Bros. was hesitant. *Superman Returns* was in development, and executives were worried that having too much of the traditional Superman mythos in *Smallville* would dilute the brand by the time the movie came out. After several negotiations, Warner Bros. agreed to let Lois appear for a four-episode arc at the beginning of the show's fourth season.

The casting director found Erica Durance, a local actress in Vancouver, where *Smallville* was filmed. Durance was originally from Calgary and moved to British Columbia after high school to pursue acting.* Vancouver had a substantial television production industry, and Durance landed gigs on shows like *Tru Calling* and *Andromeda* before joining *Smallville*. Executive producer Kelly Souders later recalled, "There were a lot of wonderful actresses who came in for the role but I remember the entire writing staff watching her tape and just saying, that's her. She had everything. She had attitude but she was loveable and brought all of it in her audition tape."

Durance's introduction to the series picked up on the events of the previous season's finale, which had ended chaotically. Chloe was apparently killed in a home explosion, and Clark left the farm to learn about his destiny from an AI based on his Kryptonian father, Jor-El. Season four began with Lois driving to Smallville; Chloe was her cousin, and Lois had suspicions about her mysterious death and came to investigate. As Lois neared the town, a lightning bolt struck the road and she veered off into a cornfield, where she found a newly returned, amnesiac Clark. She took him to the local hospital and ditched him as quickly as she could.†

Lois later learned that Clark was friends with Chloe and might know something about her death, so she went to the Kent farm to talk to him, inviting herself in and helping herself to a cup of coffee. Lois was talkative and direct to the point of rudeness, but she was a woman on a mission. The episode was fittingly titled "Crusade." Once Clark's memory was restored, they teamed up to investigate Chloe's death, even though Lois made clear that "my dad raised me to be independent and self-sufficient."

When military troops chased them away from the wreckage of Chloe's home, Lois grappled with a soldier, ultimately flipping him on the ground and knocking him out with a kick to the head. She later broke into a local military base to find more information about the explosion. Clark surreptitiously used his powers to help out with the investigation, but Lois proved herself capable of handling things

---

* You can hear a slight Alberta accent throughout Durance's run on *Smallville*, most noticeably in her soft *a*'s.
† Margot Kidder appeared in Durance's first episode, though the two didn't share any scenes. Teri Hatcher later guest-starred in the show's final season as Lois's mother.

on her own. Ultimately, they found out that Chloe was alive, and together Lois and Clark took down the villain who'd captured her.

Resolving the various cliff-hangers took up half of Lois's four-episode arc. In her third episode, she was set to return to Metropolis to start college but found out that she was a few credits short of a high school diploma and had to enroll at Smallville High. When Chloe suggested that she could write for the newspaper to get an extracurricular credit, Lois replied, "The last thing I want to be is a reporter." But more credits meant she could leave town sooner, so she signed on and quickly got into the job. Lois's story on teenage plastic surgery made the front page, and when Chloe left the paper in the next episode under the influence of a Kryptonite-infused love potion, Lois took over the newspaper and also found the potion's antidote. Clark had Lex pull some strings to get Lois into college early, partly as thanks for fixing the love potion mess and partly out of annoyance. Lois didn't particularly care for Clark, and he wasn't keen on her either. He told Lana, "She's bossy, she's stuck up, she's rude! I can't stand her."

Durance's first run was over, but she returned throughout the season. While at college, she'd been going to the local bars at night in her pajamas and bunny slippers and winning money drinking football players under the table. The university kicked her out, and she tricked Clark into asking her to move in with his family at the farm. She ended up staying with the Kents through the last third of the season.

Over the course of her first year, Durance's Lois was often a bit of a pest, but endearingly so and with a good heart. She went over well with viewers, and Warner Bros. let *Smallville* make her a series regular beginning in season five. For the next few years, she was a tertiary member of the ensemble, but she had some big moments despite her small role. She became Jonathan Kent's campaign manager when he ran for the state senate, and later was Martha Kent's chief of staff when she became a US senator. Lois eventually ended up in Metropolis as a reporter for the *Metropolis Inquisitor*, a tabloid newspaper, but a visit to her cousin Chloe at the *Daily Planet* changed her fate as *Smallville*'s seventh season began.

In the aftermath of the destruction of a local dam, Lois had seen what she believed to be an alien spaceship before falling unconscious, and the *Daily Planet*'s new editor overheard her telling Chloe about her investigation into the ship. He was intrigued and offered her a job if she could prove it was real. Clark and Chloe both knew that the spaceship belonged to Clark's Kryptonian cousin Kara Zor-El and tried to dissuade Lois from pursuing the story, but she was undeterred. She'd become a relentless crusader over the years, and she was used to stubbornly chasing down the truth despite her friends' incredulity. In the end, while Lois's article didn't have enough evidence to be printed, the editor told her, "Your prose leaps off the page like a Bengal tiger," and he hired her anyway.

Millar and Gough left the show after its seventh season, along with Kreuk and Rosenbaum. Lana and Luthor's departure meant that the new team of showrunners had to reorient the show as the eighth season began, and this involved a bigger role for Lois.* Clark joined the *Daily Planet*, and the two teamed up regularly. He also began patrolling the streets of Metropolis as an unseen hero known as "the Blur," and Lois was adamant that she'd get the first interview with him. She even pretended to be a costumed vigilante to get his attention, fighting crime as "Stiletto," and quite effectively.

Lois began pursuing the Blur in the hope of getting a front page story out of him, but the more she followed his exploits, the more her priorities changed. When she finally got to talk to him, instead of doing an interview she offered him her help. Lois soon became the Blur's confidante, eschewing the fame of an exclusive interview to assist him behind the scenes.

While *Smallville* often featured Lois in heroic ways, it had exploitive tendencies as well. Because Lois would do anything to get a story, she might find herself infiltrating a strip club, disguising herself as a dominatrix, or popping out of a cake dressed like a Playboy bunny. Durance usually played Lois as awkward in these situations

---

* The rise in Lois's profile also corresponded with a rise in female writers. Over each of *Smallville*'s last five seasons, more than half of each year's episodes were written or cowritten by women.

for comedic effect, but she was nonetheless scantily clad. Furthermore, from the fifth through the ninth season, the clips shown when Durance was listed in the opening credits included Lois pulling herself out of a lake in a red bikini.

Lois's relationship with Clark was better handled and avoided this objectification. It was a slow build; Lois dated other men over the years, while Clark's complicated relationship with Lana was a constant presence. Lois and Clark's romantic feelings for each other didn't emerge until the eighth season, and they didn't begin dating until the ninth. Even then it wasn't for long; Lois knew that Clark was hiding something, and her mistrust led to them breaking up as the season drew to a close. However, the Blur kissed Lois in the season finale, and she immediately realized that he was Clark.

Soon after, Lois left for a reporting gig in Africa, in part because she was frustrated that Clark still wouldn't tell her his secret and in part because she didn't want to derail his superhero career. She explained, "The last thing I would ever want is to be the one thing that holds him back or stands in the way." But she eventually realized that they were better together. When Clark finally told her that he was the Blur, Lois exclaimed, "What took you so long?!" Now fully in the know, Lois spent *Smallville*'s final season working with the Blur and his superhero team to combat the apocalyptic threat of the supervillain Darkseid.

Smallville ended in May 2011 after ten seasons. The series finale was supposed to feature the wedding of Lois and Clark, but an attack from Darkseid interrupted the ceremony. Lois spent the rest of the finale knocking out a fellow reporter, sneaking onto Air Force One, and convincing the president not to launch a nuclear attack against Darkseid that would kill millions of innocent people. The finale ended by jumping ahead seven years to find Lois as the star reporter at the *Daily Planet*, helping to cover for Clark as he flew off as Superman.

Ultimately, *Smallville* aired more than two hundred episodes. Durance appeared in more than half of them, establishing the first iconic Lois Lane of the new century.

9a

Animation Representation

The Fleischer animated shorts of the early 1940s had provided one of the best Golden Age depictions of Lois Lane, star reporter, but decades would pass before another cartoon version of the character proved anywhere near as iconic and influential. With Superman popular on the radio through the rest of the 1940s and in live action form on the *Adventures of Superman* television show in the 1950s, DC didn't pursue a new cartoon version of the Man of Steel until nearly a quarter of a century after the Fleischer shorts. These new animated projects didn't follow the Fleischers' lead with Lois, reducing her to little more than a prop to be rescued.

The New Adventures of Superman premiered on CBS in 1966 as a Saturday morning cartoon consisting of three six-minute stories produced by Filmation, a relatively new animation studio. The program brought back the stars of the radio show and Fleischer cartoons, Bud Collyer and Joan Alexander, as Superman and Lois Lane, though Julie Bennett took over the role of Lois in later seasons. With each story only running for six minutes, there wasn't a lot of time for character development, and Superman was the main focus. Lois rarely had much to do on the program other than be captured by a wide array of foes, including classic Superman villains like Lex Luthor and Toyman as well as more unusual antagonists like space aliens or a giant chimpanzee.

The program changed titles each season, adding cartoons starring other DC Comics characters when it became *The Superman/ Aquaman Hour of Adventure* in 1967, and then incorporating tales of the Caped Crusader when it became *The Batman/Superman Hour* in 1968 for its final season. In this final season, the format changed from self-contained shorts to two-part stories, so the extra time allowed Lois to at least investigate odd phenomena for a moment or two before her inevitable capture.

The program ended after three seasons, and the rights to DC Comics superheroes were soon licensed by animation giant Hanna-Barbera. They developed *Super Friends*, an animated version of the comics' Justice League that teamed up Superman, Batman and Robin, Wonder Woman, and Aquaman. *Super Friends* debuted in 1973 and ran in a variety of incarnations for the next thirteen years. Lois appeared in only a handful of episodes, voiced by Shannon Farnon, who also played Wonder Woman. She again did little but get captured and rescued.

Soon after the end of *Super Friends*, Warner Bros. launched another Saturday morning cartoon starring the Man of Steel. Simply titled *Superman*, the show began in fall 1988 and was produced by Ruby-Spears Enterprises. It blended elements of the Christopher Reeve movies with aspects of the recent John Byrne comic book relaunch, and while it only lasted for thirteen episodes it was a definite step forward in its depiction of Lois Lane.

Ginny McSwain voiced the ace reporter. Lois adored Superman, but she was also keen to track down stories no matter the danger. The series' first episode began with an homage to the iconic flying scene from *Superman: The Movie* before a robot attack in Metropolis ended the romantic flight. Superman warned Lois, "It's dangerous! Stay back!" but she muttered, "You've got to be kidding," before running into a building to follow the robot's trail.

Superman was a typical late-1980s cartoon, in that the plots and characterization were fairly basic, so Lois was still captured a lot over the thirteen-episode run, and she regularly declared that any trouble that arose was a job for Superman. Nonetheless, she displayed some of the spark that had been missing from her cartoon incarnations for some time. She raised the bar, and set up the next animated series to take the character to new heights.

Superman: The Animated Series

When Lois returned to Saturday morning cartoons in 1996, the game had changed for DC Comics superheroes. Four years earlier, Warner Bros. Animation had debuted *Batman: The Animated Series*, a stylized version of the Dark Knight's adventures. The show was dark and gritty but also fun and action packed, captivating kids and older audiences alike. Today, *Batman: The Animated Series* is considered to be one of the best animated series of all time, and it spawned a variety of spin-offs.

The first was *Superman: The Animated Series*. *Batman* producer Bruce Timm developed the program, setting it in the same fictional universe as its parent series and using the same animation style but adding some unique twists. *Superman* was a brighter show, both visually and tonally, with artistic influences ranging from the futuristic to the classic art deco stylings of the Fleischer cartoons. The show enjoyed a successful four-year run, and it is particularly well regarded for its depiction of Lois Lane.

Dana Delany, an actress known for her live action work in projects like the television show *China Beach* and the movie *Tombstone*, voiced Lois. *Superman: The Animated Series* was some of her earliest voice-acting work, and she was keen on the role. Delany grew up watching reruns of *Adventures of Superman* and bought *Superman's Girl Friend Lois Lane* at the drugstore each month throughout Lois's women's lib era. She remains a huge fan of the character to this day. For years, Delany's Twitter icon was an image of Lois from *Superman: The Animated Series*, and she still describes herself in her bio as "occasionally Lois Lane."

Delany imbued Lois with a dry sarcasm that was evident from her first appearance. After learning that Perry White had put a story about a blue angel with red wings on the front page of the *Daily Planet* instead of her own piece, she burst into his office and exclaimed, "Chief! I spent a week on the docks with rats and frizzed hair exposing the biggest gun-smuggling ring to hit this town in ten years, and what makes the front page? Some sprouty, New Age, granola-crunching fluff piece on angels. What's next, interviews with Bigfoot?" When her new partner, Clark Kent, asked her if she'd ever been to Kansas, she replied, "God, no," and managed to ditch him by the time they'd crossed the office to the elevators so that she could cover their assigned story by herself. After Clark later handled himself well during their investigation, Lois's only compliment was "You're not the rube hayseed I took you for."

Lois named Metropolis's new "angel," dubbing him Superman after the Nietzschean ideal, and landed the first interview with him. Instead of being bowled over by his mere presence, Lois stayed on task. She met all of Superman's claims with a healthy dose of skepticism; she was incredulous when he said he was from a different planet. There was a hint of flirtation, but it was all on Lois's end. Throughout the series, Lois was direct and firmly in control whenever she saw Superman. She flustered him with her straightforward advances and was never overly upset when he flew off. Nor was Lois solely interested in the Man of Steel; she dated Bruce Wayne for a while, and learned that he was Batman over the course of their relationship.

Overall, romance was more of a background element for this Lois; she didn't even kiss Superman until the series finale. She was too busy getting big stories, winning journalism awards, and tangling with supervillains. Like every version of Lois, she was captured and rescued by Superman on a regular basis, but she met each new danger with a steady calm. In one episode, she was transported into a dystopian alternate reality and was entirely unfazed by her change in surroundings. By the end of the show she'd teamed up with that universe's rebels and overthrown Lex Luthor's despotic reign.

Lois was similarly proactive when, in the series finale, Darkseid launched an attack on Earth by controlling Superman's mind. While the world thought that Superman had turned on them, Lois dug deeper and found the real story. The military thwarted Superman's attack and imprisoned him, so Lois broke into the prison to save the Man of Steel from execution and allow him to defeat Darkseid once and for all.

Superman: The Animated Series ended after three seasons but was followed by *Justice League* and then *Justice League Unlimited*, which continued in the same animated universe. As a member of the Justice League, Superman remained a major focus, but the expanded scope meant that Delany's Lois was featured in only a handful of episodes. She rarely had much to do other than call out a few questions from the sidelines, though she was always running toward the chaos at hand instead of away from it. She also played a key role in a second-season arc of *Justice League Unlimited*, despite appearing only briefly. The short scene began with Lois and Superman on a romantic picnic but quickly turned into Lois chastising Superman about the Justice League's overuse of violence and warning him that they were losing the public's trust. Superman didn't respond well initially, but he eventually saw her point and made reforms to the league.

After the end of *Justice League Unlimited*, Delany and the rest of the *Superman* cast made one last appearance on a Saturday morning cartoon when they guest-starred in the fifth-season premiere of *The Batman* in 2007. The show was a brand-new adaptation with its own continuity and style, but when producers wanted to tell a crossover story featuring the Man of Steel, they called on the iconic and beloved cast of *Superman* to reprise their roles. Delany brought her usual snark as Lois; she refused to get Clark into a press conference when he was running late, followed Superman's fight with Metallo across Gotham while everyone else ran away, and was an obstinate captive after the Black Mask kidnapped her, tripping the villain as he tried to flee Superman and Batman. She looked a little different, but she was the same Lois Lane.

DC Universe Animated Original Movies

DC Comics characters have starred in a variety of other animated TV programs over the past few years, and Lois has been a small part of that. She was played by Sirena Irwin in an episode of *Batman: The Brave and the Bold*, and comedian Maria Bamford voiced Lois in a pair of funny animated shorts that aired during DC's animation block on Cartoon Network. Apart from these appearances, however,

Lois and the Superman mythos generally haven't had a substantial animated television presence of late.

However, they've been a regular part of DC Universe Animated Original Movies, a special division of Warner Bros. Animation that produces direct-to-video films for more mature audiences. The films are often adaptations of popular comic book stories, and most of them are standalone entries featuring entirely new casts. Lois has appeared in seven of the more than twenty films that have been produced, including the movie that launched the entire line in 2007.

Superman: Doomsday was an adaptation of the famous "Death of Superman" story line, with Anne Heche voicing Lois Lane. The film barely resembled the original story, apart from Doomsday briefly killing Superman, but Lois's role was similar in that she took center stage after Superman's death. Instead of the "Reign of the Supermen," Lois was suspicious about a single new Superman. Eventually tracing him back to Lex Luthor, she broke into Luthor's building and found a Superman clone laboratory. Lois also figured out that Clark was Superman, drove a helicopter and a jeep through decimated downtown Metropolis, and single-handedly took out Lex Luthor.

Lois was voiced by several well-known actresses in subsequent films, including Emmy and Golden Globe winner Kyra Sedgwick in a small part in *Justice League: The New Frontier* and multiple Emmy nominee Christina Hendricks in an adaptation of *All-Star Superman*. Dana Delany returned to play Lois in *Justice League: The Flashpoint Paradox*, portraying an alternate-universe version of the character who was an undercover reporter in an Amazon-controlled London ruled by Wonder Woman.

Castle star Stana Katic voiced arguably the best-known animated film incarnation of Lois, thanks to the Internet's affinity for animated GIF images. Katic played Lois in *Superman: Unbound*, an adaptation of the comic book arc "Superman: Brainiac" that featured the alien conqueror attacking Metropolis.* As Brainiac taunted the captured city, Lois stared at him with an utterly blasé expression before

---

* The film was a *Castle* mini-reunion; Molly Quinn, who plays Alexis Castle, voiced Supergirl. Castle himself, Nathan Fillion, is also a regular presence in DC's movie line, having appeared in several of the films as the voice of Green Lantern.

flipping both middle fingers at him. That moment has since been immortalized in countless Twitter, Tumblr, and Facebook posts as a snarky response to annoying news or comments.

Altogether, the only female character who has appeared in more DC original movies than Lois Lane is Wonder Woman, and by a very slim margin. Much like her comic book appearances, Lois's many animated incarnations have had their highs and lows, but the last two decades have been a strong run for the character across a variety of projects.

Watching from the Sidelines

*B*ack in the comics, Superman's resurrection in the fall of 1993 meant a return to the norm across the Super-books, except for Lois Lane. Though she picked up where she left off with her engagement to Clark, there were changes. Some were cosmetic; the debut of *Lois & Clark: The New Adventures of Superman* was quickly followed by a new, Teri Hatcher–inspired haircut for Lois in the comics. In terms of story, after serving as the core of the Super-books during Superman's death, Lois stayed in the spotlight when he returned, launching a massive investigation of Lex Luthor. It became a running story line across all four series and gave Lois her biggest journalistic plot of the post-*Crisis* era.

The investigation began when Lois received a tip that LexCorp had falsely filed claims for buildings that were damaged during the Doomsday battle. Lois snuck in to get a closer look and found that they'd been deliberately sabotaged. Her insurance fraud story led to more serious allegations, and soon Lois was looking into the disappearance of LexCorp employees and possible attempted murder charges against Luthor himself. She went after him full tilt, even breaking into LexCorp headquarters on multiple occasions to track down evidence. Luthor didn't take kindly to Lois's inquiry and put pressure on the *Daily Planet*'s owner to get her fired. When losing her job didn't slow her down, Luthor had her apartment bombed. That didn't stop Lois either, and her investigation ultimately led to more startling revelations and culminated in Luthor's arrest and the destruction of LexCorp.

With Luthor taken care of, Lois then became wrapped up in more pedestrian matters. Being engaged to Superman was difficult. He regularly disappeared for extended periods of time without explanation, leaving Lois worried and confused. She'd fallen in love with Clark, but everything was now about Superman. Lois wasn't happy, and after every discussion she tried to have about it was interrupted by sirens, she ended their engagement.

The following months were acrimonious, and Lois ultimately left Metropolis to become a foreign correspondent, but things quickly turned back around. She took center stage in *Superman* #118 in a story that was ostensibly about her uncovering smugglers in the fictional country of Bhutran, but the end result was Lois standing atop a mountain and realizing what a kind and good man Clark was as she tearfully chastised herself for acting "like a jerk and an idiot!" She exclaimed, "It's like I was in a dark room and someone turned on the light for the first time in months." Her concerns were swept aside instead of actually dealt with in order to make way for the following week's *Superman: The Wedding Album*.

Marketed as "The Event of the Century!" the special oversized issue told the tale of Lois and Clark's reconciliation and expedited nuptials.* It began with Lois taking out the ringleader of Bhutran's heroin-smuggling outfit and hijacking his plane to return to Metropolis. She then amusingly thumbed her nose at most traditional wedding conventions. She expressed her disdain for her kitchenware-laden "Happy Homemaker" shower, refused to be given away at the ceremony, and decided to keep her own last name. Still, by issue's end, Lois was a married woman, and her role in the Super-books changed dramatically.

---

* The issue's release intentionally coincided with the characters' marriage on *Lois & Clark: The New Adventures of Superman*—more specifically, the actual wedding in the fourth season and not the fake-out clone wedding from season three.

Wedded Bliss

Lois and Clark's wedding in late 1996 was a pivotal moment for Lois in the post-*Crisis* era. A close examination of *Action Comics* shows that in the ten years before the wedding, Lois appeared in 68 percent of the series' issues, and in the fifteen years following the wedding this percentage remained almost exactly the same.* However, what Lois did and where shifted considerably. Before the wedding, when Lois appeared she was at work for the *Daily Planet* 77 percent of the time. After her marriage, this fell to 51 percent. Moreover, pre-marriage Lois covered a clearly specified story, rather than just chatting with her coworkers or attending staff meetings, in 51 percent of her appearances in *Action Comics*. Post-marriage, this dropped to 16 percent.

Lois's journalistic adventures were set aside in favor of her home life. The Man of Steel had a rough few years after the wedding; he temporarily lost his superpowers, then was mind-controlled by the villain Dominus, and later he was split into two Supermen. Lois's primary role was supporting Clark through his various problems and providing a sounding board for him to consider his next steps. Her own solo stories were few and far between, and when she wasn't busy furthering Superman's narrative she was doing the same for Jimmy, Perry, or Lucy, all of whom had long-running arcs in the 1990s.

Superman #146 was indicative of Lois's diminished role. The issue featured Lois prominently, a rarity for the time, but she was there solely to serve as a framing device for Superman's story. It began with Lois waiting for Superman to return from a Justice League meeting. While he should've been home hours earlier, a patient Lois explained to her cat, "That's life with **Superman**, and I wouldn't have it any other way." When Superman finally showed up, the couple sat down to dinner and Superman told Lois about his encounters with Toyman and the Prankster, with Lois peppering him with questions

---

* The actual percentage difference between Lois's appearances before and after the wedding is only 0.2 percent.

to help drive the narrative. Superman's only question about Lois's day was if she'd used his mother's recipe for the beef wellington she'd made for dinner.

In contrast, both *Lois & Clark* and *Smallville* turned Lois and Superman into a team after his secret identity was revealed and they got together. Her more prominent role in those adaptations may have been due to the input of female writers; *Lois & Clark* had several women on the writing staff, even after Deborah Joy LeVine left, and *Smallville* was a bastion of female scribes. The Super-books were not. Throughout the entirety of the post-*Crisis* era, sixty-six different people wrote issues across the line's several ongoing series. Only five of them were women, and only one, Louise Simonson, wrote more than ten issues.* Based on the stories these many men told, it seems that they just didn't know what to do with Lois.

The character continued to be pushed to the periphery, especially during the comics' biggest moments. Following the popularity of the "Death of Superman" arc, the Super-books built up to a seismic story line every couple years. One of the most expansive events of this era was "Our Worlds at War," a massive alien invasion story that began in the Superman line and spread throughout many other DC titles in 2001. All of the citizens of Metropolis, including Lois, were teleported into an alien prison camp at the beginning of the story, and were then largely forgotten until the event wrapped up.

Big, widely marketed changes to the creative lineup rarely resulted in much of a showcase for Lois either. When comic book superstars Brian Azzarello and Jim Lee took over *Superman* in 2004, sales skyrocketed, but Lois didn't show up until the ninth issue of their twelve-issue story line. In 2006, fan favorites Geoff Johns and Adam Kubert began a run on *Action Comics* with a famed cowriter: Richard Donner, the director of *Superman: The Movie*. Lois was part of the story, but in a new role; Clark and Lois briefly adopted a Kryptonian boy who escaped from the Phantom Zone, and now

---

* The rest were Barbara Kesel, Christina Weir, G. Willow Wilson, and Gail Simone. Simonson had a lengthy tenure on *Superman: The Man of Steel* in the early 1990s, and she wrote most of Lois's LexCorp investigation. She left the series two years after Lois and Clark tied the knot.

the duo were parents. Over the course of the year, Superman still spent most of his time living his usual life while also being a father, but Lois's life suddenly boiled down to taking care of their child and little else.

Throughout this era, Lois and Clark's marriage was a means to generate stories that focused on Superman. Lois created conflict so that Superman could brood and then act heroically to allow her to again realize how wonderful he was. Much of the conflict stemmed from Lois's jealousy, often of Superman's ex-girlfriends. Lori Lemaris, Clark's mermaid ex, moved in with the couple for an extended arc, causing constant unease in their relationship, while Lana Lang was a regular source of marital strife due to her clear obsession with Clark.

Lana and Lori annoyed Lois, but the only woman Lois saw as a viable threat was Wonder Woman. She was smart and beautiful and spent a lot of time with Superman on Justice League missions. In short, she had all of Lois's best qualities as well as superpowers, and that intimidated Lois. Her worries were unfounded; Wonder Woman didn't express much romantic interest in Superman nor him in her, especially after he was married. Nonetheless, she inspired fiery jealousy in Lois. When a new teenage superhero claimed to be Superman's daughter, Lois's first reaction was to yell at Superman as tears streamed down her face, "Was it **Wonder Woman?** I bet it **was** Wonder Woman."

Lois's jealousy led to many spats, but fights were a common occurrence generally. In the midst of the scandal surrounding Superman's daughter, Perry White had Clark secretly working on an exposé of Lex Luthor and neither of them told Lois about it. She was so furious at both of them when she found out that she briefly quit the *Daily Planet* for television news.*

The conclusion of "Our Worlds at War" led to an even bigger split. When Lois finally returned to Earth, she saw that her father was

---

* Lois wasn't without her own secrets. One of her longest-running story lines revolved around her secretly convincing Lex Luthor to save the *Daily Planet*; in return she promised to kill one story of his choosing at any time. The arrangement haunted her and brought additional stress to her marriage.

in trouble and called out for Superman to help him. Unfortunately, Superman was busy elsewhere, saving Wonder Woman. He didn't get to Lois in time, and her father was killed. Between Superman failing to save her father and Lois's preexisting Wonder Woman issues, Lois needed a break from her marriage. She took a trip around the world with her widowed mother to sort out her anger, an arc that yet again relegated Lois to a limited and sporadic role for several months.

After each of these fights had run its course and fulfilled its role in Superman's ongoing narrative, Lois and Clark inevitably made up. Their spats usually resulted in a suspension of amorous activities, like when Superman split into two Supermen and Lois made them both sleep on the couch. The end of a fight meant that everything went back to normal in the bedroom, as did Lois's returns from her many lengthy absences. One reunion dedicated a two page spread to the couple enjoying a candlelit bubble bath, in which Lois uttered the line, "Tonight you've **earned** the name Man of Steel . . ."

Lois and Clark's active sex life meant that Lois was often scantily clad, but this became a common occurrence for Lois in the 2000s no matter the setting. While the Super-books' writing staff was almost entirely male, there were no female artists across the entire ongoing Superman line in the post-*Crisis* era. Almost two hundred different artists worked on the books, and all of them were men. Both their gender and their art reflected the dominant trends of this period.

Over the course of the 1990s, the depiction of women in comic books had become increasingly sexualized. Female superheroes had always worn smaller outfits than their male counterparts, but artists now found ways to emphasize their bodies even more. Waists became tiny, breasts became globes, and outfits were drawn as if they were painted on. Over time, this objectified approach to female superheroes became the norm, then spread to *all* female characters. "Sexy" became the default setting for the entire gender.

Throughout the 1990s, Lois had hardly been a fashion plate. She wore big jackets and sweaters at the *Daily Planet* and baggy T-shirts at home. Lois was drawn like a normal woman, and comfort and functionality were her only concerns. Then in the 2000s, she started to wear skintight belly shirts and pants so low that her thong underwear was visible. Lois stopped waiting around for Superman in her pajamas, instead donning skimpy negligees.

Her professional attire was just as revealing. On a trip to Africa in an issue of *Action Comics*, Lois looked more like Lara Croft than an award-winning reporter. Her button-down shirt was open and tied under her bulbous breasts, her midriff was bare, and her "shorts" covered less skin than an average pair of briefs. A work trip to Eastern Europe in *Superman* #180 featured an entranced Lois striding through the moors in tiny underwear and an unbuttoned shirt that hung below her shoulder and blew back in the wind, barely covering her breasts.

Such outfits were out of character for Lois and never key to the story. They also came at a time when Lois had very little else to do across the Super-books. In many issues, her sole function was to spout a piece of exposition while wearing something exploitative and then disappear from the book. Once Lois became a "sexy" character, she was often called upon to be nothing *but* sexy.

Still, in the rare instances when Superman wasn't around and Lois could step away from her role as his wife, she returned to journalism and charged hard after big stories. There was her assignment covering the war in Umec, where she took a bullet from a sniper while trying to help a wounded American soldier. When Superman left Earth to monitor General Zod in the "New Krypton" event, Lois uncovered a massive government conspiracy, was arrested and interrogated by the military for treason, and ultimately helped save Earth from a wrathful Kryptonian deity.

Outside of the Super-books, Lois was known as the world's best and toughest reporter, and her guest appearances throughout the wider DC Comics universe reflected that. In *Birds of Prey* #102, Lois met with Barbara Gordon, who secretly led a superhero team, and a nervous Barbara thought, "I'd rather face the Joker. He's been known to give up on occasion. But Lane? Never." In a crossover with *Detective Comics* soon after Lex Luthor was elected president of the United States, Lois convinced Batman to break into the White House with her in order to track down Luthor's Kryptonite ring. Batman slipped in underground while Lois used her press pass to get into the building, snuck into a restricted area, took out security and communications, and met up with Batman.

Lois also patched things up with Wonder Woman when she was granted exclusive access to write a day-in-the-life piece on the amazing Amazon in *Wonder Woman* #170. Initially, Lois was cold and distant, approaching the story from a cynical angle. Her jealousy of Wonder Woman was foremost in her mind, and the two women weren't clicking at all. Then, instead of fighting, Lois and Wonder Woman talked about their issues over a game of pool. Wonder Woman even offered to let Lois use her golden lasso, which compels people to tell the truth, to ask her about Superman. Lois refused, because over the course of their conversation she'd come to respect and trust Wonder Woman. The issue presented a nuanced portrayal of Lois that was otherwise missing from the Super-books in this period, and today it is considered an iconic Lois Lane story. It showed her flaws but also her ability to change and grow. Lois also beat Wonder Woman at pool, which was no mean feat.

A few years earlier, Lois had even gotten to headline a book again, however briefly. In 1998, DC Comics put out a line of one-shots called "Girlfrenzy!" each of which spotlighted a different female character. Lois's story was written by Barbara Kesel and penciled by Amanda Conner; it was the only "Girlfrenzy!" issue with female creators at the helm. In the book, Lois was in northern Manitoba to write a story about ecotourism until reports of missing local children piqued her interest. Before long, she was scuba diving in frigid waters to break into a secret genetics laboratory, where she helped save the kids from a mad scientist's experiments. It was a rare solo showcase for Lois; Superman appeared in the book's first few pages and then flew off. Lois got to be the hero and land a huge scoop.

Superman again took center stage when his origins were retold in two high-profile miniseries, but because they were set prior to Lois and Clark's marriage, they gave Lois the chance to break free of her recent domestic limitations. The first new origin tale was *Superman: Birthright*, a twelve-issue miniseries that began in 2003, written by Mark Waid with art by Leinil Francis Yu and Gerry Alanguilan. Lois was introduced in the fourth issue, loudly confronting her publisher because he was being rude to Jimmy. She was already on the outs at the *Daily Planet*, having spent a lot of time traipsing around the world to track down stories about a mysterious man who performed super-feats; her peers called her research "Lois Lane's Loony Lark."

However, Lois was soon vindicated when rogue robotic choppers attacked Metropolis. Lois rushed to the roof to get a closer look, piloting the *Daily Planet*'s news helicopter herself to chase after the story. When the helicopter got damaged, she was rescued by a man in a blue suit and a red cape. The man told Lois not to be afraid, and she replied, "I'm **not**! Sky! Copters! **Artillery!** Danger! **Go go go!**" Just before she shooed him away to go stop the choppers, she stuck her business card in his hand and told him, "**Then** we talk." Lois had found her mystery man. She named him Superman and got a front page story out of it.

Instead of instant infatuation with the Man of Steel, Lois was depicted as the only person who trusted him when Lex Luthor turned the world against him. By the end of the series, she'd uncovered Luthor's sham alien invasion, broken into LexCorp, and disabled a Kryptonite weapon to help Superman again save the city.

In 2009, *Superman: Secret Origin* presented Lois as a confident, crusading journalist. Written by Geoff Johns with art by Gary Frank and Jon Sibal, the six-issue miniseries was published to rework Superman's origin story after *Infinite Crisis*, DC's continuity-twisting follow-up to *Crisis on Infinite Earths*. Lois was again introduced while yelling at someone, this time Perry White; she was furious because he refused to print a story criticizing Lex Luthor on his publisher's orders. Luthor was the most powerful man in Metropolis, and the people who owned all of the city's newspapers were terrified of him.

But Lois wasn't frightened of Luthor in the least. When she went to interview him with Clark, she declared, "I've been compiling a list of questions over the last year that **no** reporter would **dare** ask him." After a mysterious costumed hero appeared, every other newspaper called it a hoax, but Lois's story for the *Daily Planet* was titled "Mysterious Hero Saves Lives." When his existence was confirmed after he defeated one of Luthor's experiments gone awry, the other papers called him an untrustworthy menace, but Lois insisted her headline read, "Meet the City's New Savior—**Superman!**" Lois was the only reporter to whom Superman gave quotes, and she later warned him about Kryptonite when she learned that Luthor and the government planned to use it to subdue him. There was the occasional hint of attraction between Lois and Superman, but she was most passionate about sticking it to Lex Luthor. Being free of her marriage allowed Lois to care about things other than Superman.

Pushing Daisies

Superman had saved Lois with confident ease for decades, but the stakes were higher in the Modern Age once Lois and Superman were a couple. Instead of a simple rescue from a self-assured Man of Steel, Superman was wracked with angst whenever Lois was captured. Worry and heartache gave Superman an emotional arc as he battled whichever dastardly villain had nabbed Lois this time. The need to provide Superman with emotional drama often went further than marital strife or kidnappings. Sometimes, via an alternate timeline or some other contrivance, Lois was killed.

Death was nothing new for Lois. In the Silver Age, the imaginary stories in which she was married to Superman ended in her death more than once: In *Superman* #194, Lois died in a car crash as part of Lex Luthor's plan to exact revenge from his nemesis. Then in *Superman* #215, Lois was killed when a blast-ray ricocheted off of Superman's invulnerable chest in a story tellingly titled "The Sorrows of Superman."* Even in her own series, Lois's death was a footnote to a larger tale; when she died in *Superman's Girl Friend Lois Lane* #51, the rest of the book followed Superman's subsequent doomed relationships as he married and then mourned not only Lana Lang but Lori Lemaris as well.

Lois's deaths continued to serve as story fodder for other characters in the Modern Age. These tales made Lois a prop, reducing her

---

* After Lois's death, Superman was so lonely that he made a robot replica of her. When the batteries on his Lois robot died, he finally found happiness again by traveling to a different dimension and marrying that Earth's Lois Lane.

to a plot device while also removing her from the story that followed. This was a common predicament for female characters in superhero comics, so much so that it eventually spawned a critical response with its own unique terminology.

In 1999, future Super-books writer Gail Simone addressed the frequent deaths of female comic book characters by launching the website Women in Refrigerators. The title was a reference to *Green Lantern* #54, in which Kyle Rayner, the new Green Lantern, returned home to find that a villain had murdered his girlfriend, Alex DeWitt, and stuffed her dead body into his refrigerator. Simone saw this issue as part of a larger phenomenon within the superhero genre in which female characters were killed, injured, depowered, or otherwise side-lined in a heinous way, often violent and/or sexual, to further the story of a male character. Readers sent in names of other "fridged" female characters, and Simone compiled a lengthy list on the site.

Women dying in comics had been common for some time. For example, Gwen Stacy was killed in 1973, causing anguish for her boyfriend, Peter Parker, a.k.a. Spider-Man. Then in the mid-1980s, as superhero comics began to get darker, well-known female charac-ters were cast aside to inspire their male counterparts. Supergirl died in *Crisis on Infinite Earths* to give Superman the boost he needed to defeat the Anti-Monitor for good, while Batgirl was paralyzed and sexually abused by the Joker in *Batman: The Killing Joke* to push Batman's anger almost to the breaking point. Fridgings became increasingly regular in the early 1990s, a symptom of a genre written and illustrated primarily by men allowing itself to indulge in over-the-top violence.

Somewhat ironically, one of Lois's best-known deaths came in a book that was designed to respond to the growing brutality of the superhero genre. In 1996, DC Comics published *Kingdom Come*, a four-part miniseries written by Mark Waid with painted art by Alex Ross. The book was set in a future in which the Justice League had been replaced by more extreme superheroes who disregarded due process and simply killed their foes. Superman had hung up his cape years earlier when Lois and the rest of the *Daily Planet* staff were murdered in a gas attack by the Joker. When a new superhero killed the Joker instead of taking him to the authorities, the world backed his actions and turned against Superman and his seemingly antiquated ways, so Superman exiled himself to his Fortress of Solitude.

Lois and Superman were married in the world of *Kingdom Come*, and the book made clear that one of the main reasons Superman hid himself from the world was his grief over losing her. When he returned to action to take down the new heroes and right the world, the yellow background of his S-shield was replaced with a black background to reflect his continued mourning. Yet Lois was barely in the book. She was mentioned occasionally, and only appeared in the background of a flashback panel, a curl of long brown hair and an arm in a blouse amid the carnage at the *Daily Planet*. The entire story hinged on Superman losing Lois and the grief it caused him, but Lois herself was barely present.

A quasi-sequel a decade later fleshed out Lois's death in more detail, giving her a brave end in her final moments. She donned a gas mask and attacked the Joker before he fatally fractured her skull with a *Daily Planet* paperweight. But her final moments were again all about Superman. When Superman arrived and told her that he'd make the Joker pay, Lois's last words were, "No, please, don't cross that line . . . don't change who you are, not now . . . not ever," essentially setting up the stance that led to Superman's exile and later comeback. Moreover, the story of her death was told by this future Superman as he explained his tragic backstory after mysteriously arriving in the main DC universe. It was a three-page flashback amid a much larger Superman tale. The reaction to the flashback summed up its function; instead of saying anything about Lois's death, the first response was "Your pain must be so great."

Lois died several times in regular continuity as well, though these deaths were usually illusions meant to spur Superman toward anger or justice. When the Joker stole Mister Mxyzptlk's world-warping powers during the "Emperor Joker" story line in 2000, the Joker tricked Superman into thinking he'd killed Lois himself by flying too fast and snapping her neck. A heartbroken Superman took her death as a call to action and defiantly proclaimed, "I will always fight for a better world—for all the victims—for **Lois!**" Lois then "died" again in the following issue, leading to Superman's final and victorious confrontation with the Joker.

Two years later, the cover of *Action Comics* #796 read THE DEATH OF LOIS LANE! Inside, Superman found the villain Manchester Black standing over Lois's dead body, manipulating her corpse like a puppet. He wanted to push Superman to his breaking point, but Superman declared, "Vengeance isn't justice," and swore never to kill Manchester Black, only to send him to jail. Impressed by Superman's commitment to his values, Manchester Black revealed that Lois's death had been a ruse.

In the oversized anniversary special *Superman* #200 in 2004, Lois's death was the pivotal plot point in a grim vision of the future. Lois was alive for all of one page before she died in a catastrophic flood. Superman then made a deal with Lex Luthor to keep Lois cryogenically frozen until technology existed that could bring her back to life. In return, Superman retired and the world fell into chaos. When Lois was finally resurrected thousands of years later, she came back for one panel before being consumed by Brainiac and essentially killed once more, kick-starting the issue's final battle.

A year and a half later, Lois was again cavalierly slain multiple times for the "Sacrifice" story line. The villain Max Lord took over Superman's mind and made him think that Lois was murdered, first by Brainiac and then by Darkseid. Filled with rage, Superman mercilessly beat the enemies who killed his wife, but because of the mind control he was actually hitting Batman. The story was an important lead-in to *Infinite Crisis*, a massive event spanning nearly every DC title in which the modern Lois played practically no part other than to occasionally cheer on Superman.

The Golden Age Lois Lane, however, played a key role in *Infinite Crisis*. At the end of *Crisis on Infinite Earths* in 1986, the Golden Age Superman and Lois, Earth-Three's Alexander Luthor, and Earth-Prime's Superboy had survived the creation of the new DC universe by retreating to a pocket dimension. Over time, the Golden Age Lois grew old and ill, and Luthor convinced Superman that her illness was due to the corruption of the dark and violent new Earth. Luthor argued that if they restored the Golden Age Earth, Lois would be saved. Superman agreed to the plan and smashed through the wall between the pocket dimension and the main universe, leading to a massive conflict with Earth's heroes.

Being sickly and bedridden, the Golden Age Lois didn't have much to do in the rest of *Infinite Crisis*, and when her Earth was finally restored in the series' fifth issue, she died anyway. This led to a battle between the Golden Age Superman and his modern counterpart before the former realized that he'd been manipulated by Luthor and they teamed up to defeat him. Lois had kicked off the story and spurred its major turning point, but only through her illness and then her death.

After "dying" eight times in the span of six years, Lois stayed alive for a while. She died again in the *Flashpoint* crossover series in 2011, bravely defying the Amazon warlords who had conquered the British Isles in an alternate timeline. When *Earth 2*, a series set in a new alternate universe, premiered eight months later, her death was yet again a key motivator for Superman. This Earth was under attack from the hordes of Apokolips in the book's debut issue, and Metropolis was one of the first cities to fall. As Superman blasted through Parademons, hoping to buy Batman enough time to end the war once and for all, he excised his grief over losing Lois and his anger at "the **stupid**, senseless way she died."

Lois's most shocking death came in 2013, first in the form of a video game. *Injustice: Gods Among Us* was a fighting game in which hero could battle hero, and the story line behind the game began with the Joker's destruction of Metropolis. In the game's opening cinematic, a furious Superman burst into an interrogation room and lamented the deaths of his wife and his son. The Joker only mocked him in return, and the scene ended with Superman killing the Joker, the first step on the path to Superman taking over the world and starting a civil war among DC's superheroes.

A prequel comic published by DC Comics explored the death of the video game's Lois in more gruesome detail. The first issue began with the happy news that Lois was pregnant. As she went off to investigate a hot news tip, Superman met up with Batman to ask him to be the godfather. Unfortunately, Lois's tip was a setup, and the Joker murdered Jimmy Olsen and captured Lois. When Superman came to rescue her, the Joker infected him with a toxin that made him believe that Doomsday was attacking Lois. He barreled into Doomsday and took off into the sky, going straight up into space, where Doomsday couldn't breathe. But Doomsday wasn't Doomsday; it was Lois. Superman had been tricked into killing his wife and unborn child. To make matters worse, the Joker had installed a device on Lois's heart that was linked to a nuclear bomb in Metropolis. When Lois's heart stopped beating, the bomb went off.*

While Lois had died several times in the comics, the deaths were usually illusions. Not only was her death in *Injustice: Gods Among Us* real, but the entire story of the game hinged on that key moment. Moreover, while Lois's latest comic book death in *Earth 2* #1 sold around 80,000 copies, *Injustice: Gods Among Us* sold 1.3 million copies across various gaming platforms. Lois's most appalling death was also her most popular.

---

* The plot of this comic was largely set in stone by the video game, and writer Tom Taylor had very little room to change things. He later revealed that Lois's death "was the hardest thing I've ever had to write," so when he took over the *Earth 2* comic a few months later he brought back that universe's Lois in his first issue out of a desire to unfridge at least one version of the character. Lois's consciousness was loaded into a robot body, and she took on the mantle of the superhero Red Tornado.

10a

The New 52 and Beyond

In 2011, DC Comics dissolved Lois and Clark's marriage, along with its entire universe. A quarter century had passed since *Crisis on Infinite Earths* ushered in the Modern Age with a line-wide reboot, and while DC had tweaked some aspects of its heroes' backstories in 2005's *Infinite Crisis*, the top brass decided that it was time for another fresh start. The New 52 initiative,* a complete relaunch of DC's superhero line spread across fifty-two new series, wiped away vast swaths of continuity, including almost everything having to do with Superman and his corner of the universe. His marriage to Lois was one of the casualties of the reboot; all of the superheroes were younger now, and DC wanted to explore new romantic options.

Over the course of Lois and Clark's fifteen-year marriage, DC's creators had never found balance in their marital dynamic. The sentiment among the company's editors seemed to be that Lois was a bothersome appendage for the Man of Steel. At San Diego Comic-Con, editor Matt Idelson called Lois a "trophy wife" that Superman would be rid of in the new universe. DC's copublisher, Dan DiDio, had been gunning for the Super-marriage for some time. He had a plan to eliminate the marriage in *Infinite Crisis*, but it didn't come

---

* The relaunch was the result of DC's *Flashpoint* event, in which the Flash's time-traveling drastically altered the timeline and ultimately led to a new, slightly different universe after the Flash tried to set things right.

to fruition. Rebooting the entire line finally gave him the way out that he'd been looking for.

The New 52

At the dawn of DC Comics' new universe, not only was Lois not married to Clark anymore, she didn't even know that he was Superman. In fact, they weren't terribly close at all. Professionally, Lois had moved on from the *Daily Planet* and instead worked as a producer for the television news division of the media conglomerate that owned the paper. Clark left the *Daily Planet* soon after the relaunch to start his own online news venture.

Personally, Lois had a new beau, a correspondent named Jonathan Carroll who made his debut in an awkward scene in the new *Superman* #1. Clark stopped by Lois's apartment to apologize for something he'd said earlier in the day, but a shirtless Jonathan quickly appeared behind her and made sure to point out that they were "celebrating" the high ratings on Lois's latest telecast. Jonathan has appeared occasionally since then but has yet to develop much in the way of story lines or personality. Before long, Superman had a new girlfriend too. He began dating Wonder Woman a year into the New 52, and the couple launched their own joint series in fall 2013.

Without any close connections to Clark or Superman, Lois wasn't a major presence in the Super-books. Lois and Clark were friends, but both were busy with their separate lives. Lois had a slightly larger role in the first few issues of the new *Action Comics*, which were set five years in the past, when Lois and Clark were journalistic rivals, but when the book returned to the present she was relegated to the sidelines again. While she popped up here and there to spout a bit of exposition or further Clark's story in some way, she was rarely around for long.

Lois finally got a more substantial role a couple of years into the new universe, but she wasn't actually herself. She'd been taken over by Brainiac, and her subplot revolved around her adapting to her frightening new powers and wrestling with the alien's evil influence. In general, Lois has been one of the least utilized female characters across the Super-books. Wonder Woman has a large presence because of her romantic relationship with Superman, Supergirl had her own series for three years that often crossed over with the other titles, and even Lana Lang has garnered lengthy plotlines in *Action Comics*.

Throughout the wider New 52 universe, however, Lois's guest appearances highlighted different facets of the character that the Super-books ignored. She appeared occasionally in *Batman/Superman*, often teaming up with Batman to take down villains in a role that showcased her snark and confidence; when a villain tried to trick Lois in one issue, she calmly responded, "You think I'd come here unprepared for this? I'm **Lois Lane**. That means I'm **smarter** than you." Lois was in the middle of the action in *Superman Unchained*, a miniseries by the superstar team of Scott Snyder and Jim Lee, successfully crash-landing a sabotaged plane and using futuristic technology to disable a fleet of military vehicles that attacked Superman. Lois also had a recurring role in the weekly series *The New 52: Futures End*. Set in a world five years in the future, it found Lois in full investigative mode, running her own popular news site and researching the mysteries behind several missing and changed superheroes.

Lois's only solo outing in the New 52 was an oversized one-shot in 2014 titled *Superman: Lois Lane*. Written by Marguerite Bennett with art by Emanuela Lupacchino, Meghan Hetrick, and several others, the story centered on Lois investigating a drug cartel that her sister, Lucy, and Lucy's roommate were wrapped up in. Lois used her many sources to track down the mysterious cartel, freed herself after they captured her, and rescued Lucy's roommate. Superman only appeared in one panel, after Lois called him to sort out the rest of the cartel after she escaped. Lois used every tool at her disposal, including her brain and her brawn, to help her sister. Bennett said of her approach to Lois, "So much of what Lois is capable of can be seen in who she is beyond Superman. Not without, which I think implies a noticeable absence, a fault, a lack—but beyond him, head high, hair streaming, heroic in her own right, braving a superhuman world on beautifully human terms."

The one-shot appeared to be a test for the viability of a regular Lois Lane series, but the test did not go well. The issue came in

ninety-sixth place on the sales chart that month with 21,550 copies sold, an entirely inauspicious debut.* The book's price probably
didn't help matters, either; most DC books sold for $2.99, but this
oversized issue was $4.99.

While Lois hasn't landed a series yet, the future is looking bright
for women at DC in general. When the New 52 debuted, it was
roundly criticized for its treatment of women, both real and fictional.
There were only two female creators across the entire fifty-two-book
line, and as in the past, many of the female characters were oversexu-
alized. The New 52 made slight changes over the next few years, but
none substantive until late in 2014. With the success of a new *Harley
Quinn* series and a revamped *Batgirl*, both with female creators in
prominent roles and styles that broke from the usual dark and gritty
fare, DC saw a growing female audience and moved to capitalize
on it. The publisher's female creator ranks have grown substantially
since then, and in June 2015 a mini-relaunch of twenty-four new
series featured a variety of female characters headlining books that
were diverse in terms of creators, characters, and styles.

Meanwhile, Lois found herself wrapped up in another Superman
story. The massive "Truth" crossover ran through all of the Super-
books, and centered on Superman's secret identity being revealed
to the public. The person behind this revelation was Lois Lane.† In
a front page story for the *Daily Planet*, Lois declared that the Man
of Steel "secretly dwelt among us as reporter Clark Kent," adding,
"Many who once admired him now question his motives for creating a fake persona."

The article fractured her relationship with Clark. Lois had figured
out his identity after Superman's powers lessened and Clark began
displaying injuries that lined up with Superman's various battles.

---

* DC Comics' threshold for considering canceling a regular series is roughly 20,000 copies sold per month, so for the one-shot to debut so near to that line doomed its future
chances immediately.
† John Romita Jr., the artist on *Superman*, said of doing this story line in this new universe,
"There is no way of doing anything original with her unless you take what everybody else
expects her to do and don't do it. If she decides to be a bitch, let her be a bitch. That's her
prerogative. [. . .] It's time for her to say, 'You lied to me, you bastard.'"

The villain Hordr_Root had figured out his identity as well, and when Superman gave himself up to the villain after he threatened to disclose his secret, Lois revealed Superman's identity to the world to take away Hordr_Root's leverage and free Superman from his thrall. Even though she did this to save him, Clark was furious. When Lois went to apologize and told him, "I should've looked for another way. I had **no right**," Clark shut the door in her face. At a time when so many female characters received exciting new and heroic spotlights from DC Comics, Lois was not just limited to being a small piece of a massive Superman story line, she was there in an adversarial role.*

Lois Lane: Fallout

Whether married or single, old universe or new, DC's comic books have underutilized Lois for some time, but she's got top billing in a new medium. In May 2015, Switch Press released a young adult prose novel titled *Lois Lane: Fallout*. Written by Gwenda Bond, the author of the bestselling *Girl on a Wire*, the novel starred a teen Lois Lane who moved to Metropolis and immediately found herself in the middle of a massive mystery that needed investigating.

The book's announcement garnered press from all of the major entertainment outlets. *Hollywood Reporter* declared, "Step aside, Katniss: it's time for a teenage journalist to take over," while *Entertainment Weekly* mused, "So it's basically Lois Lane in a *Veronica Mars*-esque plot, which sounds like all kinds of awesome." The reviews lived up to the hype; a *Kirkus* starred review called *Lois Lane: Fallout* "a spectacular prose start for DC Comics' spectacular lady."

In an interview before the book's release, Bond described her approach to the novel, and to her writing generally, saying, "I want

---

* In October 2015, DC launched *Superman: Lois and Clark*, a series in which the pre–New 52 versions of the title characters journey to the rebooted DC universe and live there with their son, Jonathan. Superman remains a superhero and Lois a reporter, but both do so anonymously, with Lois writing investigative books as "Author X." It's an odd setup, but many fans were cheered to see the old Lois return after four years of poor treatment of the new Lois.

my protagonists to be nuanced and complex, and to put them at the center of the kinds of stories girls may not have always gotten the starring role in." *Lois Lane: Fallout* bore this out. Lois was the core of the book, driving the action and using what Bond called "her unmatched bravery and smarts" to take down the bizarre bullies who plagued her high school.

The novel began with Lois determined to stay under the radar. A military brat, Lois lived all over the world, and her inquisitive nature and inability to stay quiet in the face of injustice got her into trouble at every school she attended. With her family now settled in Metropolis for good, Lois was keen to make a positive impression in her new school. Then, just moments into her first day, Lois overheard the principal dismissing the concerns of a bullied student, and she couldn't help herself from getting involved. Her passionate advocacy for the bullied girl impressed the school's guest speaker for the day, *Daily Planet* reporter Perry White, and he offered Lois a job at the *Daily Scoop*, the paper's new website for teens.

Lois accepted, and soon launched an investigation of the bullies. They were an odd bunch, members of an online gaming community called the Warheads who had an unnatural ability to break down the will of their victims and make them join their group. Lois slowly got her fellow young reporters on board with her investigation, even though the many adults in her life, from the school principal to her parents, tried to shut it down. Even Perry put pressure on Lois to drop the project when a key witness in an earlier story retracted her statement after coercion from the Warheads. Ultimately, Lois tracked the Warheads back to a military contractor who used gaming technology to do hive-mind experimentation on the teens. Lois and her friends broke into the building and shut down the program, which freed the Warheads from the hive mind for good and ended their campaign of bullying.

Throughout the novel, Lois's dialogue was brusque, and she acted cool and detached, particularly as she became increasingly wrapped up in her investigation, but the first-person narration showed the compassion that motivated her. The contrast was an effective way to communicate both sides of the character, her tough exterior and kind interior. Lois's entire investigation was sparked by concern for a girl she didn't even know, but she went about it in a relentless and methodical fashion.

Lois Lane: Fallout showcased the classic elements of Lois in a new, modern setting. Bond surrounded her with a diverse group of friends, giving Lois her own unique supporting cast rather than relying on preexisting characters from the Superman universe. The issues that Lois dealt with, online gaming and bullying, touched on two hot-button topics very relevant to teen readers.*

The book also presented a new take on Clark Kent as the mysterious SmallvilleGuy, a friend Lois chatted with online after meeting him in an Internet forum about strange phenomena. SmallvilleGuy helped Lois with her investigation, but Lois was the undisputed star of the novel. She saw him as a partner, explaining, "We're the same [. . .] we protect people, we see what other people miss." At one point, Lois called SmallvilleGuy, "my trusty sidekick," and when he promised to tell her his true identity someday, Lois replied, "You're assuming I won't figure your secret out on my own first."

Despite the change in age and setting, Bond captured the drive and heroism that has defined Lois Lane since *Action Comics* #1 while successfully translating her into a new medium. With the comic book industry unsure of what to do with Lois, a prose novel was an effective way to introduce the character to a new generation of fans. Not only is young adult fiction a booming and rapidly growing market, it's become a major outlet for strong and compelling female characters.

After decades on the comic book sidelines, Lois is poised to shake off her supporting role and become a star in her own right. Following the success of *Lois Lane: Fallout*, a sequel is on the way, again written by Gwenda Bond. The second in a planned series, *Lois Lane: Double Down* is scheduled to hit stores in May 2016. Lois's new investigation has her looking into the intersection of politics and the criminal underworld in Metropolis, dangerous ground that becomes

---

* The hive-mind gaming angle was especially timely in the wake of the ridiculous Gamergate scandal that pervaded the online gaming world in 2014 and 2015.

even more difficult when she learns that the mob has ties with some of her colleagues at the *Daily Scoop*. It's exactly the sort of perilous, complicated situation in which Lois excels.

Conclusion

*L*ois Lane is to women in journalism as Superman is to super-heroes. Both are archetypical characters who defined a role and have remained an exemplar of it for decades. Other female reporters, real and fictional, have come and gone, but through her many comics, movies, and television shows, Lois Lane has been inspiring women and girls for more than seventy-five years. When Noel Neill toured college campuses in the 1970s, countless female students came to tell her that reading and watching Lois led them to pursue a degree in journalism; they didn't realize that it was a job that women could do until they saw Lois holding her own in a newspaper office full of men.

One of the keys to Lois's long-term appeal is the solid base at the core of her character. Lois has been the same woman since her very first appearance in *Action Comics* #1 in 1938. She was tough, she was ambitious, she was fearless, and she had very little respect for authority. Through every reboot and adaptation, these basic facts have remained the same.

However, the history of Lois Lane is a tumultuous tale about the degree to which this core of her character was buried. In the Golden Age, Lois swiftly shifted from reporter to cheerleader as she fell madly in love with the Man of Steel. The Silver Age brought romantic shenanigans and constant patronizing lessons, while the Bronze Age was one prolonged soap opera. In the Modern Age, Lois's role narrowed to marital stereotypes as she was regularly sidelined from the primary action.

Through it all, she persevered. Lois made her way to the front page of the *Daily Planet* and briefly became a herald of women's liberation and other social issues. She took down villains single-handedly in her solo adventures, exposed the criminal machinations of Lex Luthor, and bravely reported from the front lines of a danger-ous war. She was always a capable reporter; her exploits were just intermittent or relegated to the background.

Lois's constant adversary throughout the decades was Super-man. When Superman wasn't around, she got to be the hero and she excelled at it, from "Lois Lane, Girl Reporter" to "The Death of Superman." On her own, Lois is a fascinating character who fulfills the typical superhero narrative of fighting evil and catching bad guys, without the need for superpowers. Yet even in her self-titled series, almost every story revolved around Superman. While he was good for a front page scoop here and there, he was also a regular source of tears and frustration for Lois. He stole her stories, he embarrassed her, and he monopolized her time. In short, Superman is the worst thing to ever happen to Lois Lane.

At the same time, he's also the reason she exists. Lois was created to be a supporting character for the Man of Steel, and almost every comic book and adaptation that she's appeared in bears his name in some capacity. There would be no Lois Lane without Superman. The same is true for most female characters in superhero comic books: they are primarily adjuncts to the stories of male heroes.

This imbalance is not unique to superheroes. Throughout soci-ety, both in the real world and in entertainment, men's narratives are dominant. They are disproportionately represented at all major levels, and their stories monopolize the public discourse. This doesn't mean that women's stories aren't there, but they are more rare and have to be sought out. Even then, one often must dig through a lot of bad to find the good.

For decades, fans have looked beyond Superman's overwhelming presence to find Lois, and then sifted through her clichéd portrayals to locate her heroic core. In some eras, this was relatively easy, while in others the task became more difficult. Her history is complicated, and the tears and romantic strife were sometimes all-encompassing. Lois's past was fraught with limiting gender roles and sexist story lines, and her time in the spotlight was rare. But characters are more than just their past; their history is a starting point for readers to decide who they are and what they mean. After thousands of comics and multiple films and television shows, today Lois is an icon. It speaks to the strength of the character that for more than seventy-five years, her fans have been able to recognize that Lois's supposed flaws were in fact assets and find inspiration amid the absurdity.

Acknowledgments

I had a lot of wonderful and much-appreciated help putting this book together, from interviews to assistance with information and images to general support in a variety of ways. My thanks to Janelle Asselin, Cary Bates, Gwenda Bond, Mike Catron and Jean Shuster Peavy of the Joe Shuster Estate, Donna Woolfolk Cross, Philip S. Dockter, Greg Elias, Maxene Fabe Mulford, Maida Goodwin from the Sophia Smith Collection at Smith College, Martin Gray, Timothy Hodler from the *Comics Journal*, Todd Ifft from Photofest, Cal Johnston from Strange Adventures, Sean Kleefeld, Kate Leth, Paul Levitz, Hannah Means-Shannon and Rich Johnston of *Bleeding Cool*, Anne Elizabeth Moore, Jacque Nodell of *Sequential Crush*, Jim Nolt, Tamsyn O'Flynn, Denny O'Neil, Brad Ricca, Trina Robbins, John Siuntres, Sue of *DC Women Kicking Ass*, Kelson Vibber, Lori Wozney, and many others I am probably forgetting.

Everyone at Chicago Review Press has again been fantastic to work with, and I'm so glad to be back with them for my second book. Huge thanks to my editor, Yuval Taylor, for his support of the book and his thoughtful comments, and to the rest of the team: Devon Freeny, Jon Hahn, Mary Kravenas, and Meaghan Miller.

Michelle Hegarty of Modified Editing Services was enormously helpful with some tricky edits, and her work has made this a much better book.

My agent, Dawn Frederick of Red Sofa Literary, provided great insights and ideas at every step of the process, and her encouragement and unflagging enthusiasm for this project have been invaluable.

Finally, love and thanks to my parents, my sister, and the rest of my family for all of their support. None of them think I'm a weirdo for spending a year wholly steeped in Lois Lane comics, movies, and TV shows. They probably should, but they don't, and I'm grateful for it.

Source Notes

Introduction

This time, Superman was too late . . . *Adventures of Superman* #631 (October 2004).

DC Comics recently reprinted the story . . . John Byrne, Phil Jimenez, et al., *Lois Lane: A Celebration of 75 Years* (New York: DC Comics, 2013).

"She's the woman that Superman . . ." Arune Singh, "The New 'Adventures' of Lois & Clark: Greg Rucka Talks 'Adventures of Superman,'" *Comic Book Resources*, August 22, 2003, www.comicbookresources .com/?page=article&id=2623.

"Lois embodies everything about . . ." "75 Years of Lois Lane: A Chat with Bryan Q. Miller," *DC Women Kicking Ass* blog, April 22, 2013, http://dcwomenkickingass.tumblr.com/post/48624946890/75-years-of -lois-lane-a-chat-with-bryan-q-miller.

1. The Ambitious Sob Sister

Golden Age Superman stories have been collected in a number of formats over the years, including various hardcover *Archives* editions and paperback *Chronicles* volumes. These collections cover from 1938 to about the mid-1940s. Comics will be cited here with their issue number and publication date, and you can use those to find them in one of the collections listed above, unless the comic is from an unusual source, in which case that source will be cited as well. Information concerning the dawn of the Golden Age came primarily from

Superhero: The Secret Origin of a Genre by Peter Coogan, *Men of Tomorrow: Geeks, Gangsters, and the Birth of the Comic Book* by Gerard Jones, and *Comic Book Nation: The Transformation of Youth Culture in America* by Bradford Wright, though most books on the history of superheroes provide similar information. For the early history of Superman and Lois Lane in particular, I have relied on *Super Boys: The Amazing Adventures of Jerry Siegel and Joe Shuster—the Creators of Superman* by Brad Ricca, *Superman: The High-Flying History of America's Most Enduring Hero* by Larry Tye, and *Superman: The Unauthorized Biography* by Glen Weldon.

Creating a Legend

Sullivan compiled a new cast of characters . . . *Action Comics* #1 (June 1938).

Henri Duval . . . First appeared in *New Fun Comics* #6 (October 1935).

Doctor Occult . . . First appeared in ibid.

Slam Bradley . . . First appeared in *Detective Comics* #1 (March 1937).

They sold the rights to Superman . . . Gerard Jones, *Men of Tomorrow: Geeks, Gangsters, and the Birth of the Comic Book* (New York: Basic Books, 2004), 125.

"the newspaper film genre was . . ." Deac Russell, "The Fourth Estate and the Seventh Art," *Questioning Media Ethics*, ed. Bernard Rubin (New York: Praeger, 1978), 248.

"I'm going to prove I'm as good . . ." *Front Page Woman*, directed by Michael Curtiz (Warner Bros., 1935).

"scoop-hunting news hawk" . . . *Back in Circulation*, directed by Ray Enright (Warner Bros., 1937).

"the lady bloodhound with a nose . . ." Trailer for *Smart Blonde*, directed by Frank McDonald (Warner Bros., 1937).

cited specifically by Siegel . . . "Letters to the Editor," *Time*, May 30, 1988, 6–7.

"No, you wait here . . ." *Smart Blonde*, directed by McDonald.

Lois Amster was Jerry Siegel's . . . Brad Ricca, *Super Boys: The Amazing Adventures of Jerry Siegel and Joe Shuster—the Creators of Superman* (New York: Macmillan, 2013), 136–138.

"Doctor Occult" in 1935's *New Fun* . . . *New Fun Comics* #6 (October 1935).

"Yeah? You'll dance with me and like it!" . . . *Action Comics* #1 (June 1938).

making up less than a quarter . . . Claudia Dale Goldin, *Understanding the Gender Gap: An Economic History of American Women* (New York: Oxford University Press, 1990), 17.

jobs that had little room for advancement . . . Ibid., vii–viii.

FN when a female reporter got engaged . . . Kay Mills, *A Place in the News: From the Women's Pages to the Front Page* (New York: Dodd, Mead, 1988), 41.

A Rock and a Hard Place

Superman stopped her from being executed . . . *Action Comics* #2 (July 1938).

Superman swooped in and grabbed Lois . . . *Action Comics* #5 (October 1938).

"All the credit should go to Superman!" . . . *Action Comics* #26 (July 1940).

"He was colossal!" . . . *Action Comics* #9 (February 1939).

"What manner of being are you?" . . . *Action Comics* #2 (July 1938).

"Oh, I could kiss you! . . ." *Action Comics* #5 (October 1938).

"But when will I see you again? . . ." *Action Comics* #6 (November 1938).

"I'm going to see him again! . . ." *Action Comics* #7 (December 1938).

"Poor Lois! Still giving out advice . . ." *Superman* #18 (September/October 1942).

When Clark was late for work . . . *Superman* #19 (November/December 1942).

When Lois was made editor for a day . . . *Superman* #18 (September/October 1942).

"spineless worm" . . . *Action Comics* #5 (October 1938).

"Oh, how I hate Clark Kent! . . ." *Superman* #3 (Winter 1939/1940).

"Thanks for a swell news story!" . . . *Action Comics* #47 (April 1942).

"Just be satisfied that Superman . . ." *Action Comics* #42 (November 1941).

Superman left Lois tied to a chair . . . *Action Comics* #64 (September 1943).

put Lois in a hypnotic trance . . . *Action Comics* #33 (February 1941).

Clark knocked Lois unconscious . . . See *Action Comics* #31 (December 1940); *Superman* #7 (November/December 1940); and *Superman* #13 (November/December 1941) for examples.

Clark had already knocked out Lois . . . *Superman* #4 (Spring 1940).

"They are remarkable only because . . ." Ishbel Ross, *Ladies of the Press: The Story of Women in Journalism by an Insider* (New York: Harper, 1936), 42.

An average big-city newspaper . . . Howard Good, *Girl Reporter: Gender, Journalism, and the Movies* (Lanham, MD: Scarecrow Press, 1998), 48.

"You could have cut the ice . . ." Nan Robertson, *The Girls in the Balcony: Women, Men, and the "New York Times"* (New York: Random House, 1992), 61.

roughly fifteen thousand women were writing . . . Good, *Girl Reporter*, 48.

World War II quickly changed that . . . Robertson, *Girls in the Balcony*, 63.

The Tide Turns

Lois boldly stepped in front of speeding police . . . *Superman* #11 (July/August 1941).

When an explosion ripped through . . . *Action Comics* #31 (December 1940).

"You'll not get one scrap of information . . ." *Action Comics* #26 (July 1940).

When she was tied to a chair . . . *Superman* #14 (January/February 1942).

a troubled Lois later tossed and turned . . . *Superman* #3 (Winter 1939/1940).

a boy told Lois about abuses . . . *Action Comics* #27 (August 1940).

"Never mind me!—Save those . . ." *Superman* #6 (September/October 1940).

"weak-kneed pantywaist" . . . *Superman* #8 (January/February 1941).

When Clark was too timid to talk his way . . . *Action Comics* #32 (January 1941).

When Perry White sent Lois and Clark . . . *Superman* #32 (January/February 1945).

Lois got her first front page story . . . *Action Comics* #27 (August 1940).

"Why do you always manage to come out . . ." *Action Comics* #48 (May 1942).

Perry White warned Clark "to wake up . . ." *Action Comics* #85 (June 1945).

"Lois, love has kicked me in the face . . ." "Lois Lane, Girl Reporter" newspaper strip. The strips weren't published uniformly, so the date of publication can vary depending on the newspaper. It was from late 1943 or early 1944. For more information see Allan Holtz, "Obscurity of the Day: Lois Lane, Girl Reporter," *Stripper's Guide* blog, January 11, 2007, http://strippersguide.blogspot.com/2007/01/obscurity-of-day-lois-lane-girl.html; and Sean Kleefeld, "On History: Lois Lane, Girl Reporter," *Kleefeld on Comics* blog, January 14, 2014, www.kleefeldoncomics.com/2014/01/on-history-lois-lane-girl-reporter.html.

"Gosh, Miss Lane, you're an elegant . . ." *Superman* #28 (May/June 1944).

lit mob goons' pants on fire . . . *Superman* #37 (November/December 1945).

beat up a gang of swindlers . . . *Superman* #34 (May/June 1945).

pelted pirates with watermelons . . . *Superman* #36 (September/October 1945).

FN Clark Kent reported on female police officers . . . *Superman* #108 (September 1956).

Lois was hit by a truck and dreamed that . . . *Action Comics* #60 (May 1943).

Thinking she was Superwoman, Lois . . . *Superman* #45 (March/April 1947).

1a. Joe Shuster's Lost Lois

They ultimately settled the suit . . . Glen Weldon, *Superman: The Unauthorized Biography* (New York: John Wiley & Sons, 2013), 74.

When the musical *It's a Bird* . . . Ricca, *Super Boys*, 271.

Lost Love

Two key texts for this section were Brad Ricca's *Super Boys*, which covers the life of Joe Shuster in detail, and Craig Yoe's *Secret Identity: The Fetish Art of Superman's Co-creator Joe Shuster*, which explores and reprints Joe Shuster's fetish art from the 1950s.

"To me she was Lois Lane" . . . Tom Andrae, Geoffrey Blum, and Gary Coddington, "Of Superman and Kids with Dreams: A Rare Interview with the Creators of Superman; Jerry Siegel and Joe Shuster," *Nemo: The Classic Comics Library* 2 (August 1983): 6–19.

A decade after they parted ways . . . Ricca, *Super Boys*, 226–228.

"gross neglect of duty . . ." Larry Tye, *Superman: The High-Flying History of America's Most Enduring Hero* (New York: Random House, 2012), 121.

"The Bride Wore Leather" . . . Ted Rand, "The Bride Wore Leather," *Nights of Horror* #7 (New York: Malcla Publishing Company, 1954).

"Satan's Doorway" . . . Gar King, "Satan's Doorway," *Nights of Horror* #10 (New York: Malcla Publishing Company, 1954).

"Patriarch of Sin" . . . Gavin Moore, "Patriarch of Sin," *Nights of Horror* #13 (New York: Malcla Publishing Company, 1954).

red ants poured into honey-smeared . . . Gar King, "Satan's Playground," *Nights of Horror* #3 (New York: Malcla Publishing Company, 1954).

a striking resemblance to Clark . . . Ron Winton, "Eternal Bondage," *Nights of Horror* #9 (New York: Malcla Publishing Company, 1954).

a Lex Luthor look-alike . . . Burt Dwyer, *Rod Rule* (Chicago: Landry Press, 1954).

Jimmy Olsen's double . . . Gar King, "Never Been Kissed," *Nights of Horror* #3 (New York: Malcla Publishing Company, 1954).

"most of the women look like Lois . . ." Craig Yoe, *Secret Identity: The Fetish Art of Superman's Co-creator Joe Shuster* (New York: Abrams Comic-Arts, 2009), 21.

Shuster married once . . . Ricca, *Super Boys*, 286–288.

2. Lois Lane on Screen, Part 1

The Adventures of Superman Radio Show

Parts of *The Adventures of Superman* radio show are collected in purchasable form here and there, but the vast majority of the series is available in several locations online. I primarily used the *Old Time Radio Superman Show* podcast at Talk Shoe, www.talkshoe.com/tc/11773.

At its peak, *The Adventures of Superman* was heard . . . Tye, *Superman*, 83.

"Well, Mr. Star Reporter, couldn't you . . ." "The Atomic Beam Machine," *The Adventures of Superman* (radio), episode 7 (February 26, 1940).

sent to do a story on a prison . . . "Left to Be Killed," *The Adventures of Superman* (radio), episode 15 (March 15, 1940).

Alexander bought a wig to disguise herself . . . Tye, *Superman*, 87.

Collyer in particular was happy about . . . Bruce Scivally, *Superman on Film, Television, Radio and Broadway* (Jefferson, NC: McFarland & Company, 2008), 19.

she was kidnapped to be framed for murder . . . "Dr. Blythe's Confidence Gang, Part 2," *The Adventures of Superman* (radio), episode 109 (September 5, 1945).

sent out on stories to capture the "women's angle" . . . "Left to Be Killed," *The Adventures of Superman.*

Lois phoned in the prison break story . . . "Mystery of Dyerville, Part 1," *The Adventures of Superman* (radio), episode 20 (March 27, 1940).

"star girl reporter" . . . "The Dragon's Teeth, Part 2," *The Adventures of Superman* (radio), episode 158 (February 12, 1941).

people they talked to were always familiar with Clark . . . "The Ghost Car, Part 2," *The Adventures of Superman* (radio), episode 314 (February 11, 1942).

When Lois learned about a museum's plan . . . "The Scarlet Widow, Part 1," *The Adventures of Superman* (radio), episode 1111 (September 26, 1945).

returned to the public eye thanks to a mention . . . Steven D. Levitt and Stephen J. Dubner, *Freakonomics: A Rogue Economist Explores the Hidden Side of Everything*, rev. ed. (New York: William Morrow, 2006), 57–59.

"exposé of fanatical and un-American bigotry" . . . "Clan of the Fiery Cross, Part 5," *The Adventures of Superman* (radio), episode 1297 (June 14, 1946).

FN "lamebrains and diseased minds" "Clan of the Fiery Cross, Part 13," *The Adventures of Superman* (radio), episode 1305 (June 26, 1946).

FN a way for the folks at the top to make vast sums of money . . . "Clan of the Fiery Cross, Part 14," *The Adventures of Superman* (radio), episode 1306 (June 27, 1946).

Lois appeared in just two of the sixteen . . . They were episodes 8 and 9, broadcast June 19 and 20, 1946.

Fleischer Studios / Famous Studios Cartoons

The cartoon shorts are available on a variety of videos and DVDs because they are in the public domain, though the quality varies; the best version is probably on Warner Home Video's *Max Fleischer's Superman, 1941–1942.* They're also all on YouTube.

Fleischer Studios proposed a budget of $100,000 . . . Tye, *Superman*, 94.

the cartoon was seen by over twenty million . . . Ibid., 95.

"But, Chief, I'd like the chance to crack . . ." *Superman* (a.k.a. *The Mad Scientist*), directed by Dave Fleischer (Fleischer Studios, 1941).

When a dinosaur came to life at a museum . . . *The Arctic Giant*, directed by Dave Fleischer (Fleischer Studios, 1942).

Clark told Lois to stay put as he called . . . *The Mechanical Monsters*, directed by Dave Fleischer (Fleischer Studios, 1941).

when the *Daily Planet* sent the duo to cover . . . *Volcano*, directed by Dave Fleischer (Fleischer Studios, 1942).

"And miss the best story in year? Swell chance!" . . . *Arctic Giant*, directed by Fleischer.

a train carrying a billion dollars in gold . . . *Billion Dollar Limited*, directed by Dave Fleischer (Fleischer Studios, 1942).

After a machine gone haywire pulled an asteroid . . . *The Magnetic Telescope*, directed by Dave Fleischer (Fleischer Studios, 1942).

When a gorilla escaped from the local zoo . . . *Terror on the Midway*, directed by Dave Fleischer (Fleischer Studios, 1942).

her captors suspended her over a vat . . . *Mechanical Monsters*, directed by Fleischer.

"You showed plenty of courage getting . . ." *Arctic Giant*, directed by Fleischer.

one ended with an irate Hitler . . . *Jungle Drums*, directed by Dan Gordon (Famous Studios, 1943).

Lois snuck into the test flight . . . *Japoteurs*, directed by Seymour Kneitel (Famous Studios, 1942).

Lois didn't have much to do . . . *Showdown*, directed by I. Sparber (Famous Studios, 1942).

trapped in a Japanese prison . . . *Eleventh Hour*, directed by Dan Gordon (Famous Studios, 1942).

"It's really a great story, Lois" . . . *The Underground World*, directed by Seymour Kneitel (Famous Studios, 1943).

Adventures of Superman Television Show

Both serials and the television show are available in DVD sets. I've referred to them by chapter/episode here.

even theaters that didn't usually show serials . . . Jim Harman and Donald F. Glut, *The Great Movie Serials: Their Sound and Fury* (New York: Routledge, 1973), 206–215.

Lois snuck into a mine after an explosion . . . "Depths of the Earth," *Superman*, directed by Spencer Gordon Bennett and Thomas Carr (Columbia, 1948).

ditching him on the side of the road . . . "The Reducer Ray," *Superman*, directed by Bennett and Carr.

letting him borrow her car and then reporting . . . "Superman's Dilemma," *Superman*, directed by Bennett and Carr.

An exclusive interview turned into a kidnapping . . . "Irresistible Force," *Superman*, directed by Bennett and Carr.

when she followed up on a tip she stole from Clark . . . "Into the Electric Furnace," *Superman*, directed by Bennett and Carr.

they collaborated on a plan to have Lois . . . "Superman Crashes Through," *Atom Man vs. Superman*, directed by Spencer Gordon Bennett (Columbia, 1950).

Lois decided that Luthor was on the level . . . "Atom Man's Heat Ray," *Atom Man vs. Superman*, directed by Bennett.

"Isn't he wonderful?" . . . "Ablaze the Sky" and "Rocket of Vengeance," *Atom Man vs. Superman*, directed by Bennett.

"It was easy, for Superman" . . . "Atom Man Strikes," *Atom Man vs. Superman*, directed by Bennett.

Some say that Alyn wasn't interested . . . Larry Thomas Ward, *Truth, Justice, & the American Way: The Life and Times of Noel Neill, the Original Lois Lane* (Los Angeles: Nicholas Laurence Books, 2003), 66.

others that Alyn wasn't happy with the money . . . Scivally, *Superman on Film*, 39.

the producers wanted to go in a new direction . . . Tye, *Superman*, 132.

after the producers considered more than three hundred . . . Scivally, *Superman on Film*, 47.

"Well, babe, this is it: the bottom of the barrel" . . . Tye, *Superman*, 134.

Reeves also insisted that they share top billing . . . Jason Hofius and George Khoury, *Age of TV Heroes* (Raleigh, NC: TwoMorrows, 2010), 27.

"I can get out of the way by myself . . ." *Superman and the Mole Men*, directed by Lee Sholem (Lippert Pictures, 1951).

Each episode was budgeted at only $15,000 . . . Weldon, *Superman*, 93.

Reeves had a photographic memory . . . Tye, *Superman*, 136.

Hamilton often needed his scripts right in front of him . . . Les Daniels, *Superman: The Complete History* (San Francisco: Chronicle Books, 1999), 95.

a felonious married couple learned that Clark . . . "The Stolen Costume," *Adventures of Superman* (TV), season 1, episode 13, directed by Lee Sholem (Warner Bros., 1952).

Coates got in a little too close . . . Tye, *Superman*, 137.

When smugglers who were transporting criminals . . . "Night of Terror," *Adventures of Superman* (TV), season 1, episode 6, directed by Lee Sholem (Warner Bros., 1952).

she testified in the trial of a mob boss . . . "The Mind Machine," *Adventures of Superman* (TV), season 1, episode 8, directed by Lee Sholem (Warner Bros., 1952).

"And do nothing? Not me" . . . "Rescue," *Adventures of Superman* (TV), season 1, episode 9, directed by Thomas Carr (Warner Bros., 1952).

"I'm a big girl now, Clark . . ." "The Runaway Robot," *Adventures of Superman* (TV), season 1, episode 17, directed by Thomas Carr (Warner Bros., 1953).

"I played her tough and direct" . . . Scivally, *Superman on Film*, 49.

"one of the strongest women characters . . ." Allan Asherman, interviewed in "From Inkwell to Backlot," on *Adventures of Superman: The Complete First Season* (Warner Bros., 2006), DVD.

"tough, independent woman" . . . Gary Grossman, interviewed in "From Inkwell to Backlot."

Coates dyed her hair blonde . . . Tye, *Superman*, 142.

turned down twice her original salary . . . Jake Rossen, *Superman vs. Hollywood: How Fiendish Producers, Devious Directors, and Warring Writers Grounded an American Icon* (Chicago: Chicago Review Press, 2008), 73.

Coates's family had a history of alcoholism . . . Tye, *Superman*, 146.

they simply called her up and offered her the part . . . Scivally, *Superman on Film*, 54.

Neill had a particular affinity for the role . . . "Meet TV's Lois Lane" in *Superman's Girl Friend Lois Lane* #7 (February 1959).

"softened the role to the point of wide-eyed innocence" . . . Tom De Haven, *Our Hero: Superman on Earth* (New Haven, CT: Yale University Press, 2010), 108.

"turned it all to pudding" . . . Tye, *Superman*, 146.

watched by 91 percent of households . . . Sam Kashner and Nancy Schoenberger, *Hollywood Kryptonite: The Bulldog, the Lady, and the Death of Superman* (New York: St. Martin's Press, 1996), 41.

"You all right, kids?" . . . For example, see "The Deadly Rock," *Adventures of Superman* (TV), season 4, episode 11, directed by Harry Gerstad (Warner Bros., 1956).

Lois just responded with a resigned look . . . "The Man Who Could Read Minds," *Adventures of Superman* (TV), season 2, episode 3, directed by Thomas Carr (Warner Bros., 1953).

"Well, let's face it, we're cave people . . ." "Through the Time Barrier," *Adventures of Superman* (TV), season 3, episode 1, directed by Harry Gerstad (Warner Bros., 1955).

Lois and Jimmy captured a bad guy . . . "Beware the Wrecker," *Adventures of Superman* (TV), season 2, episode 20, directed by George Blair (Warner Bros., 1954).

Jimmy got arrested in a small town . . . "The Bully of Dry Gulch," *Adventures of Superman* (TV), season 3, episode 10, directed by George Blair (Warner Bros., 1955).

a cast and crew photo from the middle . . . Ward, *Truth, Justice, & the American Way*, 77.

"I'm Lois Lane. I'm a reporter . . . "The Wedding of Superman," *Adventures of Superman* (TV), season 4, episode 8, directed by Philip Ford (Warner Bros., 1956).

FN Neill wasn't allowed to be involved in case . . . Rossen, *Superman vs. Hollywood*, 33.

Lois couldn't even be happy that she got an exclusive . . . "Superman's Wife," *Adventures of Superman* (TV), season 6, episode 9, directed by Lew Landers (Warner Bros., 1958).

she cleverly suggested using a chimney vent . . . "Olsen's Million," *Adventures of Superman* (TV), season 3, episode 7, directed by George Blair (Warner Bros., 1955).

she wrote an editorial encouraging women to . . . "The Big Freeze," *Adventures of Superman* (TV), season 4, episode 3, directed by Harry Gerstad (Warner Bros., 1956).

2a. A Real-Life L.L.

Leonore Lemmon

"She wanted to be sure I had no designs . . ." Kashner and Schoenberger, *Hollywood Kryptonite*, 4–5.

"a very great gal" . . . Noel Neill, interviewed in Thomas McNulty, "Superman's Girl-Friend, Noel Neill!," *Dispatches from the Last Outlaw* blog, June 14, 2013, http://tommcnulty.blogspot.com/2013/06/supermans-girl -friend-noel-neill.html.

she was famously barred from the Stork Club . . . Tye, *Superman*, 153.

"if you wanted to have a good party, you invited . . ." "George Reeves: The Perils of a Superhero," *Biography* (A&E, February 2000).

Lemmon was a regular lunch guest of Frank Costello . . . Ibid.

In October 1958, George Reeves was in New York . . . For more information on Reeves and Lemmon's first meeting, see Leonore Lemmon, interview, May 1989, transcribed by Lou Koza, www.jimnolt.com/MAY1989.pdf.

"talk some sense into the boy" . . . "George Reeves," *E! Mysteries & Scandals* (E!, March 1998).

"She makes me feel like a boy . . ." "Perils of a Superhero," *Biography.*

FN Coates thought that the film did an awful . . . Philip Potempa, "Lois Lane Actress Disputes 'Superman' Movie Claim," *NWI Times,* February 27, 2007, www.nwitimes.com/entertainment/columnists/offbeat/lois-lane -actress-disputes-superman-movie-claims/article_e31d1ceb-7c77-5f0a -8192-228ad8b7511a.html.

Who Killed George Reeves?

"He was very up about that, and he looked . . ." "George Reeves," *E! Mysteries & Scandals.*

"George was never depressed when . . ." Jennifer M. Contino, "Noel Neill: Lois Lane Forever," *Pulse,* October 22, 2004, www.comicon.com/cgi -bin/ultimatebb.cgi?ubb=get_topic&f=36&t=002972 (site discontinued).

She ran into Reeves at a wardrobe fitting . . . McNulty, "Superman's Girl-Friend."

Reeves's body lacked the usual markings . . . E. J. Fleming, *The Fixers: Eddie Mannix, Howard Strickling and the MGM Publicity Machine* (New York: McFarland, 2004), 264.

His body was also fairly bruised . . . "Who Killed Superman?," *20/20 Downtown* (ABC, June 2000).

the spent shell from his pistol was found underneath . . . Rossen, *Superman vs. Hollywood,* 38.

Reeves's pistol had no fingerprints . . . Ibid.

she also hired someone to telephone Reeves's home . . . "Perils of a Superhero," *Biography.*

he was in a car accident after his brake lines . . . Ibid.

"The boy is dead. He's been murdered" . . . John Patterson, "Who Killed Superman?," *Guardian,* November 18, 2006, www.theguardian.com /film/2006/nov/18/features.weekend1.

FN One of Eddie Mannix's most infamous jobs . . . Fleming, *The Fixers,* 111–125.

On the night before he died, Reeves and Lemmon dined . . . "George Reeves," *E! Mysteries & Scandals.*

a look of disdain comes across her face . . . For an example, see "George Reeves," *E! Mysteries & Scandals.*

"He went with the wrong woman . . ." McNulty, "Superman's Girl-Friend."

"I just don't know what happened" . . . Contino, "Lois Lane Forever."

"I don't know who killed George Reeves . . ." Steven Younis, "Exclusive Interview with Noel Neill," Superman Homepage, February 9, 2007, www .supermanhomepage.com/tv/tv.php?topic=interviews/noel-neill2.

Coates has definitively stated . . . Potempa, "Actress Disputes 'Superman' Movie."

his blood alcohol level was 0.27 percent . . . "George Reeves," *E! Mysteries & Scandals.*

he was also on painkillers due to injuries . . . Tye, *Superman*, 157.

3. Sharing the Spotlight

Lois's Silver Age adventures are collected only in part, an unfortunate misstep on DC Comic's part. The first few issues of *Superman's Girl Friend Lois Lane* are collected in one *Archives* edition and across a few *Showcase Presents: Superman Family* volumes. Some her stories in *Superman* and *Action Comics* are also collected in Superman's various *Showcase* volumes. For more on Dr. Fredric Wertham, juvenile delinquency and comics, and the Comics Code Authority, see Amy Kiste Nyberg's *Seal of Approval: The History of the Comics Code* and Bart Beaty's *Fredric Wertham and the Critique of Mass Culture.*

Mistaken Identity

"he considered every writer to be . . ." Ken Quattro, "Woolfolk on Weisinger," *Comics Detective* blog, April 16, 2012, http://thecomicsdetective .blogspot.com/2012/04/woolfolk-on-weisinger.html.

"Come to think of it, it's mighty peculiar . . ." *Superman* #17 (July 1942).

When Lois noticed that the supposedly . . . *Superman* #81 (March/April 1953).

When Clark was unfazed by a bullet . . . *Superman* #84 (September/October 1953).

When Clark disappeared from the Prankster's . . . *Superman* #87 (February 1954).

"So that's the explanation! I-I . . ." *Action Comics* #139 (December 1949).

"Since Lois is impulsive, impetuous . . ." Response to a letter in *Action Comics* #248 (January 1959).

"If he told her he was really Superman . . ." Response to a letter in *Action Comics* #250 (March 1959).

FN Lois reluctantly teamed up with Lana . . . *Superman* #78 (September/ October 1952).

Learning Her Lesson

a "gut feeling" that a Lois Lane series . . . Guy H. Lillian III, "Mort Weisinger: The Man Who Wouldn't Be Superman," *Amazing World of DC Comics* 7 (July 1975).

top-five comic throughout the 1960s . . . For the full sales numbers, see John Jackson Miller, "Comic Book Sales by Year," Comichron, www.comichron .com/yearlycomicssales.html.

only 18 percent of the comics released that month . . . To tabulate these numbers, I relied on data from Mike's Amazing World of Comics, www.mikesamazingworld.com, which has comprehensive listings of comics releases going back decades.

The chart above shows the percentage . . . To tabulate these numbers, I simply counted and then charted the names of letter writers in *Superman's Girl Friend Lois Lane* comics. I did the same for *Action Comics*; *Superman's Pal, Jimmy Olsen*; and *Wonder Woman*. If you'd like to see the raw data, contact me online (http://thanley.wordpress.com) and I'll gladly send it along.

"I'll have to teach her a lesson for using . . ." *Superman's Girl Friend Lois Lane* #1 (March/April 1958).

Superman secretly helped a caveman . . . *Superman's Girl Friend Lois Lane* #19 (August 1960).

an experimental youth ray slowly de-aged . . . *Superman's Girl Friend Lois Lane* #10 (July 1959).

Lois joined the army . . . *Superman's Girl Friend Lois Lane* #6 (January 1959).

"What an idea! The staff will be delighted . . ." Ibid.

"Gosh, I wish I could save Superman . . ." *Superman's Girl Friend Lois Lane* #4 (September/October 1958).

Superman turned his corrective attention to another . . . *Superman's Girl Friend Lois Lane* #14 (January 1960).

"Finally, her expression of grief when I broke up . . ." *Superman's Girl Friend Lois Lane* #2 (May/June 1958).

"You little idiot! I warned you . . ." *Superman's Girl Friend Lois Lane* #16 (April 1960).

"I'm afraid Lois will always be confused!" . . . *Superman's Girl Friend Lois Lane* #4 (September/October 1958).

"Lois will never know whose magic . . ." *Superman's Girl Friend Lois Lane* #8 (April 1959).

As Lois celebrated getting a front page scoop . . . *Superman's Girl Friend Lois Lane* #6 (January 1959).

"If you don't believe me, Superman will . . ." *Superman's Girl Friend Lois Lane* #17 (May 1960).

"Women! Even a Superman can't . . ." *Superman's Girl Friend Lois Lane* #16 (April 1960).

"But it'll have to remain Clark's secret . . ." *Superman's Girl Friend Lois Lane* #10 (July 1959).

3a. Corporal Punishment

"If you ask me, Lois is a big headache . . ." Letter in *Superman's Girl Friend Lois Lane* #5 (November/December 1958).

"What would our writers do for plots . . ." Response to a letter in *Superman's Girl Friend Lois Lane* #9 (May 1959).

A Lesson She Won't Forget

"Dear Editor: Lois Lane is constantly . . ." Letter in *Superman's Girl Friend Lois Lane* #21 (November 1960).

Lois had arranged to stay in Superman's . . . *Superman's Girl Friend Lois Lane* #14 (January 1960).

"Dear Editor: I represent the 'North Shore . . .'" Letter in *Superman's Girl Friend Lois Lane* #24 (April 1961).

"Dear Editor: A number of readers have . . ." Letter in *Superman's Girl Friend Lois Lane* #26 (July 1961).

"Dear Editor: Everybody keeps asking . . ." Letter in *Superman's Girl Friend Lois Lane* #27 (August 1961).

"Dear Editor: Although I am a great fan . . ." Letter in *Superman's Girl Friend Lois Lane* #30 (January 1962).

4. Romantic Rivals

"AMBITION: To become Mrs. Superman . . ." For example, see *Wonder Woman* #98 (May 1958).

"If I could only find a way to win . . ." *Superman's Girl Friend Lois Lane* #1 (March/April 1958).

"The treatment of love-romance stories . . ." 1955 Comics Code, in Amy Kiste Nyberg, *Seal of Approval: The History of the Comics Code* (Jackson: University Press of Mississippi, 1998), 168.

"Superman believes that a wife's place . . ." Response to a letter in *Superman's Girl Friend Lois Lane* #22 (January 1961).

Keeping Up Appearances

"Newspaper reporting is my first love . . ." *Superman* #58 (May/June 1949).

She paid $150 for a designer dress . . . *Superman* #23 (July/August 1943).

she had Superman move a mountain . . . *Action Comics* #159 (August 1951).

"I knew Lois never wore old hats . . ." *World's Finest* #64 (May/June 1953).

"What if Superman, the man I love . . ." *Superman's Girl Friend Lois Lane* #5 (November/December 1958).

When Lois was hypnotized into . . ." *Superman's Girl Friend Lois Lane* #13 (November 1959).

Her increased brain size resulted . . . *Superman's Girl Friend Lois Lane* #27 (August 1961).

Weisinger put together a contest . . . *Giant Lois Lane Annual* #1 (Summer 1962).

FN "arrange for her to have an abortion . . ." Weldon, *Superman*, 49.

Lois's hairstyle contest attracted more than . . . *Superman's Girl Friend Lois Lane* #41 (May 1963).

"A TON of Laughs" . . . *Superman's Girl Friend Lois Lane* #4 (September/ October 1958).

Lois kissed Cosmic Man . . . *Action Comics* #258 (November 1959).

feigned interest in Mental Man . . . *Action Comics* #272 (January 1961).

agreed to marry Futureman . . . *Superman* #121 (May 1958).

Achilles . . . *Superman's Girl Friend Lois Lane* #40 (April 1963).

Robin Hood . . . *Superman's Girl Friend Lois Lane* #22 (January 1961).

Leonardo da Vinci . . . *Superman's Girl Friend Lois Lane* #37 (November 1962).

"Lois Lane of Earth! The time . . ." *Superman's Girl Friend Lois Lane* #18 (July 1960).

"What a fickle heartbreaker . . ." *Superman's Girl Friend Lois Lane* #35 (August 1962).

"How dare you throw them out . . ." *Superman's Girl Friend Lois Lane* #19 (August 1960).

"I'm mad about Superman, and . . ." *Superman's Girl Friend Lois Lane* #39 (February 1963).

Lana Lang, That Brazen Hussy

A teenage Lois actually met Lana . . . *Adventure Comics* #261 (June 1959).

"So that's the hussy who will be . . ." *Superboy* #90 (July 1961).

Lana's first appearance was relatively . . . *Superman's Girl Friend Lois Lane* #7 (February 1959).

Superman took her to Lana's house . . . *Superman's Girl Friend Lois Lane* #10 (July 1959).

"You did this—for the girl you consider . . ." *Superman's Girl Friend Lois Lane* #11 (August 1959).

"That scheming hussy egged me on . . ." *Superman's Girl Friend Lois Lane* #12 (October 1959).

"We'll be perfect ladies while fighting . . ." *Superman's Girl Friend Lois Lane* #21 (November 1960).

Lana used a Kryptonian weapon to send . . . *Superman's Girl Friend Lois Lane* #33 (May 1962).

Lois framed Lana for murder . . . *Superman's Girl Friend Lois Lane* #59 (August 1965).

she had secretly traveled back to ancient Greece . . . *Superman's Girl Friend Lois Lane* #40 (April 1963).

"If I could stop carrying the torch for Superman . . ." *Superman's Girl Friend Lois Lane* #31 (February 1962).

When Betty got some money . . . *Archie's Girls Betty and Veronica* #51 (March 1960).

Veronica paid a doctor to tell Archie . . . *Archie's Girls Betty and Veronica* #85 (January 1963).

Betty disrupted Veronica's date with Archie . . . *Archie's Girls Betty and Veronica* #87 (March 1963).

Veronica launched a campaign to knock some sense . . . *Archie's Girls Betty and Veronica* #116 (August 1965).

FN Veronica attempted a teased hairdo . . . *Archie's Girls Betty and Veronica* #85 (January 1963).

FN Betty and Veronica learned that a 1920s . . . *Archie's Girls Betty and Veronica* #98 (February 1964).

"Dear Editor: In my opinion, Lois Lane is . . ." Letter in *Superman's Girl Friend Lois Lane* #34 (July 1962).

"Dear Editor: I think Lana Lang would make . . ." Letter in *Superman's Girl Friend Lois Lane* #38 (January 1963).

Superman temporarily lost his superpowers . . . *Superman's Girl Friend Lois Lane* #38 (January 1963).

The responses filled two letter columns . . . *Superman's Girl Friend Lois Lane* #40 (April 1963) and #41 (May 1963).

"Dear Editor: I'm thoroughly disgusted . . ." Letter in *Superman's Girl Friend Lois Lane* #43 (August 1963).

"Dear Editor: I can prove you are anti-Lana . . ." Letter in *Superman's Girl Friend Lois Lane* #46 (January 1964).

"But it reads 'To Lois and Lana,' not . . ." Letter in *Superman's Girl Friend Lois Lane* #74 (May 1967).

When the duo threw a party for Superman . . . *Action Comics* #309 (February 1964).

4a. Cry for Help

She wept at the end of her first . . . *Superman's Girl Friend Lois Lane* #1 (March/April 1958).

When Lois had to leave Metropolis . . . *Superman's Girl Friend Lois Lane* #16 (April 1960).

Lois burst into tears when her alphabet . . . *Superman's Girl Friend Lois Lane* #1 (March/April 1958).

"W-Will that glorious day ever . . ." *Superman's Girl Friend Lois Lane* #15 (February 1960).

"WHY?!! Why did I ever defy Superman . . ." *Superman's Girl Friend Lois Lane* #16 (April 1960).

"I knew that though Superman would . . ." *Superman's Girl Friend Lois Lane* #13 (November 1959).

Imaginary Stories

Clark proposed to Lois . . . *Superman's Girl Friend Lois Lane* #19 (August 1960).

"I'm sorry our adoption of Supergirl . . ." *Superman's Girl Friend Lois Lane* #20 (October 1960).

"a married woman's place is in the home!" . . . *Superman's Girl Friend Lois Lane* #23 (February 1961).

Sick of the world not knowing she was . . . *Superman's Girl Friend Lois Lane* #25 (May 1961).

Lana married Superman . . . *Superman's Girl Friend Lois Lane* #26 (July 1961).

Lois married Lex Luthor . . . *Superman's Girl Friend Lois Lane* #34 (July 1962).

They returned to the old formula . . . *Superman's Girl Friend Lois Lane* #51 (August 1964).

Tracking Her Tears

"Don't you think it's time Lois Lane gave . . ." Letter in *Superman's Girl Friend Lois Lane* #9 (May 1959).

"I think it's awful the way you insult women . . ." Letter in *Superman's Girl Friend Lois Lane* #16 (April 1960).

"Dear Editor: Why do you persist . . ." Letter in *Superman's Girl Friend Lois Lane* #22 (January 1961).

"I am sick and tired of the way Superman . . ." Letter in *Superman's Girl Friend Lois Lane* #45 (November 1963).

5. Lois Lane's Brief Feminist Revolution

Very few *Superman's Girl Friend Lois Lane* stories from the early 1970s are reprinted in collected editions. You can find them here and there—the infamous "I Am Curious (Black)" story is in the recent *Lois Lane: A Celebration of 75 Years* collection—but the vast majority remain available only in their original form.

To say that Mort Weisinger was fired . . . Mark Evanier, "From the E-Mailbag," *News from ME* blog, June 22, 2013, www.newsfromme.com/2013/06/22 /from-the-e-mailbag-184/.

Esquire magazine polled college students . . . Bradford Wright, *Comic Book Nation: The Transformation of Youth Culture in America* (Baltimore: Johns Hopkins University Press, 2001), 223.

Wonder Woman gave up her superpowers . . . This era began in *Wonder Woman* #178 (September/October 1968) and lasted for four years.

Diversifying the Super-World

FN "Well, Tonto, ol' kimosavee . . ." *MAD Magazine* #38 (March 1958).

"Lois—you must give up that Indian papoose . . ." *Superman's Girl Friend Lois Lane* #110 (May 1971).

including members of Metropolis's Latino community . . . *Superman's Girl Friend Lois Lane* #111 (July 1971).

the Swedish left-wing art film . . . *I Am Curious (Yellow)*, directed by Vilgot Sjöman (Janus Films, 1967).

"It's important that I live the next 24 hours . . ." *Superman's Girl Friend Lois Lane* #106 (November 1970).

FN a Kodak advertisement on the inside cover . . . *Action Comics* #103 (December 1946).

"I been readin' about you . . ." *Green Lantern/Green Arrow* #76 (April 1970).

Lois visited Dave at his local newspaper . . . *Superman's Girl Friend Lois Lane* #114 (September 1971).

Lois met a young black woman named Julie Spence . . . *Superman's Girl Friend Lois Lane* #121 (April 1972).

the intrepid African American reporter Melba Manton . . . *Superman's Girl Friend Lois Lane* #132 (July 1973).

teamed up to rescue Wonder Woman . . . *Superman's Girl Friend Lois Lane* #136 (January/February 1974).

"Don't get uptight about women refusing to sit . . ." *Superman's Girl Friend Lois Lane* #114 (September 1971).

Hear Her Roar

Lois broke up with him and moved to Coral City . . . *Superman's Girl Friend Lois Lane* #80 (January 1968) and #81 (February 1968).

She became a volunteer nurse . . . *Superman's Girl Friend Lois Lane* #74 (May 1967).

She learned how to fight as well . . . *Superman's Girl Friend Lois Lane* #78 (October 1967).

joining a motorcycle gang . . . *Superman's Girl Friend Lois Lane* #83 (May 1968).

Lois romanced Comet the Super-Horse . . . *Superman's Girl Friend Lois Lane* #92 (May 1969).

she tried to fight Wonder Woman . . . *Superman's Girl Friend Lois Lane* #93 (July 1969).

Mary Jane Watson was a feisty, independent . . . First appeared in *The Amazing Spider-Man* #42 (November 1966).

Batgirl had a PhD by day and fought criminals . . . First appeared in *Detective Comics* #359 (January 1967).

Big Barda was a powerful, statuesque warrior . . . First appeared in *Mister Miracle* #4 (October 1971).

Gloria Steinem and *Ms.* magazine soon swooped in . . . Joanne Edgar, "Wonder Woman Revisited," *Ms.* 1, no. 1 (1972): 52–55.

"She was very much a feminist, and wanted Lois Lane . . ." Jon B. Cooke, "Rise & Fall of Rovin's Empire," *Comic Book Artist* 16 (December 2011): 25.

"And please, call me 'Ms.'" . . . Response to a letter in *Superman's Girl Friend Lois Lane* #125 (August 1972).

Lois's sister, Lucy, met an untimely demise . . . *Superman's Girl Friend Lois Lane* #120 (March 1972).

"wanted to push any boundaries with Lois . . ." Cary Bates, interview with the author.

"No amount of self-pity will ever bring . . ." *Superman's Girl Friend Lois Lane* #121 (April 1972).

"You're only being twice as stupid!" . . . *Superman's Girl Friend Lois Lane* #122 (May 1972).

"That was torture for me! I . . . I'll miss him . . ." *Superman's Girl Friend Lois Lane* #121 (April 1972).

"Oh, Superman! I care about you . . ." *Superman's Girl Friend Lois Lane* #122 (May 1972).

"What would you like me to do, Superman? . . ." Ibid.

they trekked up a dangerous mountain . . . *Superman's Girl Friend Lois Lane* #129 (February 1973).

they all traveled to France . . . *Superman's Girl Friend Lois Lane* #127 (October 1972).

"We women have to stick together" . . . *Superman's Girl Friend Lois Lane* #125 (August 1972).

Created by Robert Kanigher and Ross Andru . . . *Superman's Girl Friend Lois Lane* #105 (October 1970).

One story featured a women's lib protest . . . *Superman's Girl Friend Lois Lane* #123 (June 1972).

Rose worked for the campaign of . . . *Superman's Girl Friend Lois Lane* #126 (September 1972).

FN credited to Maxene Fabe . . . The author interviewed Fabe, and she was certain she hadn't written the issue.

"Uhh! She fights like a wildcat!" . . . *Superman's Girl Friend Lois Lane* #123 (June 1972).

Lois suspected that a valuable diamond . . . *Superman's Girl Friend Lois Lane* #127 (October 1972).

"Nice bit of life-saving, Lois!" . . . *Superman's Girl Friend Lois Lane* #126 (August 1972).

Lois fell in love with a new man . . . *Superman's Girl Friend Lois Lane* #132 (July 1973).

Superman taught her a lesson about . . . *Superman's Girl Friend Lois Lane* #128 (December 1972).

cheering her appointment as the book's . . . Edgar, "Wonder Woman Revisited," 55.

"That was a bomb. She was . . ." Jim Amash and Eric Nolen-Weathington, *Carmine Infantino: Penciler, Publisher, Provocateur* (Raleigh, NC: TwoMorrows, 2010), 126.

"a woman in her fifties victimized . . ." Dorothy Woolfolk, letter to Gloria Steinem, July 8, 1972, Sophia Smith Collection, Smith College Archives, Northampton, MA.

"always snickered at her behind her back" . . . Alan Kupperberg, "Dorothy Woolfolk Remembered," Alan Kupperberg personal website, www .alankupperberg.com/woolfolk.html.

"Both the writer of, and the editor . . ." Response to a letter in *Superman's Girl Friend Lois Lane* #133 (September 1973).

"Dottie Cottonman, woman's magazine editor" . . . *Wonder Woman* #204 (January/February 1973).

After Billie Jean King defeated Bobby Riggs . . . *Superman* #289 (July 1975).

5a. The Antifeminist Rebuttal

"I must agree with those readers who feel . . ." Letter in *Superman's Girl Friend Lois Lane* #126 (August 1972).

"Why must every ish [*sic*] allude to Women's Lib? . . ." Letter in *Superman's Girl Friend Lois Lane* #128 (December 1972).

"After a long absence, I recently picked up . . ." Letter in *Superman's Girl Friend Lois Lane* #125 (August 1972).

"made Lois into a human being" . . . Letter in *Superman's Girl Friend Lois Lane* #136 (January/February 1974).

"deal specifically with the new image of Lois" . . . *Superman's Girl Friend Lois Lane* #124 (July 1972).

"If the subject is so important to you . . ." Ibid.

Alexander the Great

"it's too much—I can't take it anymore!" . . . Letter in *Superman's Girl Friend Lois Lane* #124 (July 1972).

"That Lois Lane is one rotten lady! . . ." Ibid.

"Forget Women's lib, if we gave . . ." Response to a letter in *Superman's Girl Friend Lois Lane* #125 (August 1972).

"If I were you, I'd get together with . . ." Response to a letter in *Superman's Girl Friend Lois Lane* #126 (September 1972).

"some more tender moments between Superman . . ." Ibid.

"About the subject of Women's Lib . . ." Letter in *Superman's Girl Friend Lois Lane* #125 (August 1972).

"You must be going bananas!" . . . Response to a letter in ibid.

"I think Lois is making trouble . . ." Letter in *Superman's Girl Friend Lois Lane* #124 (July 1972).

"Should Lois scream about her rights . . ." Letter in *Superman's Girl Friend Lois Lane* #126 (September 1972).

"And now I am forced to give some space to . . ." *Superman's Girl Friend Lois Lane* #125 (August 1972).

"Who knows what evil lurks in the heart . . ." Response to a letter in *Superman's Girl Friend Lois Lane* #126 (September 1972).

"As for the issue being a 'mess,' it was . . ." Ibid.

Marc—on the Man's Side!

For this section, I am very much indebted to Jacque Nodell of *Sequential Crush* for her many fantastic posts on this subject as well as her correspondence.

"Let me first say that you are a fool! . . ." Response to a letter in *Young Love* #90 (December 1971).

"a movement or group of ladies . . ." Response to a letter in *Young Love* #94 (April 1972).

"Some of you beasts don't deserve . . ." Response to a letter in *Young Love* #93 (March 1972).

"The Girls Strike Back!" . . . *Young Love* #95 (May 1972).

two-page special column that printed . . . *Young Love* #98 (August 1972).

"They were using the character of Marc . . ." Jacque Nodell, "Who Do You Think You Are, Mr. America?," *Sequential Crush* blog, December 2, 2009, http://sequentialcrush.blogspot.com/2009/12/who-do-you-think -you-are-mr-america.html.

The columns were assigned to assistant editors . . . Paul Levitz, interview with the author.

the photograph that accompanied . . . Reader comment on Jacque Nodell, "Original 'Marc—on the Man's Side' Page—Young Love #119 (December 1975/January 1976)," *Sequential Crush* blog, May 17, 2011, http:// sequentialcrush.blogspot.com/2011/05/original-marc-on-mans-side-page -young.html.

"I like the way women stand up for . . ." Letter in *Young Love* #98 (August 1972).

The last issue of *Young Love* before . . . *Young Love* #100 (October 1972).

When the results were announced . . . *Young Love* #104 (June/July 1973).

6. As the *Daily Planet* Turns

In general, DC comic books from the mid-1970s through the mid-1980s are poorly collected. A few key stories get reprinted, mostly starring Batman, but the rest have been generally forgotten. DC's been digitizing chunks of its back catalog on the digital platform ComiXology, but this era remains a black hole. This is especially true for Lois Lane. None of her *Superman Family* stories have been collected, and only a couple of Superman stories in which she's tangentially involved are available in print or digitally somewhere.

The Galaxy Broadcasting System, a multimedia . . . Morgan Edge first appeared in *Superman's Pal, Jimmy Olsen* #133 (October 1970) and was a regular presence in the Super-books thereafter.

was even profiled in *Gentlemen's Quarterly* . . . Weldon, *Superman*, 151.

DC was steadily losing ground to Marvel Comics . . . Chris Tolworthy, "Marvel and DC Sales Figures," Chris Tolworthy personal website, accessed September 24, 2015, www.zak-site.com/Great-American-Novel/comic_sales.html.

A Superpowered Soap Opera

Lois and Clark were out at a business lunch . . . *Superman* #297 (March 1976).

Lois and Clark walking down the street . . . *Superman* #298 (April 1976).

openly kissing at the *Daily Planet* . . . *Superman* #304 (October 1976).

Lois was furious when she saw Clark . . . *Superman* #307 (January 1977).

"I thought you were two-timing me . . ." *Superman* #308 (February 1977).

he slyly used his heat vision . . . *Superman* #303 (September 1976).

"I've got a splitting headache . . ." *Superman* #309 (March 1977).

Clark's hasty exits prompted . . . *Superman* #310 (April 1977).

"When Clark first kissed Lois in that historic . . ." *Action Comics* #470 (April 1977).

"I'll say 'Yes' . . . without a moment's . . ." *Superman* #314 (August 1977).

"She feels so much for Superman . . ." This letter and the others mentioned appeared in *Superman* #318 (December 1977).

When Lois next appeared . . . *Superman* #316 (October 1977).

Lana Lang wasn't just back in Metropolis . . . *Superman* #317 (November 1977).

"I suppose Lois was too panic-stricken to . . ." *Superman* #319 (January 1978).

"Lois has been going after every story . . ." *Superman* #320 (February 1978).

"I ought to pull out your flaming red hair . . ." *Superman* #325 (July 1978).

"Lois, forgive me . . . for what a fool . . ." *Superman* #321 (March 1978).

Superman visited Lois's apartment . . . *Superman* #322 (April 1978).

Lana was stunned when Lois showed . . . *Superman* #325 (July 1978).

"She's so blasted casual about her affair . . ." *Superman* #331 (January 1979).

"Do you think I'm blind?—or stupid? . . ." *Superman* #332 (February 1979).

teaming up with Lois to pull an elaborate ruse . . . *Superman* #334 (April 1979).

Lana began to pursue Clark, and soon . . . *Superman* #380 (February 1983).

Lois requested an international assignment . . . *Action Comics* #542 (April 1983).

she agreed to fly off with him . . . *Action Comics* #543 (May 1983).

"The sneaky, sniveling, conniving witch!" . . . *Action Comics* #546 (August 1983).

"It wasn't you I was lashing out at . . ." *Superman* #388 (October 1983).

"As a younger reader, I'd never . . ." This letter and the others mentioned appeared in *Superman* #392 (February 1984).

Solo Adventures

the addition of "Mr. and Mrs. Superman" . . . The feature began in *The Superman Family* #195 (May/June 1979).

Lois investigated an elderly vigilante . . . *The Superman Family* #185 (September/October 1977).

He was replaced by the Human Cannonball . . . *The Superman Family* #188 (March/April 1978).

"Nice move, Lois! But I'm the super-hero . . ." *The Superman Family* #191 (September/October 1978).

"Gentlemen do not battle ladies" . . . *The Superman Family* #187 (January/February 1978).

"My world explodes whenever Nancy . . ." *The Superman Family* #193 (January/February 1979).

Lois investigated a weight-loss camp . . . *The Superman Family* #196 (July/August 1979).

she joined a corrupt roller derby team . . . *The Superman Family* #198 (November/December 1979).

"All those hopes I had for restarting my career . . ." *The Superman Family* #200 (March/April 1980).

main arc involved an amnesiac Lois . . . *The Superman Family* #203 (September/October 1980) through #206 (March/April 1981).

first issue was again heavy on Lois in her underwear . . . *The Superman Family* #212 (November 1981).

"She's smart—she's successful . . ." Began in *The Superman Family* #190 (July/August 1978).

"Before Clark Kent came to work at the *Daily Planet*. . ." Began in *The Superman Family* #195 (May/June 1979).

"trained by her cousin, Superman" . . . For this or any other of the introductions mentioned here, check out basically any comic book from the late 1970s or early 1980s in which these characters appear.

"Award-winning reporter . . . incomparable . . ." Began in *The Superman Family* #212 (November 1971).

"the emphasis is now on showing . . ." Letter in *The Superman Family* #204 (November/December 1980).

"Lois handled herself well and proved . . ." Ibid.

Whatever Happened to the Man of Tomorrow?

Their story was set in a future in which . . . *Superman* #423 (September 1986).

Lana Lang took a stand, teaming with . . . *Action Comics* #583 (September 1986).

6a. Women Writers

Louise Simonson came aboard . . . *Superman: The Man of Steel* #1 (July 1991).

Devin Grayson took over . . . *Batman: Gotham Knights* #1 (March 2000).

Becky Cloonan . . . *Batman* #12 (October 2012).

There wasn't a woman in the amazing Amazon's byline . . . *Wonder Woman* #300 (February 1983).

Tamsyn O'Flynn

Tamsyn O'Flynn grew up reading comic books . . . Profile of O'Flynn in *The Superman Family* #216 (March 1982).

Her first story had Lois stumble onto a missing . . . *The Superman Family* #214 (January 1982).

"Oh no! Don't tell me he's going to . . ." Ibid.

"Blame my insatiable curiosity—I'll try anything . . ." Ibid.

who praised her work in a 1983 article . . . Alan Moore, "Invisible Girls and Phantom Ladies," *Daredevils* 6 (June 1983): 16.

"Reporting is her job . . . her career . . ." *The Daring New Adventures of Supergirl* #2 (December 1982).

a teenage supermodel's familial problems . . . *The Daring New Adventures of Supergirl* #2 (December 1982) through #4 (February 1983).

psychic newspaper stories written . . . *The Daring New Adventures of Super-girl* #4 (February 1983).

FN The feature's main murder mystery victim . . . *The Daring New Adventures of Supergirl* #6 (April 1983) and #7 (May 1983).

"the best darned investigative reporter . . ." *The Daring New Adventures of Supergirl* #7 (May 1983).

Mindy Newell

Mindy Newell was working as a nurse . . . Mindy Newell, "How I Became a Comics Professional," ComicMix, July 25, 2011, www.comicmix .com/2011/07/25/mindy-newell-how-i-became-a-comics-professional/.

Newell approached editor Dick Giordano . . . Mindy Newell, "Not Super-man's Girlfriend!," ComicMix, October 29, 2012, www.comicmix .com/2012/10/29/mindy-newell-not-supermans-girlfriend/.

The story picked up soon after Lois's . . . *Lois Lane: When It Rains, God Is Crying* #1 (August 1986).

Newell didn't shy away from the gruesome . . . *Lois Lane: When It Rains, God Is Crying* #2 (September 1986).

editor Andy Helfer promised that another . . . Response to a letter in *Adventures of Superman* #425 (February 1987).

7. Lois Lane on Screen, Part 2: Movies

"Superman won't let me die . . ." "I'm Not Finished Yet," from *It's a Bird . . . It's a Plane . . . It's Superman!*, music by Charles Strouse and lyrics by Lee Adams.

FN "You've Got Possibilities," sung by Linda Lavin . . . Weldon, *Superman*, 140.

to generally positive reviews, but . . . Scivally, *Superman on Film*, 68.

resurrected in 1975 as a television special . . . *It's a Bird . . . It's a Plane . . . It's Superman!*, directed by Jack Regas (ABC, February 1975).

Superman: The Movie

Almost every book on the history of Superman delves into the movie in great detail, but for background information here I particularly relied on Rossen's *Superman vs. Hollywood*, Scivally's *Superman on Film*, Tye's *Superman*, and Weldon's *Superman*.

Leslie focused on Lois Lane in particular . . . Weldon, *Superman*, 181.

They worried about Spielberg's inexperience . . . Tye, *Superman*, 193.

they even screen-tested Alexander's wife's dentist . . . Barry M. Freiman, "One-on-One Interview with Producer Ilya Salkind," Superman Homepage,

accessed September 24, 2015, www.supermanhomepage.com/movies
/movies.php?topic=interview-salkind.

Big names like Barbara Streisand, Natalie Wood . . . See Tye, *Superman*,
193–196; and Weldon, *Superman*, 185.

Kidder was essentially off the grid, on a ranch . . . Nathan Rabin, "Random Roles: Margot Kidder," *AV Club*, March 3, 2009, www.avclub.com
/article/random-roles-margot-kidder-24554.

Donner was sold on her the second that she . . . Tye, *Superman*, 196.

it shattered the American weekend box office record . . . It actually didn't
break the opening weekend box office record; instead the film's popularity grew and it set a new weekend record in its third week of release.
For the numbers, see "*Superman* (1978)—Weekend," Box Office Mojo,
www.boxofficemojo.com/movies/?page=weekend&id=superman.htm.

"Goodness, don't you ever let up?" . . . *Superman: The Movie*, directed by
Richard Donner (Warner Bros., 1978).

"If I know Lois Lane, she'll not only . . ." *Superman II*, directed by Richard
Lester (Warner Bros., 1980).

FN she pulled out a revolver and shot him . . . *Superman II: The Richard
Donner Cut*, directed by Richard Donner (Warner Bros., 2006), DVD.

The change in director didn't go over well . . . Rabin, "Random Roles: Margot
Kidder."

"a front page story that's going to blow the lid . . ." *Superman III*, directed by
Richard Lester (Warner Bros., 1983).

Reeve was "really full of himself . . ." Rabin, "Random Roles: Margot Kidder."

"a dreadful piece of shit" . . . Ibid.

Clark revealed to Lois that he was Superman . . . *Superman IV: The Quest for
Peace*, directed by Sidney J. Furie (Warner Bros., 1987).

Superman Returns

The project remained in limbo for over a decade . . . For a good overview of
the failed attempts at a new Superman film, see Rossen, *Superman vs.
Hollywood*, 265–280.

Singer looked at several actresses for Lois Lane . . . Jeff Jensen, "Five
Things You Need to Know About 'Superman Returns,'" *Entertainment Weekly*, June 17, 2005, www.ew.com/article/2005/06/17
/five-things-you-need-know-about-superman-returns.

Kevin Spacey lobbied for his costar from . . . Cathy Dunkley, "WB Finds
Super Nemesis," *Variety*, January 6, 2005, http://variety.com/2005/film
/markets-festivals/wb-finds-super-nemesis-1117915886/.

"The world doesn't need a savior and neither do I" . . . *Superman Returns*,
directed by Bryan Singer (Warner Bros., 2006).

"Lois Lane has lost her dash and pizzazz" . . . Roger Ebert, review of *Superman Returns*, RogerEbert.com, June 26, 2006, www.rogerebert.com /reviews/superman-returns-2006.

Man of Steel

"I really wanted to show the violence is real . . ." Mark Hughes, "Exclusive Interview with Zack Snyder, Director of 'Batman vs. Superman,'" *Forbes*, April 17, 2014, www.forbes.com/sites/markhughes/2014/04/17 /exclusive-interview-with-zack-snyder-director-of-batman-vs-superman/.

Snyder had met with several actresses about the role . . . Kevin Jagernauth, "Updated: Olivia Wilde & Mila Kunis Also in the Mix for Lois Lane; Kristen Stewart Not Approached," Indiewire, February 2, 2011, http:// blogs.indiewire.com/theplaylist/olivia_wilde_mila_kunis_also_in_the _mix_for_lois_lane_kristen_stewart_repor.

Adams had been a fan of Lois since she watched . . . "Man of Steel Fan Q&A Event," Yahoo Movies, November 6, 2013, https://movies.yahoo.com /man-of-steel-live/.

Her audition and meeting with Snyder sold him . . . Geoff Boucher, "Superman News: Amy Adams Will Be Lois Lane," Hero Complex, March 27, 2011, http://herocomplex.latimes.com/movies/amy-adams-will-be-lois-lane/.

she muscled her way into covering an American . . . *Man of Steel*, directed by Zack Snyder (Warner Bros., 2013).

7a. Parodies and Homages

Margot Kidder took to the small screen . . . "Margot Kidder / The Chieftains," *Saturday Night Live*, season 4, episode 15, directed by Dave Wilson (NBC, 1979).

FN her monologue centered on her inability . . . "Teri Hatcher / Dave Matthews Band," *Saturday Night Live*, season 21, episode 18, directed by Beth McCarthy-Miller (NBC, 1996).

Looney Loises

One of the earliest parodies of Superman . . . *The Mouse of Tomorrow*, directed by Eddie Donnelly (Terrytoons, 1942).

Looney Tunes tackled similar ground . . . *Super-Rabbit*, directed by Chuck Jones, Looney Tunes (Warner Bros., 1943).

Pearl nonchalantly powdered her nose . . . *The Perils of Pearl Pureheart*, directed by Eddie Donnelly, Mighty Mouse (Terrytoons, 1949).

worked on needlepoint while . . . *Beauty on the Beach*, directed by Connie Rasinski, Mighty Mouse (Terrytoons, 1950).

a photojournalist named Vicki Vale . . . *Batman* #49 (October/November 1948).

Lana Lang appeared as Superboy's . . . *Superboy* #10 (September/October 1950).

FN a female reporter named Iris West . . . *Showcase* #4 (September/October 1956).

"Yawn! Another pearl necklace . . ." "Superduperman!," *MAD Magazine* #4 (April/May 1953).

"I simply won't go out with a poor excuse . . ." *The Ernie Kovacs Show*, directed by Barry Shear (July 2, 1956).

"TV's top reporter" . . . "Zot, Part 1," *Underdog*, season 1, episode 9 (Total Television, 1964).

FN Sweet Polly was voiced by Amy Adams . . . *Underdog*, directed by Frederik Du Chau (Disney, 2007).

"How wonderful!" . . . "Fearo, Part 1," *Underdog*, season 1, episode 17 (Total Television, 1964).

"Oh, how thrilling! . . . "The Bubbleheads, Part 1," *Underdog*, season 1, episode 25 (Total Televison, 1964).

Sweet Polly even got to be the one who . . . See "The Bubbleheads, Part 3" (season 1, episode 27, 1965), "The Magnet Men, Part 3 (season 2, episode 11, 1965), and "The Vaccum Gun, Part 3" (season 3, episode 35, 1967).

Melody Lane, a fellow reporter . . . Reprinted in Gilbert Shelton, *The Best of Wonder Wart-Hog* (London: Knockabout, 2013), 4, 14.

"Oh, Stupey, it's just divine . . ." *Not Brand Echh* #7 (April 1968).

Shelton introduced a reporter named Lois Lamebrain . . . *Zap! Comix* #4 (1969), reprinted in Shelton, *Best of Wonder Wart-Hog*, 449–450.

"one loses control over one's muscles" . . . Larry Niven, "Man of Steel, Woman of Kleenex," *Knight: The Magazine for the Adult Male* 7, no. 8 (December 1969).

"getting rid of all this pent-up sex rage" Claire Litton, "No Girls Allowed! Crumb and the Comix Counterculture," *Pop Matters*, January 23, 2007, www.popmatters.com/feature/no-girls-allowed-crumb-and-the -comix-counterculture/.

"Y'know, if you were wearing glasses . . ." "Superduperman," *MAD Magazine* #208 (July 1979).

"You're deliberately avoiding him!! . . ." "Superduperman II," *MAD Magazine* #226 (October 1981).

8. A Whole New World

The Byrne era of the Super-books is fairly well collected in the *Superman: The Man of Steel* paperback series, and the "Death of Superman" arc has been collected a variety of times, with new reissues of the popular story line typically coming out every few years. The issues in between are more hit and miss, but the digital archive for this era on ComiXology is growing at a steady rate.

John Byrne's New Lois Lane

before long Wolfman was out and Byrne . . . Wolfman lasted for a year, and Byrne took over with *Adventures of Superman* #436 (January 1988).

editor Andrew Helfer felt unneeded and left . . . Daniels, *Superman*, 161.

"I wanted Lois to be a three-dimensional character . . ." Ibid., 160.

When Lois first appeared, she was on board an experimental . . . *Man of Steel* #1 (October 1986).

"As good as got, Chief! Tell the rewrite . . ." *Man of Steel* #2 (October 1986).

"Attaway t'go, Mr. White! . . ." *World of Metropolis* #1 (August 1988).

"the best darn reporter this paper . . ." *World of Metropolis* #2 (September 1988).

a new reporter named Clark Kent showed up . . . *Man of Steel* #2 (October 1986).

referred to him as "swine" and . . . *Man of Steel* #4 (November 1986).

"the weasel who beat me to the first . . ." *Superman* #1 (January 1987).

"You big jerk! You and Kent have been . . ." *Action Comics* #597 (February 1988).

"You know full well how much I desire you . . ." *Man of Steel* #4 (November 1986).

She went undercover to find a wanted extortionist . . . *Action Comics* #600 (May 1988).

She broke into a paramilitary camp to rescue . . . *Adventures of Superman* #439 (April 1988).

"Where the heck did you pick up . . ." *Superman* #1 (January 1987).

Romance Blooms

Superman had a brief dalliance with Wonder Woman . . . *Action Comics* #600 (May 1988).

the relationship soured when Delgado . . . *Adventures of Superman* #450 (January 1989).

Lois stopped by his apartment that evening . . . *Superman* #11 (November 1987).

Even when Cat tried to be friendly with Lois . . . *Adventures of Superman* #431 (August 1987).

Byrne was displeased by his perceived lack . . . Michael Thomas, "John Byrne: The Hidden Answers," *Comic Book Resources*, August 22, 2000, www.comicbookresources.com/?page=article&id=151.

Lois cried for her lost friend . . . *Superman* #29 (March 1989).

she even asked him on a date so that . . . *Adventures of Superman* #464 (March 1990).

she gave him a big hug and agreed to . . . *Superman* #43 (May 1990).

"Maybe you want this relationship to proceed . . ." *Superman* #44 (June 1990).

going to the hairdresser to get a new look . . . *Superman* #45 (July 1990).

"I've thought this over for a long time . . ." *Superman* #50 (December 1990).

Clark revealed to Lois that he was Superman . . . *Action Comics* #662 (February 1991).

"In my heart I think I've known . . ." *Superman* #53 (March 1991).

When Superman finally returned . . . *Action Comics* #665 (May 1991).

Lois considered whether this was the sort . . . *Superman* #59 (September 1991).

"What's your problem, anyway? . . ." *Superman: The Man of Steel* #7 (January 1992).

Lois battled the nearly nude princess . . . *Superman* #62 (December 1991).

In the apartment next to her fiancé's . . . *Superman: The Man of Steel* #16 (October 1992).

"Still, if I'm lucky, this might turn into . . ." *Superman: The Man of Steel* #8 (February 1992).

Doomsday

While brainstorming a replacement story line . . . Tye, *Superman*, 244.

He escaped from a subterranean capsule . . . *Superman: The Man of Steel* #18 (December 1992).

The Justice League tried to stop him . . . *Justice League of America* #69 (December 1992).

Superman finally landed the decisive blow . . . *Superman* #75 (January 1993).

While she showed her bravery when she and Jimmy . . . Ibid.

She returned to the *Daily Planet* offices . . . *Adventures of Superman* #498 (January 1993).

she went and stood together with her friends . . . *Superman: The Man of Steel* #20 (February 1993).

She'd been scared to reach out to the Kents . . . Ibid.

She tracked the source of the flood . . . *Superman: The Man of Steel* #21 (March 1993).

Needing more firepower, Lois teamed up with Supergirl . . . *Superman* #77 (March 1993).

"HOLD IT RIGHT THERE, BUSTER!!!" . . . *Action Comics* #687 (June 1993).

Lois met the Metropolis Kid . . . *Adventures of Superman* #501 (June 1993).

"The others seem to have Superman's face . . ." *Superman: The Man of Steel* #23 (July 1993).

She asked him to prove he was Superman . . . *Superman* #78 (June 1993).

"I wish I had that much confidence in . . ." *Adventures of Superman* #503 (August 1993).

Lois knew he was a fake . . . *Action Comics* #690 (August 1993).

"I don't trust the cyborg, Perry . . ." *Superman: The Man of Steel* #25 (September 1993).

yet another Superman emerged from . . . *Superman* #81 (September 1993).

8a. Lucy Lane, Riot Grrrl

Investigating Lucy Lane

Bizarro cured her temporary blindness . . . *Man of Steel* #5 (December 1986).

she was shot by Deathstroke the Terminator . . . *Superman* #68 (June 1992).

and then turned into a vampire . . . *Superman* #70 (August 1992).

she saw him at a shelter where she was . . . *Action Comics* #673 (January 1992).

"But what about Superman? He's fighting . . ." *Adventures of Superman* #515 (August 1994).

Young women in the alternative punk scene . . . For more on the riot grrrl movement, see Sara Marcus, *Girls to the Front: The True Story of the Riot Grrrl Revolution* (New York: Harper Perennial, 2010); Lisa Darms and Kathleen Hanna, *The Riot Grrrl Collection* (New York: The Feminist Press at CUNY, 2014); and Nadine Monem, *Riot Grrrl: Revolution Girl Style Now!* (London: Black Dog Publishing, 2007).

FN Lois Lane made it to the cover . . . *Riot Grrrl* 6, in Marcus, *Girls to the Front*, 17.

resembled the early days of Bratmobile . . . Marcus, *Girls to the Front*, 55–74.

FN the Riot Grrrls had a top-ten hit . . . *Adventures of Superman* #533 (March 1996).

FN were playing a homecoming dance . . . *Action Comics* #739 (November 1997).

"taking the lead, taking responsibility . . ." *Adventures of Superman* #521 (March 1995).

They even thought about becoming superheroes . . . Ibid.

"Yes . . . asking me out at a moment's . . ." *Adventures of Superman* #535 (June 1996).

Lucy met him while visiting the *Daily Planet* . . . *Action Comics* #712 (August 1995).

attending a Pearl Jam concert together . . . *Action Comics* #720 (April 1996).

a Gallup poll found that only 48 percent . . . Frank Newport, "In U.S., 87% Approve of Black-White Marriage, vs. 4% in 1958," Gallup, July 25, 2013, www.gallup.com/poll/163697/approve-marriage-blacks-whites.aspx.

Ron's sister made it very clear . . . *Superman: The Man of Steel* #77 (March 1998).

"This is a nightmare! It can't be true! . . ." *Superman: The Man of Steel* #83 (September 1998).

left the clinic with pamphlets about . . . *Superman: The Man of Tomorrow* #11 (Fall 1998).

Lucy got a desk job at the airline . . . *Action Comics* #751 (February 1999).

took a job at a bank just so that . . . *Action Comics* #752 (March 1999).

Lucy and Ron got married . . . *Adventures of Superman* #584 (November 2000).

Lucy had a baby boy a few months later . . . *Adventures of Superman* #587 (February 2001).

She and a toddler Sam appeared briefly . . . *Adventures of Superman* #633 (December 2004).

Scarlet Witch, a former member of the Avengers . . . *House of M* #1 (August 2005).

Jean Loring, the ex-wife of the Atom . . . *Identity Crisis* #7 (February 2005).

Superwoman was revealed to be Lucy Lane . . . *Supergirl* #40 (June 2009).

Ron and their son were gone without explanation . . . *Supergirl Annual* #1 (November 2009).

she remained a crazed zealot . . . *Supergirl* #59 (February 2011).

9. Lois Lane on Screen, Part 3: Television

Alexander Salkind and syndication company Viacom . . . Freiman, "Producer Ilya Salkind."

Noel Neill did make a guest appearance . . . "Paranoia," *Superboy*, season 4, episode 6, directed by David Nutter (Viacom, 1991).

"was out of this world. She was . . ." Freiman, "Producer Ilya Salkind."

Warner Bros. filed a lien against . . . Scivally, *Superman on Film*, 119.

Lois & Clark: The New Adventures of Superman

she didn't read the few comic books . . . "From Rivals to Romance: The Making of *Lois & Clark*," on *Lois & Clark: The New Adventures of Superman; The Complete First Season* (Warner Bros., 2006), DVD.

LeVine found her woman right away when . . . "Deborah Joy LeVine," *Comic Book Central Podcast*, episode 5 (December 20, 2013), http://comicbook central.libsyn.com/comic-book-central-episode-5-deborah-joy-le-vine.

"They're real . . . and they're spectacular" . . . "The Implant," *Seinfeld*, season 4, episode 19, directed by Tom Cherones (Sony, 1993).

Hatcher was so keen to get the role that . . . "From Rivals to Romance."

"I wanted her to be an astute businesswoman . . ." Ibid.

almost called *Lois Lane's Daily Planet* . . . Weldon, *Superman*, 256.

"I nailed 'em cold!" . . . "Pilot," *Lois & Clark*, season 1, episode 1, directed by Robert Butler (Warner Bros., 1993).

writing exposés on corrupt congressmen . . . "Honeymoon in Metropolis," *Lois & Clark*, season 1, episode 11, directed by James A. Contner (Warner Bros., 1993).

faulty nuclear plants . . . "The Man of Steel Bars," *Lois & Clark*, season 1, episode 9, directed by Robert Butler (Warner Bros., 1993).

She went undercover as a nightclub singer . . . "I've Got a Crush on You," *Lois & Clark*, season 1, episode 6, directed by Gene Reynolds (Warner Bros., 1993).

refused to stop looking into a murder . . . "Witness," *Lois & Clark*, season 1, episode 13, directed by Mel Damski (Warner Bros., 1994).

federal agents showed up at the *Daily Planet* . . . "Strange Visitor (from Another Planet)," *Lois & Clark*, season 1, episode 2, directed by Randall Zisk (Warner Bros., 1993).

Lois believed that a man convicted of murder . . . "The Ides of Metropolis," *Lois & Clark*, season 1, episode 15, directed by Philip Sgriccia (Warner Bros., 1994).

She refused a spot in Luthor's protected . . . "All Shook Up," *Lois & Clark*, season 1, episode 12, directed by Felix Enriquez Alcala (Warner Bros., 1994).

"This is going to make an incredible story . . ." "Fly Hard," *Lois & Clark*, season 1, episode 19, directed by Philip Sgriccia (Warner Bros., 1994).

She stole Clark's leads . . . "Neverending Battle," *Lois & Clark*, season 1, episode 3, directed by Gene Reynolds (Warner Bros., 1993).

threw elbows to get to the pay phone . . . "All Shook Up," *Lois & Clark*.

didn't put much effort into stories that . . . "Pheromone, My Lovely," *Lois & Clark*, season 1, episode 10, directed by Bill D'Elia (Warner Bros., 1993).

"You've both been writing about . . ." "Illusions of Grandeur," *Lois & Clark*, season 1, episode 14, directed by Michael W. Watkins (Warner Bros., 1993).

She ultimately decided not to marry Luthor . . . "The House of Luthor," *Lois & Clark*, season 1, episode 21, directed by Alan J. Levi (Warner Bros., 1994).

they were still irked that Lois's name came first . . . "Deborah Joy LeVine," *Comic Book Central Podcast*.

the Prankster . . . "The Prankster," *Lois & Clark*, season 2, episode 4, directed by James Hayman (Warner Bros., 1994).

Metallo . . . "Metallo," *Lois & Clark*, season 2, episode 10, directed by James Bagdonas (Warner Bros., 1995).

the two began dating midway through . . . "The Phoenix," *Lois & Clark*, season 2, episode 13, directed by Philip Sgriccia (Warner Bros., 1995).

Clark decided to tell Lois that he was Superman . . . "And the Answer Is . . . ," *Lois & Clark*, season 2, episode 22, directed by Alan J. Levi (Warner Bros., 1995).

"Who's asking, Clark or Superman?" . . . "We Have a Lot to Talk About," *Lois & Clark*, season 3, episode 1, directed by Philip Sgriccia (Warner Bros., 1995).

She even took the superhero reins . . . "Ultra Woman," *Lois & Clark*, season 3, episode 7, directed by Mike Vejar (Warner Bros., 1995).

Lois proposed to Clark early in the season . . . Ibid.

the wedding took place soon after . . . "I Now Pronounce You . . . ," *Lois & Clark*, season 3, episode 15, directed by Jim Pohl (Warner Bros., 1996).

their plans were nearly thwarted by the maniacal . . . "Swear to God, This Time We're Not Kidding," *Lois & Clark*, season 4, episode 3, directed by Michael Lange (Warner Bros., 1996).

Lex Luthor's fiendish son . . . "Faster than a Speeding Vixen," *Lois & Clark*, season 4, episode 17, directed by Neal Ahern (Warner Bros., 1997).

that mischievous imp from the fifth dimension . . . "Twas the Night Before Mxymas," *Lois & Clark*, season 4, episode 11, directed by Mike Vejar (Warner Bros., 1996).

Lois became interim editor of the *Daily Planet* . . . "Stop the Presses," *Lois & Clark*, season 4, episode 10, directed by Peter Ellis (Warner Bros., 1996).

in a two-parter she was able to beat . . . "The People vs. Lois Lane," *Lois & Clark*, season 4, episode 6, directed by Robert Ginty, and "Dead Lois Walking," *Lois & Clark*, season 4, episode 7, directed by Chris Long (Warner Bros., 1996).

They closed the finale with a cliff-hanger . . . "The Family Hour," *Lois & Clark*, season 4, episode 22, directed by Robert Ginty (Warner Bros., 1997).

FN Producer Brad Buckner and writer Tim Minear later revealed . . . Craig Byrne, "Brad Buckner: Executive Producer, Season 3–4," KryptonSite, August 2003, www.kryptonsite.com/loisclark/buckner2003.htm; *Lois & Clark* FAQ, RedBoots.net, accessed September 24, 2015, www.redboots .net/lc-faq/Q31.htm.

Smallville

After plans for a show about a young Bruce Wayne . . . Paul Simpson, *Smallville: The Official Companion, Season 1* (London: Titan Books, 2004), 8–9.

breaking the WB's ratings record with its premiere . . . "Smallville's Super Debut—a WB Ratings Bonanza!," Superman Homepage, October 18, 2001, www.supermanhomepage.com/news/2001-news/2001-news-tv.php?topic=2001-news-tv/1018i.

After several negotiations, Warner Bros. agreed . . . Craig Byrne, *Smallville: The Official Companion, Season 4* (London: Titan Books, 2007), 138–140.

"There were a lot of wonderful actresses . . ." Jami Philbrick, "'Smallville: Homecoming" 200th Episode Q&A," MovieWeb, October 15, 2010, http://movieweb.com/smallville-homecoming-200th-episode-qa/.

Chloe was apparently killed in a home explosion . . . "Covenant," *Smallville*, season 3, episode 22, directed by Greg Beeman (Warner Bros., 2004).

Season four began with Lois driving to Smallville . . . "Crusade," *Smallville*, season 4, episode 1, directed by Greg Beeman (Warner Bros., 2004).

FN Teri Hatcher later guest-starred in the show's . . . "Abandoned," *Smallville*, season 10, episode 8, directed by Kevin G. Fair (Warner Bros., 2010).

When military troops chased them away . . . "Gone," *Smallville*, season 4, episode 2, directed by James Marshall (Warner Bros., 2004).

"The last thing I want to be is a reporter" . . . "Facade," *Smallville*, season 4, episode 3, directed by Pat Williams (Warner Bros., 2004).

Lois took over the newspaper and also found . . . "Devoted," *Smallville*, season 4, episode 4, directed by David Carson (Warner Bros., 2004).

"She's bossy, she's stuck up, she's rude! . . ." "Gone," *Smallville*.

she'd been going to the local bars at night . . . "Recruit," *Smallville*, season 4, episode 13, directed by Jeannot Szwarc (Warner Bros., 2005).

She became Jonathan Kent's campaign manager . . . "Fanatic," *Smallville*, season 5, episode 10, directed by Michael Rohl (Warner Bros., 2006).

Martha Kent's chief of staff . . . "Fragile," *Smallville*, season 5, episode 18, directed by Tom Welling (Warner Bros., 2006).

a reporter for the *Metropolis Inquisitor* . . . "Sneeze," *Smallville*, season 6, episode 2, directed by Paul Shapiro (Warner Bros., 2006).

"Your prose leaps off the page like a Bengal . . ." "Kara," *Smallville*, season 7, episode 2, directed by James Conway (Warner Bros., 2007).

She even pretended to be a costumed . . . "Stiletto," *Smallville*, season 8, episode 19, directed by Kevin G. Fair (Warner Bros., 2009).

instead of doing an interview she offered . . . Ibid.

infiltrating a strip club . . . "Exposed," *Smallville*, season 5, episode 6, directed by Jeannot Szwarc (Warner Bros., 2005).

disguising herself as a dominatrix . . . "Supergirl," *Smallville*, season 10, episode 3, directed by Mairzee Almas (Warner Bros., 2010).

popping out of cake dressed like . . . "Charade," *Smallville*, season 9, episode 18, directed by Brian Peterson (Warner Bros., 2010).

Lois and Clark's romantic feelings . . . "Bride," *Smallville*, season 8, episode 10, directed by Jeannot Szwarc (Warner Bros., 2008).

they didn't begin dating . . . "Crossfire," *Smallville*, season 9, episode 6, directed by Michael Rohl (Warner Bros., 2009).

her mistrust led to them breaking up . . . "Hostage," *Smallville*, season 9, episode 20, directed by Glen Winter (Warner Bros., 2010).

she immediately realized that he was . . . "Salvation," *Smallville*, season 9, episode 21, directed by Greg Beeman (Warner Bros., 2010).

Lois left for a reporting gig in Africa . . . "Lazarus," *Smallville*, season 10, episode 1, directed by Kevin G. Fair (Warner Bros., 2010).

"The last thing I would ever want is to be . . ." "Shield," season 10, episode 2, directed by Glen Winter (Warner Bros., 2010).

"What took you so long?!" . . . "Isis," *Smallville*, season 10, episode 5, directed by James Marshall (Warner Bros., 2010).

Lois spent the rest of the finale knocking out . . . "Finale," *Smallville*, season 10, episodes 21–22, directed by Kevin G. Fair and Greg Beeman (Warner Bros., 2011).

9a. Animation Representation

villains like Lex Luthor . . . "The Deadly Dish," *The New Adventures of Superman*, season 1, episode 18 (Warner Bros., 1966).

Toyman . . . "The Toys of Doom," *The New Adventures of Superman*, season 1, episode 14 (Warner Bros., 1966).

space aliens . . . "The Robot of Riga," *The New Adventures of Superman*, season 1, episode 9 (Warner Bros., 1966).

a giant chimpanzee . . . "The Chimp Who Made It Big," *The New Adventures of Superman*, season 1, episode 7 (Warner Bros., 1966).

"It's dangerous! Stay back!" . . . "Destroy the Defendroids / The Adoption," *Superman*, season 1, episode 1 (Warner Bros., 1988).

Superman: The Animated Series

Batman: The Animated Series is considered to be . . . The show ranked seventh on *TV Guide*'s list of the greatest cartoons of all time, and third on IGN's list: Rich Sands, "*TV Guide Magazine*'s 60 Great Cartoons of All Time," *TV Guide*, September 24, 2013, www.tvguide.com/news/greatest-cartoons-tv-guide-magazine-1071203/; "The Top 25 Animated Series for Adults," IGN, July 15, 2013, www.ign.com/articles/2013/07/15/top-25-animated-shows-for-adults?page=5.

Delany grew up watching reruns of . . . Andy Khouri, "*Superman: The Animated Series* Star Dana Delany on Lois Lane's 75th Birthday," *Wired*, July 8, 2013, www.wired.com/2013/07/lois-lane-dana-delany/.

she still describes herself in her bio as "occasionally Lois Lane" . . . Dana Delany's Twitter page, accessed September 24, 2015, https://twitter.com/danadelany.

"Chief! I spent a week on the docks . . ." "The Last Son of Krypton, Part 2," *Superman: The Animated Series*, season 1, episode 2, directed by Scott Jeralds and Curt Geda (Warner Bros., 1996).

"You're not the rube hayseed I took you for" . . . Ibid.

Lois named Metropolis's new "angel" . . . "The Last Son of Krypton, Part 3," *Superman: The Animated Series*, season 1, episode 3, directed by Bruce Timm and Dan Riba (Warner Bros., 1996).

she dated Bruce Wayne for a while . . . "World's Finest, Parts 1–3," *Superman: The Animated Series*, season 2, episodes 16–18, directed by Toshihiko Masuda (Warner Bros., 1997).

didn't even kiss Superman until the series finale . . . "Legacy, Part 2," *Superman: The Animated Series*, season 4, episode 3, directed by Dan Riba (Warner Bros., 2000).

winning journalism awards . . . "Target," *Superman: The Animated Series*, season 2, episode 7, directed by Curt Geda (Warner Bros., 1997).

she was transported into a dystopian . . . "Brave New Metropolis," *Superman: The Animated Series*, season 2, episode 12, directed by Curt Geda (Warner Bros., 1997).

Lois broke into the prison . . . "Legacy, Part 2," *Superman: The Animated Series*.

she was always running toward the chaos . . . "Clash," *Justice League Unlimited*, season 2, episode 7, directed by Dan Riba (Warner Bros., 2005).

She also played a key role . . . "Question Authority," *Justice League Unlimited*, season 2, episode 9, directed by Dan Riba (Warner Bros., 2005).

crossover story featuring the Man of Steel . . . "The Batman/Superman Story, Part 1," *The Batman*, season 5, episode 1, directed by Vinton Heuck (Warner Bros., 2007).

DC Universe Animated Original Movies

She was played by Sirena Irwin in an episode . . . "Battle of the Superheroes!," *Batman: The Brave and the Bold*, season 3, episode 5, directed by Ben Jones (Warner Bros., 2011).

comedian Maria Bamford voiced Lois . . . "Lois" and "Bizarro," *Tales of Metropolis*, directed by Will Patrick (Warner Bros., 2013).

Lois was suspicious about a single new Superman . . . *Superman: Doomsday*, directed by Lauren Montgomery, Bruce Timm, and Brandon Vietti (Warner Bros., 2007), DVD.

Golden Globe award winner Kyra Sedgwick . . . *Justice League: The New Frontier*, directed by David Bullock (Warner Bros., 2008), DVD.

Emmy nominee Christina Hendricks . . . *All-Star Superman*, directed by Sam Liu (Warner Bros., 2011), DVD.

Dana Delany returned to play Lois . . . *Justice League: The Flashpoint Paradox*, directed by Jay Oliva (Warner Bros., 2013), DVD.

Stana Katic voiced arguably the best-known . . . *Superman: Unbound*, directed by James Tucker (Warner Bros., 2013), DVD.

That moment has since been immortalized . . . Just google "Lois Lane middle finger gif" and you'll find it.

10. Watching from the Sidelines

This era is fairly well collected, though several of said collections are currently out of print. Key collections relevant to this chapter include Geoff Johns and Phil Jimenez, *Infinite Crisis* (2008); Geoff Johns and Gary Frank, *Superman: Secret Origin* (2011); Geoff Johns and Richard Donner, *Superman: Last Son of Krypton* (2013); Jeph Loeb and J. M. DeMatteis, *Superman: Emperor Joker* (2007); Jeph Loeb and Joe Casey, *Superman: Our Worlds at War* (2006); James Robinson and Greg Rucka, *Superman: Nightwing & Flamebird*, vol. 2 (2010); Greg Rucka and Mark Verheiden, *Superman: Sacrifice* (2006); Greg Rucka and Matthew Clark, *Superman: Unconventional Warfare* (2005); and Mark Waid and Leinil Francis Yu, *Superman: Birthright* (2005). The vast majority of the Super-books from 2000 on are available digitally via ComiXology; availability is more hit and miss through the 1990s.

Teri Hatcher–inspired haircut . . . *Superman: The Man of Steel* #27 (November 1993).

a massive investigation of Lex Luthor . . . Began in ibid.

Lois was looking into the disappearance . . . *Superman* #86 (February 1994).

breaking into LexCorp headquarters on multiple . . . Ibid.; *Adventures of Superman* #509 (February 1994); *Superman: The Man of Steel* #34 (June 1994).

put pressure on the *Daily Planet*'s owner . . . *Superman* #89 (May 1994).

Luthor had her apartment bombed . . . *Adventures of Superman* #512 (May 1994).

culminated in Luthor's arrest . . . *Action Comics* #700 (June 1994).

she ended their engagement . . . *Action Comics* #720 (April 1996).

the end result was Lois standing atop . . . *Superman* #118 (December 1996).

It began with Lois taking out the ringleader . . . *Superman: The Wedding Album* (December 1996).

decided to keep her own last name . . . *Adventures of Superman* #541 (December 1996).

Wedded Bliss

A close examination of *Action Comics* . . . To find these numbers, I tallied Lois's appearances and what she was doing in every issue of *Action Comics* from John Byrne taking over the title in 1986 to the beginning of the New 52 in 2011. I didn't include the year that *Action Comics* went weekly, because Superman was barely in the book during that time.

"That's life with Superman . . ." *Superman* #146 (July 1999).

teleported into an alien prison camp . . . *Superman: The Man of Steel* #115 (August 2001).

Lois didn't show up until the ninth issue . . . *Superman* #212 (February 2005).

now the duo were parents . . . *Action Comics* #845 (January 2007).

Lori Lemaris, Clark's mermaid ex . . . *Adventures of Superman* #532 (February 1996).

Lana Lang was a regular source . . . Lana was creepily obsessed with Clark. She named her son after him in *Superman: The Doomsday Wars* #1 (November 1998), and left her husband because she still had feelings for Clark in *Action Comics* #819 (November 2004).

"Was it Wonder Woman? I bet it was . . ." *Superman* #192 (June 2003).

She was so furious at both of them . . . *Superman* #194 (August 2003).

FN secretly convincing Lex Luthor to save . . . *Superman* #151 (December 1999).

she saw that her father was in trouble . . . *Action Comics* #781 (September 2001).

She took a trip around the world . . . Began in *Superman* #176 (January 2002).

like when Superman split into two Supermen . . . *Superman: The Man of Tomorrow* #10 (Winter 1998).

"Tonight you've earned the name Man of Steel . . ." *Superman* #159 (August 2000).

skintight belly shirts . . . *Superman* #222 (December 2005).

pants so low that her thong underwear . . . *Adventures of Superman* #644 (November 2005).

instead donning skimpy negligees . . . For examples, see *Superman* #219 (September 2005); *Superman* #654 (September 2006); and *Action Comics* #848 (May 2007).

Her button-down shirt was open . . . *Action Comics* #772 (December 2000).

A work trip to Eastern Europe . . . *Superman* #180 (May 2002).

her assignment covering the war in Umec . . . *Adventures of Superman* #627 (June 2004).

was arrested and interrogated . . . *Action Comics* #884 (February 2010).

helped save Earth from a wrathful . . . *Action Comics* #888 (June 2010).

"I'd rather face the Joker. He's been known . . ." *Birds of Prey* #102 (March 2007).

Lois convinced Batman to break into . . . *Detective Comics* #756 (May 2001).

Lois also patched things up with Wonder Woman . . . *Wonder Woman* #170 (July 2001).

Lois was in northern Manitoba . . . *GirlFrenzy! Superman: Lois Lane* (June 1998).

loudly confronting her publisher . . . *Superman: Birthright* #4 (December 2003).

"I'm not! Sky! Copters! Artillery! . . ." Ibid.

She named him Superman and . . . *Superman: Birthright* #5 (January 2004).

uncovered Lex Luthor's sham alien invasion . . . *Superman: Birthright* #11 (August 2004).

Lois was again introduced while yelling . . . *Superman: Secret Origin* #3 (January 2010).

"I've been compiling a list of questions . . ." *Superman: Secret Origin* #4 (March 2010).

Lois was the only reporter to whom Superman gave . . . *Superman: Secret Origin* #5 (May 2010).

later warned him about Kryptonite when . . . *Superman: Secret Origin* #6 (October 2010).

Pushing Daisies

Lois died in a car crash . . . *Superman* #194 (February 1967).

Lois was killed when a blast-ray . . . *Superman* #215 (April 1969).

Even in her own series, Lois's death . . . *Superman's Girl Friend Lois Lane* #51 (August 1964).

Gail Simone addressed the frequent deaths of female . . . Gail Simone, Women in Refrigerators, March 1999, http://lby3.com/wir/.

returned home to find that a villain had murdered . . . *Green Lantern* #54 (August 1994).

Gwen Stacy was killed in 1973 . . . *The Amazing Spider-Man* #121 (June 1973).

Supergirl died in *Crisis on Infinite Earths* . . . *Crisis on Infinite Earths* #7 (October 1985).

Batgirl was paralyzed and sexually abused . . . Alan Moore and Brian Bolland, *Batman: The Killing Joke* (New York: DC Comics, 1988).

Lois and the rest of the *Daily Planet* staff . . . *Kingdom Come* #2 (June 1996).

only appeared in the background of a flashback panel . . . Ibid.

"No, please, don't cross that line . . ." *JSA Kingdom Come Special: Superman* #1 (January 2009).

"I will always fight for a better world . . ." *Superman: The Man of Steel* #105 (October 2000).

Lois then "died" again in the following . . . *Action Comics* #770 (October 2000).

Superman found the villain Manchester Black . . . *Action Comics* #796 (December 2002).

Lois's death was the pivotal plot point in . . . *Superman* #200 (February 2004).

Lois was murdered, first by Brainiac . . . *Superman* #219 (September 2005).

and then by Darkseid . . . *Action Comics* #829 (September 2005).

Luthor convinced Superman that her illness . . . *Infinite Crisis* #2 (January 2006).

when her Earth was finally restored . . . *Infinite Crisis* #5 (April 2006).

She died again in the *Flashpoint* crossover . . . *Flashpoint: Lois Lane and the Resistance* #3 (October 2011).

"the stupid, senseless way she died" . . . *Earth 2* #1 (July 2012).

a furious Superman burst into an interrogation . . . *Injustice: Gods Among Us*, directed by Ed Boon (NetherRealm Studios, Warner Bros. Interactive Entertainment, 2013), video game.

The first issue began with the happy news . . . *Injustice: Gods Among Us, Year One* #1 (January 2013).

Superman had been tricked into killing . . . *Injustice: Gods Among Us, Year One* #3 (January 2013).

FN Lois's death "was the hardest thing I've ever . . ." Vaneta Rogers, "'Unfridging Lois' Just One of the Surprises Tom Taylor Plans for DC's *Earth 2*," *Newsarama*, November 22, 2013, www.newsarama.com/19662-unfridging -lois-just-one-of-the-surprises-tom-taylor-plans-for-dc-s-earth-2.html.

FN Lois's consciousness was loaded into a robot body . . . *Earth 2* #17 (January 2014).

Earth 2 #1 sold around 80,000 copies . . . John Jackson Miller, "May 2012 Comic Book Sales Figures," Comichron, www.comichron.com /monthlycomicssales/2012/2012-05.html.

Injustice: Gods Among Us sold 1.3 million . . . "Injustice: Gods Among Us," VGChartz, accessed September 24, 2015, www.vgchartz.com /game/71001/injustice-gods-among-us/.

10a. The New 52 and Beyond

editor Matt Idelson called Lois a "trophy wife" . . . Alan Kistler, "SDCC 2011: The Mood of DC Fans at Comic-Con," *Newsarama*, July 25, 2011,

www.newsarama.com/8088-sdcc-2011-the-mood-of-dc-fans-at-comic
-con.html.

DC's copublisher, Dan DiDio, had been gunning for . . . Rich Johnston,
"When Dan DiDio Planned to Kill Superman's Marriage to Lois Lane—
and Lots of Young Justice Members!," *Bleeding Cool*, January 29, 2015,
www.bleedingcool.com/2015/01/19/dan-didio-planned-kill-supermans
-marriage-lois-lane-lots-young-injustice-members/.

The New 52

The comics of the New 52 era are extremely well collected in a variety of
ordered volumes, and all of them are available digitally through ComiXology.

Lois had moved on from the *Daily Planet* and . . . *Superman* #1 (November
2011).

Clark left the *Daily Planet* soon after . . . *Superman* #13 (December 2012).

Jonathan quickly appeared behind her . . . *Superman* #1 (November 2011).

He began dating Wonder Woman . . . *Justice League* #12 (October 2011).

the couple launched their own joint . . . *Superman/Wonder Woman* #1
(December 2013).

She'd been taken over by Brainiac . . . Began in *Superman Annual* #2 (September 2013).

"You think I'd come here unprepared . . ." *Batman/Superman* #13 (October
2014).

crash-landing a sabotaged plane . . . *Superman Unchained* #3 (October 2013).

using futuristic technology to disable . . . *Superman Unchained* #7 (July 2014).

running her own popular news site . . . Began in *The New 52: Futures End*
#1 (July 2014).

the story centered on Lois investigating a drug . . . *Superman: Lois Lane* #1
(April 2014).

"So much of what Lois is capable of can be seen . . ." Tony Guerrero, "Exclusive
Interview: Marguerite Bennett on *Lois Lane* One-Shot & *Joker's Daughter* One-Shot," Comic Vine, November 8, 2013, www.comicvine.com
/articles/exclusive-interview-marguerite-bennett-on-lois-lan/1100-147543/.

The issue came in ninety-sixth place . . . John Jackson Miller, "February
2014 Comic Book Sales Figures," Comichron, www.comichron.com
/monthlycomicssales/2014/2014-02.html.

FN "There is no way of doing anything original . . ." Jeffrey Renaud, "Yang
& Romita, Jr. Expose Lois Lane in New 'Superman' Arc 'Before Truth,'"
Comic Book Resources, June 24, 2015, www.comicbookresources.com
/article/yang-romita-jr-expose-lois-lane-in-new-superman-arc-before-truth.

In a front page story for the *Daily Planet* . . . The story was on a *Daily Planet* front page that was printed up as part of a free giveaway in comic book shops in June 2015.

"I should've looked for another way . . ." *Divergence FCDB Special Edition* #1 (June 2015).

Lois Lane: Fallout

"Step aside, Katniss: it's time . . ." Graeme McMillan, "Lois Lane Is Your New YA Fiction Hero," *Hollywood Reporter*, August 26, 2014, www .hollywoodreporter.com/heat-vision/lois-lane-is-your-new-728182.

"So it's basically Lois Lane . . ." Joshua Rivera, "Lois Lane to Star in New YA Novel," *Entertainment Weekly*, August 26, 2014, www.ew.com /article/2014/08/26/lois-lane-to-star-in-new-ya-novel.

"a spectacular prose start . . ." Review of *Lois Lane: Fallout*, *Kirkus*, February 16, 2015, www.kirkusreviews.com/book-reviews/gwenda-bond /fallout-bond/.

"I want my protagonists to be nuanced . . ." Byron Brewer, "DF Interview: Gwenda Bond Gives Lois Lane the Prose Treatment," Dynamic Forces official website, February 23, 2015, https://dynamicforces.com/htmlfiles /interviews.html?showinterview=IN02231585561.

"her unmatched bravery and smarts" . . . Gwenda Bond, "The Secret Is Out . . . (!!!)," Gwenda Bond personal website, August 26, 2014, www.gwendabond .com/bondgirl/2014/08/secretisout.html.

"We're the same [. . .] we protect . . ." Gwenda Bond, *Lois Lane: Fallout* (North Mankato, MN: Switch Press, 2015), 135–136.

"my trusty sidekick" Bond, *Fallout*, 287.

"You're assuming I won't figure . . ." Bond, *Fallout*, 303.

Conclusion

When Noel Neill toured college campuses . . . Rip Pense, "A Crush More Powerful Than a Locomotive," *Los Angeles Times*, August 12, 1994, http:// articles.latimes.com/1994-08-12/news/ls-26480_1_noel-neill.

Bibliography

Adventures of Superman (TV). Seasons 1–6. Warner Bros., 2005–2006. DVD.

All-Star Superman. Directed by Sam Liu. Warner Bros., 2011. DVD.

Amash, Jim, and Eric Nolen-Weathington. *Carmine Infantino: Penciler, Publisher, Provocateur.* Raleigh, NC: TwoMorrows, 2010.

Andrae, Tom, Geoffrey Blum, and Gary Coddington. "Of Superman and Kids with Dreams: A Rare Interview with the Creators of Superman; Jerry Siegel and Joe Shuster." *Nemo: The Classic Comics Library* 2 (August 1983): 6–19.

Back in Circulation. Directed by Ray Enright. Warner Bros., 1937.

Beaty, Bart. *Fredric Wertham and the Critique of Mass Culture.* Jackson: University Press of Mississippi, 2005.

Beauty on the Beach. Directed by Connie Rasinski. Mighty Mouse. Terrytoons, 1950.

Benton, Mike. *Superhero Comics of the Silver Age: An Illustrated History.* Dallas: Taylor Publishing Company, 1991.

Binder, Otto, Curt Swan, et al. *Superman: The Man of Tomorrow Archives.* Vols. 1–3. New York: DC Comics, 2005–2014.

Binder, Otto, Kurt Schaffenberger, et al. *Superman's Girl Friend Lois Lane Archives.* Vol. 1. New York: DC Comics, 2012.

Biography. "George Reeves: The Perils of a Superhero." A&E, February 2000.

Bond, Gwenda. *Lois Lane: Fallout.* North Mankato, MN: Switch Press, 2015.

———. "The Secret Is Out . . . (!!!)." Gwenda Bond personal website, August 26, 2014. www.gwendabond.com/bondgirl/2014/08/secretisout.html.

Boucher, Geoff. "Superman News: Amy Adams Will Be Lois Lane." Hero Complex, March 27, 2011. http://herocomplex.latimes.com/movies /amy-adams-will-be-lois-lane/.

Box Office Mojo. "*Superman* (1978)—Weekend." www.boxofficemojo.com /movies/?page=weekend&id=superman.htm.

Brewer, Byron. "DF Interview: Gwenda Bond Gives Lois Lane the Prose Treatment." Dynamic Forces official website, February 23, 2015. https://dynam icforces.com/htmlfiles/interviews.html?showinterview=IN02231585561.

Brioux, Bill. *Truth and Rumors: The Reality Behind TV's Most Famous Myths*. Westport, CT: Praeger Publishers, 2008.

Byrne, Craig. "Brad Buckner: Executive Producer, Season 3–4." KryptonSite, August 2003. www.kryptonsite.com/loisclark/buckner2003.htm.

———. *Smallville: The Official Companion, Season 4*. London: Titan Books, 2007.

Byrne, John, et al. *Superman: The Man of Steel*. Vols. 1–8. New York: DC Comics, 2003–2014.

Byrne, John, Phil Jimenez, et al. *Lois Lane: A Celebration of 75 Years*. New York: DC Comics, 2013.

Cameron, Donald, Curt Swan, et al. *Showcase Presents: Superman Family*. Vols. 1–4. New York: DC Comics, 2006–2013.

Comic Book Central Podcast. "Deborah Joy LeVine." Episode 5 (December 20, 2013). http://comicbookcentral.libsyn.com/comic-book-central-episode-5 -deborah-joy-le-vine.

Contino, Jennifer M. "Noel Neill: Lois Lane Forever." *Pulse*, October 22, 2004. www.comicon.com/cgi-bin/ultimatebb.cgi?ubb=get_topic&f=36&t= 002972 (site discontinued).

Coogan, Peter. *Superhero: The Secret Origin of a Genre*. Austin: Monkey-Brain Books, 2006.

Cooke, Jon B. "Rise & Fall of Rovin's Empire." *Comic Book Artist* 16 (December 2011): 24–43.

Daniels, Les. *Superman: The Complete History*. San Francisco: Chronicle Books, 1999.

Darms, Lisa, and Kathleen Hanna. *The Riot Grrrl Collection*. New York: The Feminist Press at CUNY, 2014.

DC Women Kicking Ass blog. "75 Years of Lois Lane: A Chat with Bryan Q. Miller." April 22, 2013. http://dcwomenkickingass.tumblr.com/post/486 24946890/75-years-of-lois-lane-a-chat-with-bryan-q-miller.

De Haven, Tom. *Our Hero: Superman on Earth*. New Haven, CT: Yale University Press, 2010.

Deckard, Barbara Sinclair. *The Women's Movement: Political, Socioeconomic, and Psychological Issues*. New York: Harper & Row, 1979.

Douglas, Susan J. *Where the Girls Are: Growing Up Female with the Mass Media*. New York: Times Books, 1994.

Duncan, Randy, and Matthew J. Smith. *Icons of the American Comic Book: From Captain America to Wonder Woman*. Santa Barbara, CA: Greenwood, 2013.

Dunkley, Cathy. "WB Finds Super Nemesis." *Variety*, January 6, 2005. http://variety.com/2005/film/markets-festivals/wb-finds-super-nemesis-1117915886/.

E! Mysteries & Scandals. "George Reeves." E!, March 1998.

Ebert, Roger. Review of *Superman Returns*. RogerEbert.com, June 26, 2006, www.rogerebert.com/reviews/superman-returns-2006.

Edgar, Joanne. "Wonder Woman Revisited." *Ms.* 1, no. 1 (1972): 52–55.

Evanier, Mark. "From the E-Mailbag." *News from ME* blog, June 22, 2013. www.newsfromme.com/2013/06/22/from-the-e-mailbag-184/.

Farghaly, Nadine, Ed. *Examining Lois Lane: The Scoop on Superman's Sweetheart*. Lanham, MD: Scarecrow Press, 2013.

Fleming, E. J. *The Fixers: Eddie Mannix, Howard Strickling and the MGM Publicity Machine*. New York: McFarland, 2004.

Freiman, Barry M. "One-on-One Interview with Producer Ilya Salkind." Superman Homepage, accessed September 24, 2015. www.supermanhomepage.com/movies/movies.php?topic=interview-salkind.

"From Inkwell to Backlot." On *Adventures of Superman: The Complete First Season*. Warner Bros., 2006. DVD.

"From Rivals to Romance: The Making of *Lois & Clark*." On *Lois & Clark: The New Adventures of Superman; The Complete First Season*. Warner Bros., 2006. DVD.

Front Page Woman. Directed by Michael Curtiz. Warner Bros., 1935.

Goldin, Claudia Dale. *Understanding the Gender Gap: An Economic History of American Women*. New York: Oxford University Press, 1990.

Good, Howard. *Girl Reporter: Gender, Journalism, and the Movies*. Lanham, MD: Scarecrow Press, 1998.

Guerrero, Tony. "Exclusive Interview: Marguerite Bennett on *Lois Lane* One-Shot & *Joker's Daughter* One-Shot." Comic Vine, November 8, 2013. www.comicvine.com/articles/exclusive-interview-marguerite-bennett-on-lois-lan/1100-147543/.

Hadju, David. *The Ten-Cent Plague: The Great Comic-Book Scare and How It Changed America*. New York: Farrar, Straus and Giroux, 2008.

Harman, Jim, and Donald F. Glut. *The Great Movie Serials: Their Sound and Fury*. New York: Routledge, 1973.

Hofius, Jason, and George Khoury. *Age of TV Heroes*. Raleigh, NC: Two-Morrows, 2010.

Holtz, Allan. "Obscurity of the Day: Lois Lane, Girl Reporter." *Stripper's Guide* blog, January 11, 2007. http://strippersguide.blogspot.com/2007/01/obscurity-of-day-lois-lane-girl.html.

Hughes, Mark. "Exclusive Interview with Zack Snyder, Director of 'Batman vs. Superman.'" *Forbes*, April 17, 2014. www.forbes.com/sites/markhughes/2014/04/17/exclusive-interview-with-zack-snyder-director-of-batman-vs-superman/.

I Am Curious (Yellow). Directed by Vilgot Sjöman. Janus Films, 1967.

IGN. "The Top 25 Animated Series for Adults." July 15, 2013. www.ign.com/articles/2013/07/15/top-25-animated-shows-for-adults?page=5.

Injustice: Gods Among Us. Directed by Ed Boon. NetherRealm Studios, Warner Bros. Interactive Entertainment, 2013. Video Game.

Jacobs, Frank. *The Mad World of William M. Gaines*. Secaucus, NJ: Lyle Stuart, 1972.

Jacobs, Will, and Gerard Jones. *The Comic Book Heroes: The First History of Modern Comics from the Silver Age to the Present*. Rocklin, CA: Prima, 1997.

Jagernauth, Kevin. "Updated: Olivia Wilde & Mila Kunis Also in the Mix for Lois Lane; Kristen Stewart Not Approached." Indiewire, February 2, 2011. http://blogs.indiewire.com/theplaylist/olivia_wilde_mila_kunis_also_in_the_mix_for_lois_lane_kristen_stewart_repor.

Jensen, Jeff. "Five Things You Need to Know About 'Superman Returns.'" *Entertainment Weekly*, June 17, 2005. www.ew.com/article/2005/06/17/five-things-you-need-know-about-superman-returns.

Johns, Geoff, Richard Donner, and Adam Kubert. *Superman: Last Son of Krypton*. New York: DC Comics, 2013.

Johns, Geoff, and Gary Frank. *Superman: Secret Origin*. New York: DC Comics, 2011.

Johns, Geoff, Phil Jimenez, et al. *Infinite Crisis*. New York: DC Comics, 2008.

Johnston, Rich. "When Dan DiDio Planned to Kill Superman's Marriage to Lois Lane—and Lots of Young Justice Members!" *Bleeding Cool*, January 29, 2015. www.bleedingcool.com/2015/01/19/dan-didio-planned-kill-supermans-marriage-lois-lane-lots-young-injustice-members/.

Jones, Gerard. *Men of Tomorrow: Geeks, Gangsters, and the Birth of the Comic Book*. New York: Basic Books, 2004.

Jurgens, Dan, Jerry Ordway, et al. *The Death of Superman*. New York: DC Comics, 1993.

———. *The Return of Superman*. New York: DC Comics, 1993.

———. *Superman: The Death and Return of Superman Omnibus*. New York: DC Comics, 2013.

———. *World Without a Superman*. New York: DC Comics, 1993.

Justice League: The Flashpoint Paradox. Directed by Jay Oliva. Warner Bros., 2013. DVD.

Justice League: The New Frontier. Directed by David Bullock. Warner Bros., 2008. DVD.

Kashner, Sam, and Nancy Schoenberger. *Hollywood Kryptonite: The Bulldog, the Lady, and the Death of Superman.* New York: St. Martin's Press, 1996.

Khouri, Andy. "*Superman: The Animated Series* Star Dana Delany on Lois Lane's 75th Birthday." *Wired*, July 8, 2013. www.wired.com/2013/07/lois-lane-dana-delany/.

Kirkus. Review of *Lois Lane: Fallout.* February 16, 2015. www.kirkusreviews.com/book-reviews/gwenda-bond/fallout-bond/.

Kistler, Alan. "SDCC 2011: The Mood of DC Fans at Comic-Con." *Newsarama*, July 25, 2011. www.newsarama.com/8088-sdcc-2011-the-mood-of-dc-fans-at-comic-con.html.

Kleefeld, Sean. "On History: Lois Lane, Girl Reporter." *Kleefeld on Comics* blog, January 14, 2014. www.kleefeldoncomics.com/2014/01/on-history-lois-lane-girl-reporter.html.

Kupperberg, Alan. "Dorothy Woolfolk Remembered." Alan Kupperberg personal website. www.alankupperberg.com/woolfolk.html.

Lawson, Corrina. "The Cliffs of Insanity: Lois Lane and Comics Culture." *Geek Mom* blog, November 15, 2013. http://geekmom.com/2013/11/cliffs-insanity-lois-lane-comic-culture/.

———. "Dear DC Comics: Why Do You Keep Fridging Me?" *Wired*, March 5, 2012. http://archive.wired.com/geekdad/2012/03/loislane/.

Lemmon, Leonore. Interview, May 1989. Transcribed by Lou Koza. www.jimnolt.com/MAY1989.pdf.

Levitt, Steven D., and Stephen J. Dubner. *Freakonomics: A Rogue Economist Explores the Hidden Side of Everything.* Rev. ed. New York: William Morrow, 2006.

Lillian, Guy H., III. "Mort Weisinger: The Man Who Wouldn't Be Superman." *Amazing World of DC Comics* 7 (July 1975).

Litton, Claire. "No Girls Allowed! Crumb and the Comix Counterculture." *Pop Matters*, January 23, 2007. www.popmatters.com/feature/no-girls-allowed-crumb-and-the-comix-counterculture/.

Loeb, Jeph, Joe Casey, et al. *Superman: Our Worlds at War.* New York: DC Comics, 2006.

Loeb, Jeph, J. M. DeMatteis, et al. *Superman: Emperor Joker.* New York: DC Comics, 2007.

Lois & Clark FAQ. RedBoots.net, accessed September 24, 2015. www.redboots.net/lc-faq/Q31.htm

Lois & Clark: The New Adventures of Superman. Seasons 1–4. Warner Bros., 2005–2006. DVD.

Man of Steel. Directed by Zack Snyder. Warner Bros., 2013.

Marcus, Sara. *Girls to the Front: The True Story of the Riot Grrrl Revolution.* New York: Harper Perennial, 2010.

Max Fleischer's Superman, 1941–1942. Warner Bros., 2009. DVD.

McMillan, Graeme. "Lois Lane Is Your New YA Fiction Hero." *Hollywood Reporter,* August 26, 2014. www.hollywoodreporter.com/heat-vision /lois-lane-is-your-new-728182.

McNulty, Thomas. "Superman's Girl-Friend, Noel Neill!" *Dispatches from the Last Outlaw* blog, June 14, 2013. http://tommcnulty.blogspot .com/2013/06/supermans-girl-friend-noel-neill.html.

Miller, John Jackson. "Comic Book Sales by Year." Comichron. www .comichron.com/yearlycomicssales.html.

———. "February 2014 Comic Book Sales Figures." Comichron. www .comichron.com/monthlycomicssales/2014/2014-02.html.

———. "May 2012 Comic Book Sales Figures." Comichron. www.comichron .com/monthlycomicssales/2012/2012-05.html.

Mills, Kay. *A Place in the News: From the Women's Pages to the Front Page.* New York: Dodd, Mead, 1988.

Monem, Nadine. *Riot Grrrl: Revolution Girl Style Now!* London: Black Dog Publishing, 2007.

Moore, Alan. "Invisible Girls and Phantom Ladies." *Daredevils* 6 (June 1983): 15–18.

Moore, Alan, and Brian Bolland. *Batman: The Killing Joke.* New York: DC Comics, 1988.

Moore, Alan, and Curt Swan. *Superman: Whatever Happened to the Man of Tomorrow?* New York: DC Comics, 2009.

Mouse of Tomorrow, The. Directed by Eddie Donnelly. Terrytoons, 1942.

Napier, Claire. "All Star Lois Lane: Superman, Icons, Personhood and Love." *Women Write About Comics* blog, September 6, 2013. http:// womenwriteaboutcomics.com/2013/09/06/all-star-lois-lane-superman -icons-personhood-and-love/.

New Adventures of Superman, The. Warner Bros., 2007. DVD.

Newell, Mindy. "How I Became a Comics Professional." ComicMix, July 25, 2011. www.comicmix.com/2011/07/25/mindy-newell-how-i-became -a-comics-professional/.

———. "Not Superman's Girlfriend!" ComicMix, October 29, 2012. www.comicmix.com/2012/10/29/mindy-newell-not-supermans -girlfriend/.

Newport, Frank. "In U.S., 87% Approve of Black-White Marriage, vs. 4% in 1958." Gallup, July 25, 2013. www.gallup.com/poll/163697/approve -marriage-blacks-whites.aspx.

Nights of Horror. Issues 1–16. New York: Malcla Publishing, 1954.

Niven, Larry. "Man of Steel, Woman of Kleenex." *Knight: The Magazine for the Adult Male* 7, no. 8 (December 1969).

Nodell, Jacque. "Original 'Marc—On the Man's Side' Page—Young Love #119 (December 1975/January 1976)." *Sequential Crush* blog, May 17, 2011. http://sequentialcrush.blogspot.com/2011/05/original-marc-on -mans-side-page-young.html.

———. "Who Do You Think You Are, Mr. America?" *Sequential Crush* blog, December 2, 2009. http://sequentialcrush.blogspot.com/2009/12/who -do-you-think-you-are-mr-america.html.

Nyberg, Amy Kiste. *Seal of Approval: The History of the Comics Code.* Jackson: University Press of Mississippi, 1998.

Old Time Radio Superman Show podcast. Talk Shoe, 2008–2015. www .talkshoe.com/tc/11773.

Patterson, John. "Who Killed Superman?" *Guardian*, November 18, 2006. www.theguardian.com/film/2006/nov/18/features.weekend1.

Pense, Rip. "A Crush More Powerful Than a Locomotive." *Los Angeles Times*, August 12, 1994. http://articles.latimes.com/1994-08-12/news /ls-26480_1_noel-neill.

Perils of Pearl Pureheart, The. Directed by Eddie Donnelly. Mighty Mouse. Terrytoons, 1949.

Philbrick, Jami. "'Smallville: Homecoming' 200th Episode Q&A." MovieWeb, October 15, 2010. http://movieweb.com/smallville-homecoming -200th-episode-qa/.

Potempa, Philip. "Lois Lane Actress Disputes 'Superman' Movie Claim." *NWI Times*, February 27, 2007. www.nwitimes.com/entertainment /columnists/offbeat/lois-lane-actress-disputes-superman-movie-claims /article_e31d1ceb-7c77-5f0a-8192-228ad8b7511a.html.

Quattro, Ken. "Woolfolk on Weisinger." *Comics Detective* blog, April 16, 2012. http://thecomicsdetective.blogspot.com/2012/04/woolfolk-on -weisinger.html.

Rabin, Nathan. "Random Roles: Margot Kidder." *AV Club*, March 3, 2009. www.avclub.com/article/random-roles-margot-kidder-24554.

Renaud, Jeffrey. "Yang & Romita, Jr. Expose Lois Lane in New 'Superman' Arc 'Before Truth.'" *Comic Book Resources*, June 24, 2015. www.comicbookresources.com/article/yang-romita-jr-expose-lois-lane -in-new-superman-arc-before-truth.

Ricca, Brad. *Super Boys: The Amazing Adventures of Jerry Siegel and Joe Shuster—the Creators of Superman.* New York: Macmillan, 2013.

Rivera, Joshua. "Lois Lane to Star in New YA Novel." *Entertainment Weekly,* August 26, 2014. www.ew.com/article/2014/08/26/lois-lane-to-star-in-new-ya-novel.

Ro, Ronin. *Tales to Astonish: Jack Kirby, Stan Lee, and the American Comic Book Revolution.* New York: Bloomsbury, 2004.

Robbins, Trina. *The Great Women Superheroes.* New York: Kitchen Sink Press, 1996.

Robertson, Nan. *The Girls in the Balcony: Women, Men, and the "New York Times."* New York: Random House, 1992.

Robinson, James, Greg Rucka, et al. *Superman: Nightwing & Flamebird.* Vol. 2. New York: DC Comics, 2010.

Rogers, Vaneta. "'Unfridging Lois' Just One of the Surprises Tom Taylor Plans for DC's *Earth 2.*" *Newsarama,* November 22, 2013. www.newsarama.com/19662-unfridging-lois-just-one-of-the-surprises-tom-taylor-plans-for-dc-s-earth-2.html.

Ross, Ishbel. *Ladies of the Press: The Story of Women in Journalism by an Insider.* New York: Harper, 1936.

Rossen, Jake. *Superman vs. Hollywood: How Fiendish Producers, Devious Directors, and Warring Writers Grounded an American Icon.* Chicago: Chicago Review Press, 2008.

Rucka, Greg, Matthew Clark, et al. *Superman: Unconventional Warfare.* New York: DC Comics, 2005.

Rucka, Greg, Mark Verheiden, et al. *Superman: Sacrifice.* New York: DC Comics, 2006.

Russell, Deac. "The Fourth Estate and the Seventh Art." *Questioning Media Ethics,* edited by Bernard Rubin. New York: Praeger, 1978. 232–248.

Sands, Rich. "*TV Guide Magazine's* 60 Great Cartoons of All Time." *TV Guide,* September 24, 2013. www.tvguide.com/news/greatest-cartoons-tv-guide-magazine-1071203/.

Saturday Night Live. "Margot Kidder/The Chieftains." Season 4, episode 15. Directed by Dave Wilson. NBC, 1979.

———. "Teri Hatcher/Dave Matthews Band." Season 21, episode 18. Directed by Beth McCarthy-Miller. NBC, 1996.

Schwartz, Alvin, Kurt Swan, et al. *Showcase Presents: Superman.* Vols. 1–4. New York: DC Comics, 2005–2008.

Scivally, Bruce. *Superman on Film, Television, Radio and Broadway.* Jefferson, NC: McFarland & Company, 2008.

Shelton, Gilbert. *The Best of Wonder Wart-Hog.* London: Knockabout, 2013.

Smallville. Seasons 3–10. Warner Bros., 2004–2010. DVD.

Smart Blonde. Directed by Frank McDonald. Warner Bros., 1937.

Smith, Don E., Jr. "De-Constructing a Tabloid Caricature." Superman Homepage, January 2009. www.supermanhomepage.com/tv/tv.php?topic=interviews/janalanhenderson1.

Siegel, Jerry, and Joe Shuster. *Superman Archives.* Vols. 1–8. New York: DC Comics, 1997–2010.

———. *The Superman Chronicles.* Vols. 1–10. New York: DC Comics, 2006–2012.

———. *Superman: The Action Comics Archives.* Vols. 1–5. New York: DC Comics, 1998–2007.

Simone, Gail. Women in Refrigerators, March 1999. http://lby3.com/wir/.

Simpson, Paul. *Smallville: The Official Companion, Season 1.* London: Titan Books, 2004.

Singh, Arune. "The New 'Adventures' of Lois & Clark: Greg Rucka Talks 'Adventures of Superman.'" *Comic Book Resources,* August 22, 2003. www.comicbookresources.com/?page=article&id=2623.

Superboy. Season 4. Warner Bros., 2013. DVD.

Superman: Doomsday. Directed by Lauren Montgomery, Bruce Timm, and Brandon Vietti. Warner Bros., 2007. DVD.

Superman Homepage. "Smallville's Super Debut—a WB Ratings Bonanza!" October 18, 2001. www.supermanhomepage.com/news/2001-news/2001-news-tv.php?topic=2001-news-tv/1018i.

Superman Returns. Directed by Bryan Singer. Warner Bros., 2006.

Superman: The Animated Series. Season 1–3. Warner Bros., 2005–2006. DVD.

Superman: The Movie. Directed by Richard Donner. Warner Bros., 1978.

Superman: The Theatrical Serials Collection. Directed by Spencer Gordon Bennett and Thomas Carr. Warner Bros., 2006. DVD.

Superman II. Directed by Richard Lester. Warner Bros., 1980.

Superman II: The Richard Donner Cut. Directed by Richard Donner. Warner Bros., 2006. DVD.

Superman III. Directed by Richard Lester. Warner Bros., 1983.

Superman IV: The Quest for Peace. Directed by Sidney J. Furie. Warner Bros., 1987.

Superman: Unbound. Directed by James Tucker. Warner Bros., 2013. DVD

Super-Rabbit. Directed by Chuck Jones. Looney Tunes. Warner Bros., 1943.

Thomas, Michael. "John Byrne: The Hidden Answers." *Comic Book Resources,* August 22, 2000. www.comicbookresources.com/?page=article&id=151.

Tolworthy, Chris. "Marvel and DC Sales Figures." Chris Tolworthy personal website, accessed September 24, 2015. www.zak-site.com/Great-American-Novel/comic_sales.html.

20/20 Downtown. "Who Killed Superman?" ABC, June 2000.

Tye, Larry. *Superman: The High-Flying History of America's Most Enduring Hero*. New York: Random House, 2012.

Underdog. Directed by Frederik Du Chau. Disney, 2007.

Underdog: The Complete Series. Shout! Factory, 2012. DVD.

VGChartz. "Injustice: Gods Among Us." Accessed September 24, 2015. www.vgchartz.com/game/71001/injustice-gods-among-us/.

Waid, Mark, and Leinil Francis Yu. *Superman: Birthright*. New York: DC Comics, 2005.

Ward, Larry Thomas. *Truth, Justice, & the American Way: The Life and Times of Noel Neill, the Original Lois Lane*. Los Angeles: Nicholas Laurence Books, 2003.

Weldon, Glen. *Superman: The Unauthorized Biography*. New York: John Wiley & Sons, 2013.

Wertham, Fredric. *Seduction of the Innocent*. New York: Rinehart & Company, 1954.

Williams, J. P. "All's Fair in Love and Journalism: Female Rivalry in *Superman*." *Journal of Popular Culture* 24, no. 2 (Fall 1990): 103–112.

Wolk, Douglas. *Reading Comics: How Graphic Novels Work and What They Mean*. Cambridge, MA: Da Capo Press, 2008.

Woolfolk, Dorothy. Letter to Gloria Steinem, July 8, 1972. Sophia Smith Collection, Smith College Archives, Northampton, MA.

Wright, Bradford. *Comic Book Nation: The Transformation of Youth Culture in America*. Baltimore: Johns Hopkins University Press, 2001.

Yahoo Movies. "Man of Steel Fan Q&A Event." November 6, 2013. https://movies.yahoo.com/man-of-steel-live/.

Yoe, Craig. *Secret Identity: The Fetish Art of Superman's Co-creator Joe Shuster*. New York: Abrams ComicArts, 2009.

Younis, Steven. "Exclusive Interview with Noel Neill." Superman Homepage, February 9, 2007. www.supermanhomepage.com/tv/tv.php?topic=interviews/noel-neill2.

Index

*Daring New Adventures of Super-
    girl, The*, 137–39
Dark Knight film franchise, 154
Darkseid (character), 199, 204, 221
Davis, Bette, 4
DC Comics
    attempts at relevancy, 117, 132
    and Comics Code Authority, 54
    licensing rights, 79
    litigation against, 19, 24
    management changes, 93, 171
    and Modern Age of comics,
        165–66
    New 52 initiative, 225–26
    rebooting of series, 186
    serialization, 118
    Superman's importance to, 12
DC Universe Animated Original
        Movies, 206
"Death of Superman" arc, 206, 212
DeFalco, Tom, 127, 128–29
Delany, Dana, 203, 205, 206
Delgado, Jose (character), 170
Desanex, Philbert (character), 161
Detective Comics, 2
DeWitt, Alex (character), 219
Dexter, Sheila (character), 78–79
DiDio, Dan, 225–26
Ditko, Steve, 19
diversity efforts, 95–99
Dobrotka, Ed, 16
Donner, Richard, 145, 150, 212
Doomsday (character), 176, 223
Drucker, Mort, 162
Dubner, Stephen J., 28
Durance, Erica, 195–96, 197,
        198–99

Earth 2 series, 222, 223
Earth-Two, 165n

Ebert, Roger, 153
Edge, Morgan (character), 117,
        122–23
Eisner Awards, viii
Elliott, Jordan (Superman alias),
        133
Ellsworth, Whitney, 40, 54, 77n
Emory, Thomas, 65
Eradicator (character), 171, 178,
        179n

Fabe, Maxene, 106n, 135
Famous Studios, 32
fans
    as coconspirators, 63–64
    fondness for Lois, 122
    frustration with patriarchy, 92
    gender of, 58–59, 228
    and Lois vs. Lana rivalry, 84–86
    on Lois's capability, 131–32
    maturity of, 122
Farnon, Shannon, 202
Farrell, Glenda, 4
female characters
    feminist influence on, 101–2
    and gender stereotypes, 6n, 126
    inferiority to men, 17, 28, 234
    killing off of, 185–86, 219
    lack of strong roles, 183
    objectification of, 21, 76, 131,
        214–15, 228
    popularity of, 4, 11
    See also gender roles
feminism, 92, 101–2, 109, 112–13
Filmation, 201
Finger, Bill, 8n, 19
Flash, the (character), 54, 159n,
        225n
Flashpoint series, 222, 225n
Fleischer, Dave, 29

Also from Chicago Review Press

**Wonder Woman
Unbound**
**The Curious History
of the World's Most
Famous Heroine**
Tim Hanley
978-1-61374-909-8
$18.95 (CAN $22.95)
*Also available in e-book
formats*

With her golden lasso and her bullet-deflecting bracelets, Wonder Woman is a beloved icon of female strength in a world of male superheroes. But this close look at her history portrays a complicated heroine who is more than just a female Superman. When they debuted in the 1940s, Wonder Woman comics advocated female superiority and the benefits of matriarchy; her adventures were also colored by bondage imagery and hidden lesbian leanings. In the decades that followed, Wonder Woman fell backward as American women began to step forward. Ultimately, Wonder Woman became a feminist symbol in the 1970s, and the curious details of her past were quickly forgotten. Exploring this lost history adds new dimensions to the world's most beloved female character, and *Wonder Woman Unbound* delves into her comic book and its spin-offs as well as the motivations of her creators to showcase the peculiar journey of a twentieth-century icon.

Superman vs. Hollywood
How Fiendish Producers, Devious Directors, and Warring Writers Grounded an American Icon
Jake Rossen
978-1-55652-731-9
$16.95 (CAN $18.95)
Also available in e-book formats

For the first time, one book unearths all the details of Superman's turbulent adventures in Tinseltown, from his radio serial through the 2006 film *Superman Returns*. Based on extensive interviews with producers, screenwriters, cast members, and crew, *Superman vs. Hollywood* spills the beans on Marlon Brando's eccentricities; the challenges of making Superman appear to fly; the casting process that at various points had Superman being played by Sylvester Stallone, Neil Diamond, Nicolas Cage, Ashton Kutcher, and even Muhammad Ali; and the Superman movies, fashioned by such maverick filmmakers as Kevin Smith and Tim Burton, that never made it to the screen.

Stan Lee and the Rise and Fall of the American Comic Book
Jordan Raphael and Tom Spurgeon
978-1-55652-541-4
$16.95 (CAN $25.95)
Also available in e-book formats

The face of Marvel Comics and the cocreator of Spider-Man, the X-Men, the Fantastic Four, and hundreds of other colorful heroes, Stan Lee is known as a dazzling writer, a skilled editor, a relentless self-promoter, a credit hog, and a huckster—a man equal parts P. T. Barnum and Walt Disney. This book, based on interviews with Stan Lee and dozens of his colleagues and contemporaries, as well as extensive archival research, is at once a professional history, an appreciation, and a critical exploration of Stan Lee and his many accomplishments.

Heroes in the Night
Inside the Real Life Superhero Movement
Tea Krulos
978-1-61374-775-9
$16.95 (CAN $18.95)
Also available in e-book formats

Heroes in the Night traces journalist Tea Krulos's journey into the strange subculture of Real Life Superheroes, random citizens who have adopted comic book–style personas and hit the streets to fight injustice. Some concentrate on humanitarian or activist missions—helping the homeless, gathering donations for food banks, or delivering toys to children—while others actively patrol their neighborhoods looking for crime to fight. By day, these modern Clark Kents work as dishwashers, pencil pushers, and executives in Fortune 500 companies. But by night they become heroes for the people. Through historic research and extensive interviews, Krulos shares not only their shining, triumphant moments, but also some of their ill-advised, terrifying disasters.

Leaving Mundania
Inside the Transformative World of Live Action Role-Playing Games
Lizzie Stark
978-1-56976-605-7
$16.95 (CAN $18.95)
Also available in e-book formats

"With humor, intelligence, and more than a little bravery, Lizzie Stark guides us into the vast subculture of larping, where lawyers become vampire hunters and systems analysts turn into knights. Hilarious, honest, and enlightening, *Leaving Mundania* reminds us how thin the boundaries are between the roles we play and the selves we believe ourselves to be."
—Stacey Richter, Pushcart Prize–winning author of *My Date with Satan* and *Twin Study: Stories*

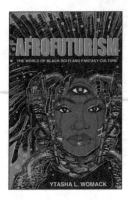

Afrofuturism
The World of Black Sci-Fi and Fantasy Culture
Ytasha L. Womack
978-1-61374-796-4
$16.95 (CAN $18.95)
Also available in e-book formats

In this hip, accessible primer to the music, literature, and art of Afrofuturism, author Ytasha Womack introduces readers to the burgeoning community of artists creating Afrofuturist works, the innovators from the past, and the wide range of subjects they explore. From the sci-fi literature of Samuel Delany, Octavia Butler, and N. K. Jemisin to the musical cosmos of Sun Ra, George Clinton, and the Black Eyed Peas' will.i.am, to the visual and multimedia artists inspired by African Dogon myths and Egyptian deities, the book's topics range from the "alien" experience of blacks in America to the "wake up" cry that peppers sci-fi literature, sermons, and activism.

The Cartoon Music Book
Daniel Goldmark and Yuval Taylor, editors
978-1-55652-473-8
$18.95 (CAN $28.95)
Also available in e-book formats

The popularity of cartoon music, from Carl Stalling's work for Warner Bros. to Disney sound tracks and *The Simpsons*' song parodies, has never been greater. This lively and fascinating look at cartoon music's past and present collects contributions from well-known music critics and cartoonists, and interviews with the principal cartoon composers. Here Mark Mothersbaugh talks about his music for *Rugrats*, Alf Clausen about composing for *The Simpsons*, Carl Stalling about his work for Walt Disney and Warner Bros., Irwin Chusid about Raymond Scott's work, Will Friedwald about *Casper the Friendly Ghost*, Richard Stone about his music for *Animaniacs*, Joseph Lanza about *Ren and Stimpy*, and much, much more.